Lecture Notes in Computer Science 2006

Edited by G. Goos, J. Hartmanis and J. van Leeuwen

T0230311

Springer
Berlin
Heidelberg
New York
Barcelona
Hong Kong
London
Milan
Paris
Singapore
Tokyo

Reiner Dumke   Alain Abran (Eds.)

New Approaches in Software Measurement

10th International Workshop, IWSM 2000
Berlin, Germany, October 4-6, 2000
Proceedings

 Springer

Series Editors

Gerhard Goos, Karlsruhe University, Germany
Juris Hartmanis, Cornell University, NY, USA
Jan van Leeuwen, Utrecht University, The Netherlands

Volume Editors

Reiner Dumke
Universitat Magdeburg, Institut für Verteilte Systeme
Universitätsplatz 2, 39106 Magdeburg, Germany
E-mail: dumke@ivs.cs.uni-magdeburg.de

Alain Abran
Universite du Quebec á Montreal
C.P. 8888, Succ. Centre-Ville, Montreal, Quebec, Canada
E-mail: abran.alain@uquam.ca

Cataloging-in-Publication Data applied for

Die Deutsche Bibliothek - CIP-Einheitsaufnahme

New approaches in software measurement : 10th international workshop ;
proceedings / IWSM 2000, Berlin, Germany, October 4 - 6, 2000. Reiner
Dumke ; Alain Abran (ed.). - Berlin ; Heidelberg ; New York ;
Barcelona ; Hong Kong ; London ; Milan ; Paris ; Singapore ; Tokyo :
Springer, 2001
   (Lecture notes in computer science ; Vol. 2006)
   ISBN 3-540-41727-3

CR Subject Classification (1998): D.2, K.6.3

ISSN 0302-9743
ISBN 3-540-41727-3 Springer-Verlag Berlin Heidelberg New York

Springer-Verlag Berlin Heidelberg New York
a member of BertelsmannSpringer Science+Business Media GmbH
' Springer-Verlag Berlin Heidelberg 2001
Printed in Germany

Typesetting: Camera-ready by author, data conversion by PTP Berlin, Stefan Sossna
Printed on acid-free paper   SPIN 10782298   06/3142   5 4 3 2 1 0

Preface

Software measurement is one of the key technologies employed to control and manage the software development process. Research avenues such as the applicability of metrics, the efficiency of measurement programs in industry, and the theoretical foundations (of software engineering?) have been investigated to evaluate and improve modern software development areas such as object-orientation, component-based develop-ment, multimedia systems design, reliable telecommunication systems etc.

In the tradition of our software measurement research communities, the German Computer Science Interest (GI) Group on Software Measurement and the Canadian Interest Group in Software Metrics (CIM) have attended to these concerns in recent years. Initially, research initiatives were directed at the definition of new methods of software measurement and the validation of these methods themselves. This was then followed by more and more investigation into practical applications of software measurement and key findings in this area of software engineering have been published in:

! Dumke/Zuse: Theory and Practice of Software Measurement, 1994

! Ebert/Dumke: Software-Metriken in der Praxis, 1996

! Lehner/Dumke/Abran: Software Metrics - Research and Practice in Software Measurement, 1997

! Dumke/Abran: Software Measurement - Current Trends in Research and Practice, 1999

We would also like to mention that the proceedings of the Lac Supérieur workshop have been made available on the web at www.lrgl.uqam.ca?

This new book includes the proceedings of the 10th Workshop on Software Measurement held in Berlin in October 2000. It is a collection of theoretical studies in the field of software measurement as well as experience reports on the application of software metrics in Canadian, Belgian, Chinese, Spanish, Italian, English, and German companies and universities.

Some of the papers and reports describe new kinds of measurements for object-oriented systems and further improvements to the Function Point method. Others address specific aspects in the software development (requirements engineering, customer satisfaction, and agents economy) and the improvement of the software process itself. Finally, the improvement of the software measurement process itself was investigated and new approaches were discussed.

The book will be of interest to software engineering researchers, as well as to practitioners in the areas of project management and quality improvement programs, for both software maintenance and software development in general.

The members of the program committee were:

Alain Abran, University of Quebec in Montreal, Canada

Manfred Bundschuh, DASMA, Germany

Jean-Marc Desharnais, CIM Montreal, Canada

Reiner Dumke, University of Magdeburg, Germany

Christof Ebert, Alcatel Antwerp, Belgium

Tracy Hall, University of Hertfordshire, UK

Franz Lehner, University of Regensburg, Germany

Claus Lewerentz, TU Cottbus, Germany

Rini van Solingen, IESE Kaiserslautern, Germany

Andreas Schmietendorf, T-Nova Berlin, Germany

Harry Sneed, SES Munich/Budapest, Hungary

Charles Symons, SMS, London, UK

Hans van Vliet, University of Amsterdam, The Netherlands

Horst Zuse, TU Berlin, Germany

We also extend our thanks to Mrs. Doerge for the preparation of the unified layout and Springer-Verlag for their helpful cooperation.

December 2000   Reiner R. Dumke
                                                           Alain Abran

Table of Contents

Software Measurement of Special Aspects

Improving the Software Measurement Process

Impact of Inheritance on Metrics for Size, Coupling, and Cohesion in Object-Oriented Systems

Dirk Beyer, Claus Lewerentz, and Frank Simon

Software Systems Engineering Research Group
Technical University Cottbus, Germany
(db|cl|simon)@informatik.tu-cottbus.de

Abstract. In today's engineering of object oriented systems many different metrics are used to get feedback about design quality and to automatically identify design weaknesses. While the concept of inheritance is covered by special inheritance metrics its impact on other classical metrics (like size, coupling or cohesion metrics) is not considered; this can yield misleading measurement values and false interpretations. In this paper we present an approach to work the concept of inheritance into classical metrics (and with it the related concepts of overriding, overloading and polymorphism). This is done by some language dependent *flattening* functions that modify the data on which the measurement will be done. These functions are implemented within our metrics tool *Crocodile* and are applied for a case study: the comparison of the measurement values of the original data with the measurement values of the flattened data yields interesting results and improves the power of classical measurements for interpretation.

1   Introduction

The measurement of object oriented systems seems to be a powerful tool for the qualitative assessment (cf. [5]). The availability of about 200 object oriented metrics [14] – i.e. metrics which are defined on object oriented systems -- and many books that consider the measurement of object oriented software, confirm this assumption. In general, these metrics can be classified into coupling, cohesion and size metrics. Inheritance is covered as a separate concept with its own metrics (e.g. *depth of inheritance, number of children, number of parents,* cf. [9]). However, most metrics for size, coupling and cohesion within the object oriented area ignore inheritance.

This paper shows another view: we demonstrate the impact of inheritance on other classical metrics, like size, coupling or cohesion metrics. The basic idea is the following: imagine a class A with 20 public methods, and a class B that inherits from class A and adds 15 additional public methods. Ignoring inheritance might yield the interpretation that class A is greater or even more complex than class B (as suggested by the measurement values for *number of public methods*: 20 for class A and 15 for class B). This is false when considering the functional size of a class as the set of

R. Dumke and A. Abran (Eds.): IWSM 2000, LNCS 2006, pp. 1-17, 2001.
© Springer-Verlag Berlin Heidelberg 2001

methods that a client class can use. This set remains unchanged for class A but increases to 35 methods for class B.

To examine this phenomenon in more detail we have to consider in depth the concept of inheritance and all concepts that might be touched by it, i.e. overriding, overloading and polymorphism. The idea of representing a class as it really is, i.e. considering all inherited attributes and operations, was introduced by Meyer [10]: his function *flat* constructs the flat representation of a class. In the field of object oriented measurement this concept is called *inheritance context* [3]: it allows for a selection of superclasses to be flattened into a subclass. With respect to measurement this includes flattening the associations between classes: Particularly in polymorph structures client classes are often coupled only with the interface class. Subclasses of the interface class are not coupled with the client class. Upon using the flattening process every client class with the possibility of calling operations of any subclass, is now also coupled with it.

Although it is very straight forward to consider flattening in measurement it had not been yet examined in detail, but nearly mentioned as a theoretic possibility (cf. [1], Section 4.2.4) or treated by various rare used metrics without a substantial knowledge of their behaviour or implementation details (e.g. *number of methods overridden by a subclass, number of methods inherited by a subclass, or number of methods added by a subclass*, cf. [9]). One point might be the necessity of adjusting the concept of flattening to each of the special programming languages with respect to the inheritance related concepts of overriding, overloading and polymorphism. This task is not easy, especially for C++.

This paper gives a brief overview of how the flattening has to work for C++ projects. For more details of how multiple inheritance or inheritance chains is treated see [13].

By applying flattening to large C++ systems we want to examine two points:
1. How are measurement values of classical size, coupling and cohesion metrics changed; and,
2. How can the quantitative analysis of the flattening itself be interpreted (e.g. how many methods, attributes or associations have to be copied into a subclass).

This examination is done by calculating five classical metrics for a case study. Firstly we use the usual technique, i.e. we ignore the inheritance structure; and secondly we flatten all classes before measuring them. We show that there are clear differences between the two approaches and that the quantitative analysis of the flattening itself gives many important hints for understanding the system.

This paper is structured as follows: in Section 2, the basic concepts of overloading, overriding and polymorphism are explained with respect to our flattening functions. We give an overview of these concepts for the language C++ and introduce some corresponding flattening functions. Section 3 shows the impact of flattening on measurement values of five classical metrics, and Section 4 explains how the quantitative analysis of the flattening itself can be interpreted to get a better understanding of the system and some worth suggestions for restructuring. The paper closes with a summary.

2   Overloading, Overriding, and Polymorphism in C++

Extending the simple addition of functionality into subclasses (cf. Section 1), we have to consider the concepts of overloading, overriding and polymorphism, because they might not only add but also modify functionality. These concepts only occur, if two method names (without considering parameters) are identical. Attributes can not be overloaded but they can be overridden in some cases (see below). Such situation where two members (either attributes or methods) with the same name (either locally declared or inherited) are visible in one class we call *name conflict*.

In the following, we discuss overloading, overriding and polymorphism separately for attributes and methods, and we distinguish the cases where name conflicts occur and where the name is unique.

For each situation we define a special flattening function which copies some members, i.e. methods or attributes, into a subclass with respect to some given rules. All flattening functions have three parameters: a superclass, the class where to copy members into and which is a direct subclass of the superclass, and the type of inheritance.

2.1   Attributes without Conflicting Names

Without name conflicts for attributes, the technique of flattening classes within an inheritance structure is simple: the attributes of a superclass are copied into all subclasses, if they are still visible there, which depends on the attribute's visibility.

Before defining the flattening function for attributes with unique names we have to think about **wrapped attributes,** which are attributes that are not directly accessible, i.e. they have the visibility private, but they are accessible by visible get and set methods. The encapsulation principle of object oriented design advises against the direct access to any attribute. The recommended construction is to access these attributes by special get methods and set methods. Our consideration of attributes above is blind to attributes used in this way, although ignoring these attributes within the subclass does not reflect the real situation: imagine a class A with 10 private attributes and each attribute has one get method and one set method. If then a class B inherits from this class and does not add, modify or delete anything there would be no reason why class A and class B should be considered as different. However, if measured separately, this would happen if no flattening or even if our previous flattening function would be applied. Therefore, also these wrapped attributes have to be considered for the flattening process. This kind of visibility we call *invisible* (i.e. not visible but indirectly accessible) in contrast to *inaccessible* (i.e. not visible and not accessible).

Now we are able to define the flattening function for attributes that do not have name conflicts:

> **flatten_unique_attribute_names** *(superclass, subclass, inheritance type)*: This flattening version copies all attributes (visible and invisible ones) of the *superclass* into the *subclass* if an attribute with the same name does not exist in the *subclass*. The attribute's visibility in the target class depends on the *inheritance type* and the *attribute's visibility*.

2.2   Attributes with Conflicting Names

In some cases overriding of attributes exists: If a subclass defines an attribute with the same name as a visible attribute of a superclass, the subclass' attribute overrides the superclass' attribute, i.e. it is no longer directly accessible but only by the use of the scope operator. For the later effect on measurement, it has to be decided, whether also attributes that are accessible only by explicitly using the scope operator have to be considered or not. For the purpose of this paper, which is to show the impact of inherited members on measurement values, we do not consider the use of members via the scope operator because of the following reasons:

1. For static members it is applicable to all classes independently of any inheritance relation between them.
2. The re-definition of an attribute within a subclass is a deliberate decision. Using the scope operator bypasses this decision. We can not really imagine examples in which the use of both attributes, the inherited via scope operator and the re-defined one, might make much sense.
3. In real-life applications we analysed (cf. [7]) the scope operator is not used very frequently.
4. Using the scope operator increases the dependencies between the particular classes. The reuse of a class is much more difficult because it is not sufficient to reproduce all use-relations and inheritance relations but it is necessary to adapt all code using the scope operator to the new environment.

Because of this we do not need to define a further flattening function for attributes that have the same name, because if two such attributes exist, the one of the superclass can be ignored.

2.3   Methods without Conflicting Names

The flattening function for methods with unique names is similar to the flattening function for attributes with unique names: the methods of a superclass are copied into the subclass if they are still visible there.

As done for attributes we have to think about *wrapped methods*, which are methods that are not directly accessible, i.e. they have the visibility private, but are accessible through other visible methods. This concept of private auxiliary methods is often used to extract some specific functionality. For our purpose all private methods that are used by a non-private method have to be considered for the flattening process. Their visibility within the target class is changed to *invisible*. Now we can define the flattening function for methods that do not have name conflicts:

> **flatten_unique_method_names** (*superclass, subclass, inheritance type*): This flattening version copies all methods (visible and invisible ones) of the *superclass* into the *subclass* if no method with the same name exists in the *subclass*. The method's visibility in the target class depends on the *inheritance type* and the *method's visibility*.

2.4   Methods with Conflicting Names

Methods within a subclass can overload (for the definition of similar operations in different ways for different data types or numbers) or override (for a redefinition of a method) a method of a superclass. It overrides if the *signatures* [11] are identical and it overloads if the names are equal but at least one parameter is different (for details cf. [13]).

With respect to inheritance there is a very important point to remember if dealing with overriding and overloading in C++: a method in a subclass will override all methods with the same name from the superclass, but not overload them! So, whenever two methods from two classes in an inheritance relation have the same name, the flattening function must not copy the method from the superclass into the subclass and, therefore, there is no need for an additional flattening function.

2.5   Polymorphic Use-Relations

In this section we deal with *polymorphism*, in particular *run-time polymorphism* (in contrast to *compile-time polymorphism* that can be achieved by overloading and that can be solved by the compiler) (cf. [12]). The technique to implement this kind of polymorphism is called *late binding*. This means that the determination which version of a function is called when a message with appropriate name occurs is made at run time and is based on the caller's object type. In C++ this type of late binding is only possible if an object is accessed via pointer (or via reference, which is an implicit pointer, [12], pp. 341) and if the called method is declared `virtual`.

If considering polymorphic structures it is not always possible to decide at compile-time which function will be executed at run-time. Due to this, the static analysis of polymorphic use-relations between classes is often reduced to use-relations between superclasses [8].

Because the static analysis of source code always considers only potential of use and not the actual frequency of use, there should be a function *flatten_polymorphic_use_relations* that copies the use-relations into all methods of the subclass that could be executed by calling a method in a superclass. This flattening function depends not only on the superclass and subclass but also on the class that uses methods of the superclass [13].

The corresponding flattening function is defined as follows:

---

flatten_polymorphic_use_relations (*superclass, subclass, inheritance's type*): This flattening version adds use-relations that cover calls of the client class to public methods of the subclass. This is done in the following way:

A use-relation between a method m_{usingc} of the client class and a public method m_{subc} of the subclass is added if

the inheritance's type is public,

- m_{usingc} uses the method m_{superc} declared in the superclass,
- m_{superc} is defined as virtual,
- m_{superc} is overridden or implemented by m_{subc} within the subclass.

---

3   Impact of Flattening on Size, Coupling, and Cohesion Metrics

The flattening functions are implemented within the metrics tool *Crocodile* ([8], [13]) that allows to measure large object oriented systems and to apply the flattening functions. This section demonstrates the impact of the flattening process on some typical object oriented metrics. At first we describe a case study in detail and give a quantitative overview how much information was added to the flattened version. Afterwards we explain very briefly some typical metrics (two size, one coupling and two cohesion metrics) that we used for our exploration. Some diagrams show the differences between the measurement values of the normal and the flattened source code data. Afterwards we analyse these value changes in detail and give some specific interpretations, which show, that the values obtained from the flattened version reflect the intuition more appropriately than the traditional values.

3.1   Description of the Case Study

As case study, we used the source code of the Crocodile metrics tool itself. We know the sources in detail and so we are able to evaluate the results; it is written completely in C++; it uses inheritance -- which is not true for all C++ projects, especially for those originally written in C -- ; it is based on a GUI framework; and it uses a library for data structures. This integration of external components is typical for today's software products and demonstrates the necessity of a selection mechanism for the flattening process because not all superclasses have to be flattened in all subclasses [13].

The analysed system consists of 113 files and 57 classes. It has a maximum inheritance depth of 4, has 18 inheritance relations, and does not use multiple inheritance.

These numbers showed to be invariant against the flattening functions because no classes, files, or inheritances are added. The table below gives a quantitative overview about the classes: the first column describes the kind of considered objects, the second counts its occurrences in the original data, the third counts its occurrences in the flattened data and the last shows the percentage increase of the occurrences in the flattened data.

Table 1. Quantitative overview on original and flattened sources

	Original sources	Flattened sources	% Increase
Methods	589	706	+20%
Attributes	226	314	+39%
Use_Method_Relations	666	692	+4%

To demonstrate the impact of the flattening process on the measurement values for classical metrics we chose five typical object oriented metrics, i.e. two size metrics, one use-based coupling metric and two use-based cohesion metrics. In Sections 3.2. to 3.4. we show how the values for these classical metrics change by our flattening functions. In Sections 4.2. to 4.4. we interpret these changes in detail and give some specific interpretations.

3.2   Impact of Flattening on Size Metrics

Two widespread-used size metrics for object oriented source code are the *number of methods (NoM,* cf. *NOM* in [4], *number of instance methods* in [9]) as indicator for functional size and the *number of attributes (NoA,* cf. *NOA* in [4], *number of instance variables* in [9]) as indicator for size of encapsulated data.

The impact of flattening on the metric *NoM* is shown by the distribution of the proportional changes within the system (cf. Figure 1). The x-axis is divided into intervals of percentage of the measurement value changes before and after flattening; the y-axis shows the count of classes having a measurement value change within the interval. As displayed the measurement values remain unchanged for 39 classes (0% changing of the values). These are exactly the classes that have not any superclass. On the other side the range of change is between 101 and 200 percent for 12 classes and between 1401 and 1500 percent for one other class !

The same kind of diagram for the metric *NoA* is shown in Figure 2; to be able to display proportional changes also for classes having no attributes before flattening, we set these proportional changes to the value: *number of added attributes* * 100.

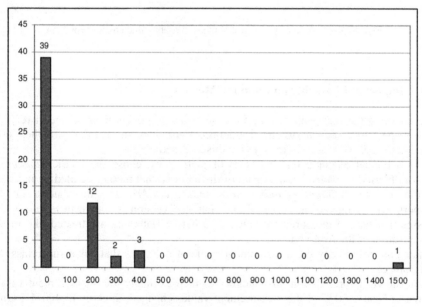

Fig. 1. Distribution of proportional measurement value changes for NoM

As in the previous Figure the values did not change for 39 classes because they have not any superclass. The other values are changed a lot again.

As demonstrated for both metrics, *number of methods (NoM)* and *number of attributes (NoA),* it is clear that size metrics are very sensitive to our flattening process: Over 31 % of the measured values changed, one up to 2.900 % ! Thus, ignoring inheritance for size metrics might yield misleading numbers which in turn might yield false interpretations. Some classes which seem to be very small (and thus easy to understand and to maintain) are in fact very large (and thus difficult to understand and to maintain) because they get (and need) a lot of functionality and data from their superclasses.

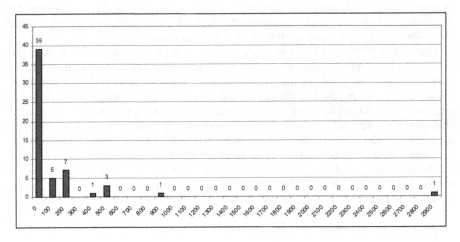

Fig. 2. Distribution of proportional measurement value changes for NoA

3.3   Impact of Flattening on Coupling Metrics

The coupling between entities – in our case classes – covers their degree of relation with respect to a special system abstraction. Very often the entities plus their use-relation (e.g. *RFC* or *fan-out* in [4]) give this abstraction.

As a typical example for this class of metrics we chose the metric *number of externally used methods*, i.e. the count of distinct external methods called by methods within a class (*efferent coupling to methods, effCM*). The distribution of the proportional changes of the original and flattened version is shown in Figure 3; the classes that have a measurement value of 0 before flattening are treated like in the visualisation of the *NoA* values.

For this metric only the measurement value of one class that has a superclass did not change.

As shown before, also in this category of metrics, many low measurement values increase: Nearly 30 % of the measurement values changed, three up to 400 % ! Only upon using the flattening functions the usual reduction of coupling to superclasses within an inheritance relation is extended to coupling to the subclasses. Because use-based coupling is an important indicator for class understanding and class clustering (e.g. into subsystems, cf. [7]) these changes of measurement values have a strong impact. Thus, ignoring inheritance for coupling metrics might give a misleading picture of a system which again might suggest false restructuring actions.

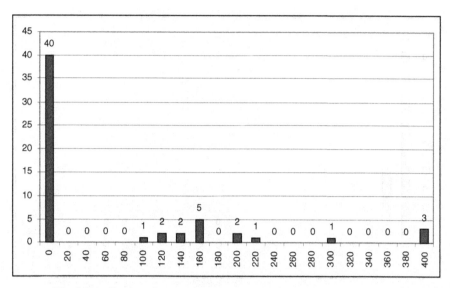

Fig. 3. Distribution of proportional measurement value changes for effCM

3.4   Impact of Flattening on Cohesion Metrics

The third important category of metrics for object oriented systems is the area of cohesion, i.e. to which degree the members of an entity belong together. We examine two different types of cohesion for two different abstraction levels: at first we use the well-known inner class cohesion measure *LCOM* [2], which assumes cohesion within a class to be based only on attribute use-relations. Secondly we use a generic distance based cohesion concept developed at our metrics research team [6]. Here we instantiated it on the class level in such a way that cohesion between classes is based on method-to-method use-relations plus method-to-attribute use-relations: The more two classes use from each other the smaller is their distance.

For the *LCOM* measure, we got the distribution diagram of the measurement value changes as displayed in Figure 4. Again, the increase of the measurement values is obvious, which suggests a weaker class cohesion. However, the validation of this result within the system can not be made: The problem is the very specific point of view to cohesion for *LCOM*, i.e. cohesion is based only on attribute use-relations: Due to flattening many methods are copied into the subclass. With them, the used private attributes are copied as wrapped attributes. Of course no newly implemented method within the subclass has direct access to this attribute, i.e. the *LCOM* value increases. The solution to consider only non-wrapped attributes within subclasses also increases the *LCOM* values because then some methods do not use any attribute of the subclass.

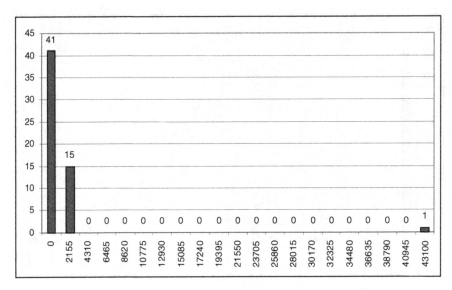

Fig. 4. Distribution of proportional measurement value changes for LCOM

The main result of these measurement changes is that attribute-based cohesion decreases heavily for classes having at least one superclass.

The opposite -- which is an increase of cohesion -- is the result of the second view on cohesion: The changes of the measurement values can not be displayed as above because the cohesion measurement values are not measured for classes but for pairs of classes, which for example can be used as geometric distances within a visualisation (cf. Section 4.4). The flattening of one class X might change all measurement values of class pairs where X is part of. For the given 57 classes there exist 57^2 values. The frequency of relative changes for the two versions is displayed within Figure 5.

Most distances remain unchanged (2995) or increase only minimal (122; cumulated within the interval]0.05..0] to 3117). The most obvious changes are the decreases of distances (~4% of the distances), i.e. the cohesion increases. This comes from the added coupling to subclasses. Ignoring this fact might yield the false interpretation that a class X is only cohesive to a used superclass Y but not to Y's subclasses, which in turn might suggest the false subsystem creation, i.e. to separate Y's subclasses from class X.

On the other side, the flattening can also decrease cohesion: If a class X heavily interacts with the whole functionality of a class Y that has a superclass, one might assume a high degree of cohesion. The flattening process, however, reveals that class X uses only a little part of the functionality of class Y because the latter one inherits a lot of functionality from its superclass. Thus, cohesion decreases.

As shown in this section, also cohesion metrics are sensible to the flattening process. Thus, ignoring inheritance for cohesion metrics might give a misleading impression about the cohesion of the system.

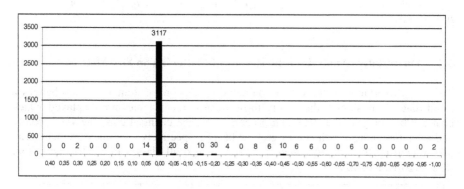

Fig. 5. Frequency of relative changes for class cohesion metric within both versions

4   Quantitative Analysis of the Flattening Process Itself

The last section demonstrates how heavily the flattening process changes several kinds of software measures and how misleading the separate consideration of inheritance for the other metrics might be. In this section we do not examine only the value changes over the whole system but try to interpret them; additionally, we try to interpret value changes for single classes that might give additional information. Thus, the quantitative analysis of the flattening functions itself -- i.e. how many members gets a subclass -- can be seen as a new kind of metrics that gives a new kind of information.

At first we try to interpret the value changes for the whole system. Afterwards for every metric we show a ranking list of the classes for which the flattening process changed the values most, and give an interpretation.

4.1   Quantitative Analysis of the Overall Flattening Results

While flattening the following observations were conspicuous: None of the added methods is a wrapped method and only 13 of the added attributes are wrapped attributes. This has the following reasons:

1. In many cases inheritance is used to create type hierarchies, i.e. the superclass is used as abstract class or only even as interface for subclasses.
2. The partial implementations within the superclasses use some private attributes but never private methods: the functionality of methods that are flattened into subclasses is low and does not need any private auxiliary method but only some private attributes.

Thus, it is possible to characterise the pre-dominant use of inheritance within a system by only analysing these numbers. This kind of analysis is not possible with any typical inheritance metric like *depth of inheritance, number of children* or *number of parents* (cf. [9]).

4.2   Quantitative Analysis of the Results of Flattening on Size Metrics

To get an overview on the effects on some specific measurement value changes a trend diagram is shown: there only those measurement values are displayed which changed by applying the flattening process. For each changed class the value before and after flattening are shown in grey or black respectively. The measurement pairs are ordered by their relative increase. We renamed all classes in all diagrams from `class1` to `class57`.

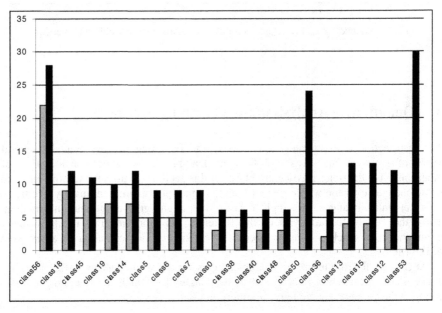

Fig. 6. Measurement values of NoM before and after the flattening process

In Figure 6 we contrast the measurement values of the non-flattened classes with the flattened classes for the metric *NoM*. We only discuss the results for the classes with the most extreme values. The highest relative increase is 15: `class53` has 2 methods before the flattening process and has 30 methods after the flattening process. This class is a subclass of the parser class *FlexLexer* that comes with the *flex* library package and defines the interface of the class for the lexical analyser. In fact, our subclass does not add or modify anything but defines its own constructor and destructor. In this case, inheritance is used only to change the given class name. Thus, the flattened version corresponds to our knowledge that `class53` is a very large class that offers a lot of functionality.

The same measurement visualisation is used for the metric *NoA* in Figure 7:

as for *NoM*, the impact of flattening is clear: 12 classes of the non-flattened version that seem to be anomalous --because they have no attributes (classes 0, 36, 38,

`40, 48, 5, 6, 7, 13, 14, 15, 53)` -- are changed in a way that they have at least one attribute, i.e. they seem to be more than only a container of functions. On the other side, there are two classes with 29 attributes (classes `53` and `56`): Both classes again belong to the parser functionality of the analysed system: A thorough analysis of this situation revealed, that the inheritance used is very debatable and should be renovated.

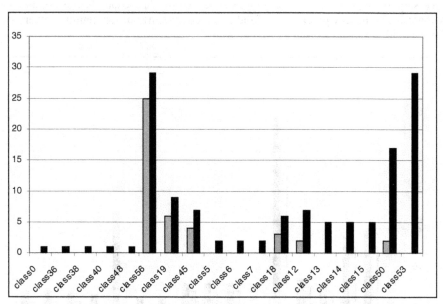

Fig. 7. Measurement values of NoA before and after the flattening process

4.3   Quantitative Analysis of the Flattening Process on Coupling Metrics

As above we contrast the value changes of the non-flattened classes (grey bars) to the flattened classes (black bars) for the metric *effCM* (cf. Figure 8).

It is very interesting that the measurement value of `class5` increases to 49 (before 34): This class is used for the calculation of a special cohesion concept that is integrated into the analysed system. It calculates the cohesion values by using a lot of interfaces. There are many different kinds of cohesion, which are all compatible to one cohesion concept, implemented by different subclasses. Thus, after flattening, the coupling is extended from the interface to all its implementations.

The highest increase occurs for classes `0, 38` and `50`: All three classes are subclasses of an abstract superclass that is partially implemented. Because this implementation is inherited by all subclasses, the subclasses get additional coupling.

Another interesting point is the increase of four classes that have no coupling at all within the non-flattened system (classes `14, 15, 18` and `45`). All four classes are abstract superclasses that have an implementation based on pure virtual methods of the same class, i.e. they have only couplings to methods of the same class. But by resolving the polymorphic structure (by adding potential use-coupling) the implemented methods of the superclass have couplings to subclasses implementing the pure virtual methods. Only the "flattened" measurement reflects the coupling to all inheritance sub-trees. Neglecting these additional couplings could yield the false clustering to separate some concrete implementations from the interface and also from a client class. This view on a system based on potential use-coupling changes measurement values in a very interesting way because it shows coupling that is not necessary for compiling (all four superclasses of the last example are compilable without including any other class of the analysed system) but for runtime (otherwise there would be linker errors).

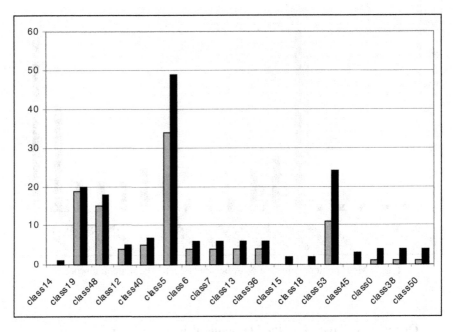

Fig. 8. Measurement values of effCM before and after the flattening process

4.4   Quantitative Analysis of the Flattening Process on Cohesion Metrics

In Figure 9 the measurement values of *LCOM* are displayed for usual and for the flattened version. As explained in Section 3.4., these value changes are not very informative because of the conceptual weakness of *LCOM*. Thus, this diagram we present only for completeness.

Much more information is available by examination of flattening for our second kind of cohesion. A 3D-visualisation (cf. [6]) based on the values calculated from the flattened version reflects better our knowledge about the measured system. Because of the difficulties to reproduce the 3D-visualisation in black/white printing, in the following we use a 2D-representation of the same data. Two classes having a shorter distance are more cohesive than two classes having a longer distance. The absolute position of a class is not interpretable but its distances from other classes. In Figure 10 this visualisation is shown for the usual system; in Figure 11 the flattened version is presented.

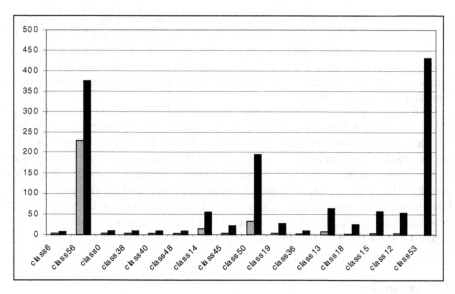

Fig. 9. Measurement values of LCOM before and after the flattening process

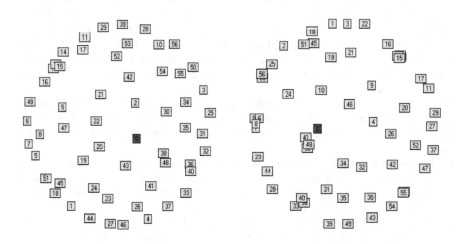

Fig. 10. Distance based cohesion before
         Flattened

Fig. 11. Distance based cohesion after
         flattened

The first impression is that the flattened version has more clusters of classes like classes {41, 48, 38 (partly hidden)}, {5, 6, 7, 8}, {55,50 (hidden)} or {56, 53 (partly hidden)}. The latter cluster is the one whose cohesion values increase most, i.e. the distance decreases from 0.958 to 0.001 (cf. the interval –0.95 to –1 within Section 3.4). This are the same classes that attracted our attention in the interpretation of the *NoM* and *NoA* values (classes 53 and 56). In fact, a class that inherits from another class and adds or modifies nearly nothing is very cohesive to its superclass because they are nearly identical. They provide the same functionality, they have the same coupling, etc.

On the other side there exists one class pair whose distance increases from 0.605 to 0.939, i.e. their cohesion decreases (class53 with class54 having no superclass, i.e. that is not mentioned in the other considerations). In this case the client class54 has an object of the subclass class53 as member and uses some functionality from it. However, class53 inherits a lot of functionality from its superclass that is not used by class54, i.e. the cohesion between class53 and class54 decreases. Unfortunately, the superclass of class53 is a reused class adapted by inheritance. A good restructuring would be to reduce at least the visibility of methods of the superclass that are not used within class53 or to reuse the class by aggregation.

5   Summary

Measuring object oriented systems without considering the possibility to distribute functionality and data over several classes within an inheritance structure is only one view. We have motivated the view in which every class is changed to its flattened presentation, i.e. inherited members are also considered, because it gives another interesting view on a system. Afterwards we have presented a concept for the programming language C++ that explains, how this flattening process should work in detail. There we concentrated on how to handle inherited attributes, inherited methods, how to resolve polymorphism, and how corresponding flattening functions have to be defined.

These concepts are implemented in the metrics engine Crocodile allowing us to get experience with our new flattening concept. Within our case study we validated our hypothesis that this new view on a system might be helpful by the following three points:

1. Within the non-flattened version, we detected many classes whose interpretation of the measurement values would be misleading. If the view on a system that is presented by the measurement values might suggest false interpretations, a further view seems to be useful.
2. With the flattened version we detected many classes that indeed showed some anomalies and that indeed would be good candidates for restructuring. Nevertheless, there also exist constraints in this version that made us marking some outliers as difficult and not necessary to change, e.g. using standard classes like *FlexLexer*.
3. Considering the differences between the measurement values of the flattened and non-flattened version produces another interesting view on a system. This information gives new insights into the kind of inheritance, e.g. if inheritance is

used only for source code sharing, for defining an interface or for creating type hierarchies.

Because of the very interesting results of this work we will investigate in porting our concepts to other object oriented languages like Java. First experiences of the application to large Java projects like JWAM (cf. http://www.jwam.de) looks very promising, especially for the visualisation within our generic cohesion concept.

References

1. Briand, L.C., Daly, J.W., Wüst, J.: A unified framework for cohesion measurement in object-oriented systems. Fraunhofer Institute for Experimental Software Engineering, Technischer Bericht ISERN-97-05 (1997)
2. Chidamber, S., Kemerer, C.: A metrics suite for object oriented design. IEEE Transactions on Software Engineering, 20(1994)6, 476-493
3. Erni, K., Lewerentz, C.: Applying design-metrics to object oriented frameworks. In: Software metrics symposium, IEEE Computer Society Press (1996) 64-74
4. Henderson-Sellers, B.: Object-oriented metrics – measures of complexity. Prentice Hall, New Jersey (1996)
5. Köhler, G., Rust, H., Simon, F.: Understanding object oriented software systems without source code inspection. Published in Proceedings of Experiences in reengineering workshop, Edited by Oliver Ciupke, Karlsruhe (1999)
6. Lewerentz, C., Löffler, S., Simon, F.: Distance based cohesion measuring. In: Proceedings of the 2nd European Software Measurement Conference (FESMA) 99, Technologisch Instituut Amsterdam (1999)
7. Lewerentz, C., Rust, H., Simon, F.: Quality - Metrics - Numbers - Consequences: Lessons learned. In: Reiner Dumke, Franz Lehner (Hrsg.): Software-Metriken: Entwicklungen, Werkzeuge und Anwendungsverfahren. Gabler Verlag, Wiesbaden (2000) pp. 51-70
8. Lewerentz, C., Simon, F.: A product metrics tool integrated into a software development environment. In: Proceedings of object-oriented product metrics for software quality assessment workshop (at 12th ECOOP), CRIM Montreal (1998)
9. Lorenz, M. Kidd, J.: Object-Oriented Software Metrics – A practical guide. Prentice Hall, New Jersey (1994)
10. Meyer, B.: Object-oriented Software construction. Prentice Hall, London (1988)
11. Meyer, B.: Object-oriented software construction. 2nd ed., Prentice Hall, London (1997)
12. Schildt, H.: C++: The Complete Reference. 3rd edition, McGraw-Hill, Berkeley (1998)
13. Simon, F., Beyer, D.: Considering Inheritance, Overriding, Overloading and Polymorphism for Measuring C++ Sources. Technical Report 04/00, Computer Science Reports, Technical University Cottbus, May (2000)
14. Zuse, H.: A framework of software measurement. de Gruyter, Berlin (1998)

Measuring Object-Orientedness: The Invocation Profile

Peter Rosner[1], Tracy Hall[2], and Tobias Mayer[1]

[1]Centre for Systems and Software Engineering, South Bank University,
Borough Rd, London SE1 0AA, UK
+44 207 815 7473
rosnerpe@sbu.ac.uk
tobias@sbu.ac.uk
[2]Department of Computer Science, University of Hertfordshire, Hatfield,
Hertfordshire, AL10 8AB, UK
hallt@herts.ac.uk

Abstract. This paper introduces the *invocation profile* as the basis for a suite of metrics to indicate the presence and mix of object-oriented mechanisms in a system written in an object-oriented language. This addresses concerns of practitioners and stakeholders that object-oriented mechanisms should be adequately exploited in such a system and gives an indication of the skills needed by developers for system enhancement and maintenance. An outline is given of plans to implement this metrics suite for systems written in Java.

1 Introduction

In this paper we describe a set of metrics based on an *invocation profile*—the counting of method invocations belonging to different invocation categories within a system written in a statically typed object-oriented programming language such as C++ or Java. The counting is of invocation occurrences in source code rather than the dynamic counting of invocations in a running system. Future work is planned to implement these metrics for systems written in Java.

Our previous work [15], [16] has surveyed existing metrics suites and concluded that, amongst other deficiencies, they fail to address adequately differences between the OO (object-oriented) paradigm and its function-oriented counterpart.

This is a serious problem. As Booch [6] points out, without the object-oriented conceptual framework, you may be programming in an OO language "...but your design is going to smell like a FORTRAN, Pascal or C application. You will have missed out on or otherwise abused the expressive power of the object-oriented language you are using for implementation. More importantly, you are not likely to have mastered the complexity of the problem at hand."

Whether a system written in an OO language is in fact utilising the object-oriented concepts of the language is therefore of interest to practitioners and stakeholders alike. Of interest also is how these concepts combine within the application code-giving, for example, an indication of the skills required in developing and maintaining the application.

R. Dumke and A. Abran (Eds.): IWSM 2000, LNCS 2006, pp. 18-28, 2001.
© Springer-Verlag Berlin Heidelberg 2001

To help address these questions—whether and how the object paradigm is being used—we propose that the invocation profile be constructed by counting and classifying method invocations within a system's source code at the method, class and system levels. Central categories within the profile are

- Procedural-type invocation
- Inheritance-based invocation
- Abstraction invocation

The components of each of these categories can be recombined into different categories to give different measures of interest within a system. These include measures of polymorphism at work; how functionality is extended via inheritance as against using remote objects; and the proportion of remote invocations that are abstract or 'pure interface'.

Our central hypothesis is that profiles at the method, class and system levels based on counts of different types of method invocation help practitioners and stakeholders address such questions as:

1. To what extent are the concepts of object-orientation used in a system?
2. To what extent is composition as against inheritance being used to enhance the functionality of a class?
3. To what extent is there programming to interface or abstract class rather than to concrete class?

2   Using the Invocation Profile

Using the invocation profile for a particular system is envisaged to be a heuristic activity—systems in different application domains, belonging to different organisations, making use of different class toolkits, and with differing expectations of re-use, cannot be expected to be directly comparable.

We therefore anticipate that the invocation profile, instead of being a direct or definitive indicator of quality, will rather be used in the pragmatic spirit of "assessment and diagnosis" [12]. We envisage the comparison of invocation profiles for systems within system type (toolkit, application, framework), application domain, and organisation. Deviations from past patterns observed in invocation profiles within such categories would prompt further investigation at the appropriate method, class or system level.

It is also envisaged that the invocation profile will be extremely useful in assessing the mix of skills required to maintain and develop a particular system. In many cases a critical factor affecting the maintainability and extendibility of methods, classes or a whole system may not be the inherent complexity of the code as measured by existing product metrics suites. It may rather be whether developers assigned to the task have mastered the OO concepts inherent in the design of the relevant methods, classes or the whole system. Henderson-Sellers [12] refers to this factor contributing to *overall* complexity as "programmer characteristics".

The invocation profile is also expected to support overall assessments of system characteristics such as modifiability and decomposability and thus aid in decisions about a system's future development direction.

In the following section we give the definitions for each type of invocation and indicate the categories into which they fit. In section 4 we outline a set of metrics based on elements of the profile. In section 5 we compare our proposed metrics with other existing approaches to object-oriented metrics. In section 6 we outline plans to implement the metrics set for systems written in Java.

3   The Invocation Profile-Definitions

Procedural-Type Invocation

A *procedural-type* invocation is one that does not cross the boundary of the current object or current class. The term is used to indicate that the invocation is conceptually similar to an in-module call to a procedure in a non-object-oriented language. For a developer with an understanding of purely procedural concepts such invocations should be easily understandable.

In the context of a judicious blend of invocation of inherited methods and message passing between objects, cohesive procedural-type invocations within a class are indeed part of a well-designed OO system. Different blends of all these features will occur within different types of application. However a predominance of procedural-type invocations over other categories at a system level should at least be cause for further investigation to establish whether there has indeed been under-use or abuse of the language's expressive power.

Also included in the procedural-type invocation category are invocations of class-wide methods (denoted by *static* in Java) and other invocations of 'global' methods.

Object-Based Invocation

An *object-based language* [19] supports the construction of systems composed of objects each embodying data and associated methods. An object incorporates the principle of abstraction/encapsulation. The functionality of the system is achieved by cooperative message passing between the objects. An object's data and methods are specified by its abstract data type, but there is no class inheritance.

An *object-based invocation* in an OO language is therefore defined to be a invocation on a remote target object where the method invoked always resides in the class to which the target object is typed in the calling method. (The term *remote* in this paper refers to an object other than the invoking object). Cases where the method invoked is located in an ancestor class, via inheritance, or else is potentially in a descendant class, via the virtual mechanism, do not therefore qualify as object-based invocations. It should be noted here that even though a method may be virtual in a class (in Java all methods are virtual), the virtual mechanism only potentially comes into play at run-time if there is at least one method with the same signature actually defined in a descendant class.

Inheritance-Based Invocation

Inheritance extends the object-based concept. Inheritance enables a new class to be derived from another. In the new class, instance variables may be added and methods may be added or replaced to give greater or altered functionality. Methods of the superclass can be overriden completely within the subclass, or else an overriding method itself can invoke its corresponding superclass method via language-specific constructs (e.g. *super* in Java). Inheritance implies self-reference—an inherited operation can refer to the receiving object (implicitly or explicitly via *this* in Java). *Inheritance-based invocation* has five flavours:

1. A descendant class directly invoking a method of an ancestor class.
2. In the case of a non-remote invocation, an ancestor class invoking a virtual method (abstract or non-abstract) which may cause actual invocation of an overriding method in a descendant class. If the virtual method is abstract, such deferred invocation in a descendant class will always occur.
3. Remote invocation of a method in a class that is ancestor to the one to which the target object is typed.
4. Remote invocation of a non-abstract virtual method in the class to which the object is typed, which may cause actual invocation of an overriding method in a descendant class.
5. Remote invocation of an abstract method in an abstract class. Note that this type of invocation is also classified under abstraction invocations (see below).

Earlier writings on object-orientation emphasised the need for a language to support both abstraction/encapsulation *and* inheritance in order for it to qualify as 'object-oriented'[6], [19]. According to Booch [6], "If a language does not provide for direct inheritance, then it is not object-oriented". According to this criteria, object-based invocations within a system written in an OO language are not exploiting the full features of the language.

However more recently writers and practitioners have placed more emphasis on *composition* rather than inheritance as a means of extending class functionality. Composition fits well within the object-based concept. It allows for run-time mixing and matching of functionality. Within the growing body of design patterns [10], [11], the composition approach predominates. (In fact Gamma et al [10] after Lieberman [14] show that composition can be used to completely replace implementation inheritance through *delegation*, trading off increased run-time flexibility against potentially worse performance and lower understandability when compared to extension via inheritance).

The result therefore has undoubtedly been a reduction in the over-reliance on implementation inheritance as an extension mechanism.

Abstraction Invocation

An *abstraction invocation* is defined as a remote invocation of an abstract method—one where only the method signature is specified for the artefact to which the target object is typed in the calling method. The actual method invoked is determined by the class of the target object at run-time. In C++ such an abstract method is termed 'a pure virtual function' [17]; in Java it is termed an 'abstract method'.

Loose coupling between classes is achieved by, for example, typing parameters and return values in methods to artefacts that are not concrete classes and performing abstract invocations on such object references. This approach, not emphasised in early OO writing and practice, is now another of the focuses within current design approaches and the design patterns already mentioned above. There is now general agreement that abstraction invocation results in systems that are more "flexible, extensible and pluggable" [9], thus achieving a major goal of object systems.

Abstraction invocations fall into two sub-categories pure interface invocations and abstract class invocations.

Pure interface invocation

In typed OO languages such as C++ or Java, it is possible to define a 'pure interface' artefact consisting only of abstract method declarations—enabling a variable, typed to the pure interface, to reference objects belonging to any conforming classes—not restricted to any one part of the class hierarchy. In C++ such a pure interface is a *specification class* composed only of pure virtual functions, the *class* construct still being used as if it were a normal class. Multiple inheritance in C++ allows a specification class to act as a pure interface for a class anywhere in the class hierarchy. In Java a special language construct *interface* is provided consisting only of abstract methods. Although a class in Java can inherit from only one other class, it can additionally implement multiple interfaces.

A *pure-interface invocation* is therefore defined as an abstract invocation via a reference to a pure interface such as a specification class in C++ or an interface in Java.

Interestingly recent advances in the software technology to build distributed heterogeneous systems fall within the approach of programming to pure interface. For example the interface definition languages for distributed systems built around the OMG's Common Object Request Broker Architecture (CORBA) and Microsoft's COM and DCOM component architectures involve the definition of pure interfaces with no method bodies. Similarly for distributed all-Java systems using Remote Method Invocation (RMI), remote methods are accessed via interface only.

Another related emerging technology has been that of software components which enable pre-built binary units of software to be configured and deployed within a system. Whilst such components need not necessarily be constructed using object-oriented technology, "object technology if harnessed carefully, is probably one of the best ways to realise component technology" [18]. Components rely on pure interface with associated strict contracts for communication.

Remote abstract invocation

Unlike a pure interface, an abstract class is tied in to the inheritance hierarchy of a system. The same mechanism for sharing of implementation via inheritance is used for providing the flexibility of enabling a reference to be bound to objects of different classes. Abstract method invocations *from within* a class have been categorised under inheritance-based invocations only.

However *remote abstract invocations*—remote invocations of abstract methods in abstract classes—have been included under both the categories abstraction invocations *and* inheritance-based invocations; while they can only be realised in the context of the inheritance features of an OO language, from the developers viewpoint they also share features in common with pure interface invocations.

Summary of Invocation-Types

Table 1 below gives a summary of the invocation types defined so far, with an allocation of a unique keyword for each type.

4   Proposed Set of Metrics

Having defined the details of our invocation profile we now define a set of metrics based upon it. It should be noted that unlike many metrics which aim to measure coupling, e.g. [1], [2], [3], [4], [8] or response-for-class, e.g. [8], our aim is to show design paradigms and approaches at work. We therefore deliberately specify counting *all* invocation occurrences (in the source code, not at run time) corresponding to an invocation type, irrespective of repetitions.

Table 1. Summary of invocation types with keywords

Type of invocation	keyword
Invocation of a method defined locally in the current class	LOCL
Remote invocation of a method which is always implemented in the class to which the target object is typed	REM
Invocation of a method defined in an ancestor class	INH
Invocation of an abstract or non-abstract method that is overriden in at least one descendant class	VIR
Remote invocation of a method which is defined in an ancestor of the target class	REMINH
Remote invocation of a method in a non-abstract class, where the method is overriden in at least one descendant class	REMV
Remote invocation of an abstract method in an abstract class	REMA
Remote invocation of a method in a pure interface	REMI

The metrics are to be applied to a specified set of application classes that in general would not include "stable classes"—that is classes in supplied and tested class libraries or infrastructure classes already tested and imported for use in the system. However detection and measurement would be applied to calls *from* the specified application classes to such stable classes.

We propose the following set of derived metrics based on such detections, although other metrics could also be derived.

1. *invocation type metrics,* giving the mix of the various control-flow paradigms at work in the application: procedural, object-based, inheritance-based, abstraction and pure interface.

2. *remote vs inherited,* the relative weight of remote method invocations against remote and inherited method invocations. This gives an indication of the extent to which the design relies on remote objects as against inherited classes for extending functionality.

3. *polymorphism ratio*, the relative weight of virtual, remote-virtual, remote-abstract and pure-interface method invocations against all non procedure-type invocations
4. *abstraction in remote*, the relative weight of abstraction invocations to all remote invocations
5. *interface in remote*, the relative weight of pure-interface invocations to all remote invocations

Each metric is applied first at the method level and then generalised to the class and system levels. Invocation-type metrics

Invocation counts

We first specify the raw counts of invocation types upon which the measures are based. For method i within class j the following counts of invocations are

all method count = $calls_{ij}$
procedural-type count $proc_{ij}$ = total in LOCL
non-inheritance object-based count ob_{ij} = total in REM
inheritance-based count inh_{ij} = total in INH, REMINH, VIR, REMV, REMA.
abstraction count abs_{ij} = total in REMA, REMI
pure interface count if_{ij} = total in REMI.

Invocation ratios

We now use these raw counts to give their ratios within all method invocations

procedural ratio $procratio_{ij}$ **=** $proc_{ij}/calls_{ij}$
object-based ratio $obratio_{ij} = ob_{ij}/calls_{ij}$
inheritance-based ratio $inhratio_{ij} = inh_{ij}/calls_{ij}$
abstraction ratio $absratio_{ij} = abs_{ij}/calls_{ij}$
pure interface ratio $ifratio_{ij} = if_{ij}/calls_{ij}$

Similarly $calls_j$, $proc_j$, ob_j, inh_j abs_j and if_j can be measured for the corresponding counts in the code for class j. The ratios for these are $procratio_j$, $obratio_j$, $inhratio_j$, $absratio_j$, $ifratio_j$.

Finally *calls*, *proc*, *ob*, *inh*, *abs* and *if*, and corresponding *procratio*, *obratio*, *inhratio*, *absratio*, *ifratio* would be the measures of counts and ratios at the system level for all classes specified for measurement.

Remote versus Inherited Metric

The metric *remote versus inherited* determines the relative weight of remote invocations against remote and inherited method invocations. Using the notation defined in the previous section, for method i within class j:

total remote invocations $remall_{ij}$ = total in REM, REMINH, REMV, REMA, REMI
total inherited invocations inh_{ij} = total in INH
remote versus inherited
$remtoinhratio_{ij} = remall_{ij}/(remall_{ij} + inh_j)$

Corresponding measures at the class level are *remall$_j$, inh$_j$, reminhratio$_j$* and at the system level they are *remall, inh, reminhratio*

Polymorphism Ratio

The *polymorphism ratio* determines the relative weight of polymorphic invocations against all non procedure-type invocations. For method i within class j

polymorphic invocations $poly_{ij}$ = total in VIR, REMV, REMA, REMI categories
non procedure-type invocations
   $nonproc_{ij} = calls_{ij} - proc_{ij}$
Ratio of polymorphic calls against all remote calls
   $polyratio_{ij} = poly_{ij}/nonproc_{ij}$

Similarly for class j there is the corresponding measure *polyratio$_j$* and at the system level it is *polyratio* .

Abstraction in Remote

The *abstraction in remote* metric determines the relative weight of abstraction invocations against all remote invocations. For method i in class j the abstraction in remote metric is given by

$$absinremote_{ij} = abs_{ij}/rem_{ij}$$

Similarly for measures *absinremote$_j$* for class j, and *absinremote* at the system level.

Interface in Remote

The *interface in remote* metric determines the relative weight of pure-interface invocations against all remote invocations. For method i within class j

$$ifaceinremote_{ij} = if_{ij}/remall_{ij}$$

Similarly for measures *ifaceinremote$_j$* for class j, and *ifaceinremote* at the system level.

5   Comparison with Other Metrics

Of the many different object-oriented design metrics suites proposed over the past ten years none provide an unambiguous way of determining the degree and mix of object-oriented concepts within a system.

Existing OO design metrics suites, the best known of which are the Chidamber & Kemerer suite [7], [8] and the MOOD metrics [1], [2], [3], [4] clearly have their roots in traditional (function-orientated) metrics. The issue of what kind of system is being measured is largely ignored.

Traditional design attributes such as coupling, cohesion and size provide much of the focus for current OO metrics. While it is undoubtedly important to assess such aspects of an OO system, alongside more OO-specific attributes such as encapsulation, abstraction and inheritance, it is also important to understand what kind of system is being measured.

Certain of the metrics do go some way towards determining the concepts being used, but can also give misleading results. For example, as we have noted the pure-interface concept, implemented in Java by means of the *interface* artefact, can be simulated in C++ using multiple inheritance of 'pure specification' classes. Such systems would likely result in high values for metrics that count ancestors or descendants yet implementation inheritance is not used at all in the pure-interface concept. This may well create confusion when analyzing the metrics results.

Likewise, OO 'coupling' metrics such as CBO [8], COF [2] and DCC [5] focus on counts of classes or methods that are targets of invocations rather than on all 'message sends'. (The 'message passing coupling' metric MPC proposed by Li and Henry [13] does however appear to be equivalent to our count of all remote invocations *remall*).

Systems with high values for coupling metrics that simply count target classes or target methods will not necessarily be systems where significant inter-object communication predominates in the design. To their credit, the proponents of these metrics have clear intentions as to what is being measured (e.g. class reusability in the case of DCC). The metrics are certainly not intended to identify the underlying OO concepts. However, assessment of such attributes is inextricably tied in to the concept or concepts being used.

Our proposed suite of metrics based on the invocation profile helps to fill this gap.

6   An Automated Tool for Java Systems

In future work we plan to build a tool for implementing, for Java-based systems, the metrics outlined in this paper. The user would specify the set of classes to be measured and each method would be parsed to detect method calls, including calls to methods in stable classes outside of the classes under measurement. The parsing mechanism will need to detect and count nested method calls, as well as calls of the form

```
super.method(), this.method().
```

Constructors will be included in the parsing. Calls to *super()* in constructors will be treated as inherited method calls. Calls to *static* class-wide methods will be treated under the LOCL category.

For remote method calls the type of the target (concrete class, abstract class, interface) will need to be deduced either from the type of the variable denoting the target object or in the case of nested method calls, via the type of the returned object from another method call.

Abstract methods will be detected via the *abstract* keyword, and pure interface methods will be those inside *interface* definitions.

7   Conclusions

We have described a proposed set of metrics we feel address more closely than existing metrics the issues of concern to those involved in the development of a system using an object-oriented programming language. Whilst not providing a direct indication of quality in a system, results from our metrics suite should prove useful in exploring and assessing the object-oriented mechanisms at work and the degree to which the power of the language is being exploited.

Our next task is to prove the usefulness of these proposals through implementing them in a tool for Java systems and applying them in practice.

References

1. Abreu, F.B., Carapuça, R.: Candidate metrics for object-orientated software within a taxonomy framework. Proc. AQUIS'93 Conference, Venice, Italy (1993)
2. Abreu, F.B., Carapuça, R.: Object-orientated software engineering: measuring and controlling the development process. Proc. 4th Int. Conf. On Software Quality, McLean, VA, USA (1994)
3. Abreu, F.B., Goulão, M., Esteves, R.: Toward the design quality evaluation of object-orientated software systems. Proc. 5th Int. Conf. On Software Quality (1995)
4. Abreu, F.B., Melo, W.: Evaluating the impact of object-orientated design on software quality. Proc. 3rd International Software Metrics Symposium (METRICS'96), IEEE, Berlin, Germany (1996)
5. Bansiya, J., Davis, C.: Automated metrics and object-orientated development. Dr Dobb's Journal, (1997)
6   Booch, G.: Object-oriented analysis and design. 2nd edition, Addison Wesley (1994)
7. Chidamber, S.R., Kemerer, C.F.: Towards a metrics suite for object-orientated design. Proc. Sixth OOPSLA Conference (1991) 197-211
8. Chidamber, S.R., Kemerer, C.F.: A metrics suite for object-orientated design. IEEE Transactions on Software Engineering, 20(1994)6, 47
9. Coad, P., Mayfield, M.: Java Design, Building Better Apps and Applets. Yourdon Press Computing Series (1999)
10. Gamma, E., Helm, R., Johnson, R., Vlissides, J.: Design Patterns, Elements of Reusable Object-Oriented Software. Addison-Wesly Professional Computing Series (1995)
11. Grand, M.: Patterns in Java. 2 Vols, Wiley (1998)
12. Henderson-Sellers, B.: Object-oriented metrics, measures of complexity. Prentice Hall (1996)
13. Li, W., Henry, S.: Object-oriented metrics that predict maintainability. J. Sys. Software (1993) 111-122
14. Lieberman, H.: Using prototypical objects to implement shared behaviour in object-oriented systems. Object-oriented Programming systems, Languages and Applications Conference Proceedings, Portland, OR, November (1986) 214-223
15. Mayer, T.G., Hall, T.: A critical analysis of current OO design metrics. Software Quality management VII: Managing Quality, C. Hawkins, G. King, M. Ross, G. Staples (Eds.), London, British Computer Society (1999) 147-160
16. Mayer, T.G., Hall, T.: Measuring OO systems: a critical analysis of the MOOD metrics. Tools 29, (Procs. Technology of OO Languages & Systems, Europe '99), R. Mitchell, A. C. Wills, J. Bosch, B. Meyer (Eds.): Los Alamitos, Ca., USA, IEEE Computer Society (1999) 108-117
17. Stroustrup, B.: The C++ Programming Language. 2nd Edition, Addison Wesley (1991)

18. Szyperski, C.: Component Software, Beyond Object-Oriented Programming. Addison Wesley (1998)
19. Wegner, P.: Concepts and paradigms of object-oriented programming. OOOPS Messenger 1(1990) 7-87

CEOS – A Cost Estimation Method for Evolutionary, Object-Oriented Software Development

Siar Sarferaz[1] and Wolfgang Hesse[2]

[1]microTOOL GmbH, Voltastr. 5, D–13349 Berlin, Germany
Tel.: +49-030-467086-0
Siar.Sarferaz@microTOOL.de

[2]FB Mathematik/Informatik, Universität Marburg, Hans Meerwein-Str.,
D-35032 Marburg, Germany
Tel.: +49-6421-282 1515, Fax: +49-6421-282 5419
hesse@informatik.uni-marburg.de

Abstract. In this article we present a method for estimating the effort of software projects following an evolutionary, object-oriented development paradigm. Effort calculation is based on decomposing systems into manageable building blocks (components, subsystems, classes), and assessing the complexity for all their associated development cycles. Most terms of the complexity calculation formulae carry coefficients which represent their individual weights ranging from factors for particular features up to general influence factors of the project environment. These coefficients can continuously be improved by statistical regression analysis.

Outstanding features of the method are its flexibility (allowing estimations for project portions of any size) and its capability to deal with dynamic adjustments which might become necessary due to changed plans during project progress. This capability reflects the evolutionary character of software development and, in particular, implies revision, use and evaluation activities.

1   Introduction

Estimating the effort and costs for software projects has turned out to be an important competition factor in the market of individual software development - mostly due to the increasing proportion of fixed-price projects demanded by the customers. Many empirical investigations have shown that time and cost budgets are frequently exceeded (cf. e.g. [4] and [12]) mostly due to too optimistic estimations. Thus an as precise as possible cost estimation is a decisive prerequisite for economical and successful software project management.

However, due to many factors of uncertainty reliable cost estimation is a very difficult task. As an immaterial and always changeable product, software is hardly to be quantified. Estimating the development effort implies taking care of many product-specific influence factors (like product complexity and quality) as well as process-specific ones (like use of methods and tools, quality of teams and organisation), which altogether increase the difficulties.

R. Dumke and A. Abran (Eds.): IWSM 2000, LNCS 2006, pp. 29-43, 2001.
© Springer-Verlag Berlin Heidelberg 2001

There are several cost estimation methods some of which have been widely disseminated and experienced (as, e.g. Function Point [1] or COCOMO [2]). Most of them follow the basic principle of *"Break down - sum up"*: The functionality of the intended system is broken down to smaller better manageable units (e.g. called "functions"), the complexity of which is estimated and then summed up and modified by one or several factors representing general system and project characteristics. Only very few methods are suited for object oriented (OO-) software development. For example, H. Sneed with his Object Point method tries to apply the basic idea of Function Points to the "OO world" [11]. Besides its well-acknowledged benefits we see three major deficits of this method:

(1) Like the Function Point method it relies on a variety of subjective assessments which are weighted by numerical coefficients given by the method in a sometimes arbitrary and doubtful way.

(2) Some of its calculation methods (as e.g. the treatment of quality influence factors) are hardly to understand and would require some revisions to be used in practice.

(3) There are no provisions for dynamic assessments and estimation adaption according to the growing knowledge and possible changes during project progress.

Traditional cost estimation methods were based on the then popular paradigms of functional decomposition and phase-driven development. Object-oriented methods have emphasised the ideas of data-based decomposition, reuse and component-driven development. Thus we have based our method on a process model (called EOS, cf. [5,6,7]) which follows the basic principles of *object orientation through all stages of development, hierarchical system architecture, component-based development cycles, software evolution through use and revision* and which emphasises a *recursive and orthogonal process structure*. This structure offers high flexibility for modular system development, use and reuse of already existing components as well as for project management but it requires rather sophisticated planning, coordinating and estimating procedures and instruments.

In the following sections we start with a short summary of our process modelling approach (section 2) and then present the CEOS method in three steps corresponding to the EOS levels of software development: class level, component level, system level (section 3). In the fourth section implementation issues are addressed and some conclusions for further work are drawn.

2   EOS – A Component-Based Approach to Software Process Modelling

In contrast to most traditional, waterfall-like software life cycle models (and even many process models for OO development as, for example, Rational's Unified Process), the EOS model does not emphasise a phase-driven but a component-oriented development approach (cf. fig. 1). Among others, this approach has the following implications:

– The principal criterion for structuring software development processes is no longer their phases (cf. the upper part of fig. 1) but a *hierarchy of system building blocks* (in EOS called *components, classes and subsystems*) representing a static view on the system architecture (cf. the lower part of fig. 1).

- Components and subsystems are the central structural units of the system architecture which are not only used to group smaller units (e.g. classes) to larger logical units but also for organisational reasons as e.g. delegation of a component to a particular person or to a small team responsible for its development and maintenance, planning of associated activities or storage and support for retrieval in a component library. Subsystems are (normally non-disjoint) collections of classes grouped together for joint execution during test and system integration.
- Each building block has its own *development cycle* consisting of four main activities called *analysis, design, implementation* and *operational use* (cf. fig. 2).
- In contrast to traditional waterfall models, new building blocks may be formed - and corresponding development cycles are enacted - at any stage of the development. A new development cycle may interrupt an already existing one or it is evolving in parallel. Concurrent development cycles are coordinated by project management with the help of *revision points*. Thus the traditional phase structure dominating one overall, system-wide development process is replaced by a collection of concurrent, individual development cycles for all building blocks under construction.

For further details cf. [5,6,7].

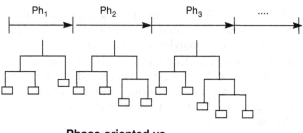

Phase oriented vs ...

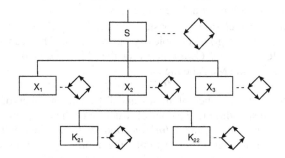

... Component oriented process structure

Fig. 1. Two approaches to structure the software process

According to the hierarchy of software building blocks, three levels of granularity can be distinguished which are also important for the following cost estimation procedures: (a) *the system level,* (b) the *component level* and (c) the *class level.*

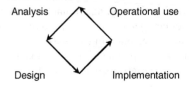

Analysis   Operational use

Design   Implementation

Fig. 2. Structure of an EOS development cycle

3   The Cost Estimation Model: General Assumptions

In this section we present our CEOS (Cost estimation for EOS project) method. It is based on a proposal of P. Nesi and T. Querci for estimating the development effort of object oriented systems [9]. Some basic assumptions of this approach are:

–   The effort needed for developing a piece of software depends on its complexity in a linear way.
–   The complexity of a software building block depends on the complexity of its *ingredients* (e.g. smaller, contained building blocks or other structural units) which can be weighted by individual *coefficients.*
–   The quality of an estimate depends on the fitness and preciseness of the used coefficients. These can continuously be improved by using "real life" data from earlier projects and statistical regression analysis techniques [10]. In a running project, data gathered from terminated phases or activities can be used to improve the current estimates.
–   Particular coefficients can be defined and used for tailoring estimates to certain segments or iterations of a development cycle.
–   For detailed calculations, a basic metric (denoted „m" in the sequel - for quantifying the program complexity) is required. This can e.g. be the well-known *LOC (Lines Of Code) metric* or the *McCabe metric.* In the sequel we use a variant of the McCabe metric:

$$MCC = |E| - |N| + 1,$$

where $|N|$ is the number of nodes and $|E|$ is the number of edges in a flow diagram corresponding to the control structure of the program.

We distinguish metrics for the *definition complexity* and the *application complexity* of classes and their attributes. For example, the application complexity is used in the metrics for inheritance, association and aggregation relationships. The (definition) complexity of a class to be developed is calculated from the complexity of its attributes and operations which may involve the application complexity of other (used) classes. The application complexity value is always less than the corresponding definition complexity value.

In order to facilitate the presentation, we start with two preliminary assumptions:
(1) For each building block, the corresponding development cycle is executed *exactly once*.
(2) We are interested in *total estimates* covering the effort for all activities of a development cycle.

These assumptions will be leveraged in later sections.

4   Metrics for the Sub-Class Layer

The following table (fig. 3) lists the metrics which are introduced in this section.

Metric	Name	Metric	Name
Attributes		**Operations**	
AC_m^{App}	Attribute Application Complexity	MC_m^{App}	Method Application Complexity
AC_m^{Def}	Attribute Definition Complexity	MC_m^{Def}	Method Definition Complexity
		MBC_m^{App}	Method Body Complexity (Application)
		MBC_m^{Def}	Method Body Complexity (Definition)
		MIC_m^{App}	Method Interface Complexity (Application)
		MIC_m^{Def}	Method Interface Complexity (Definition)
		MLA	Number of Method Local Attributes

Fig. 3. Metrics for the sub-class layer

4.1   Attribute Metrics

We define know the metrics AC_m^{App} and AC_m^{Def} to measure the complexity of attributes. The letter „m" stands for a basic metric, the abbreviations „App" and „Def" refer to application and definition complexity, respectively.

Let A : *ClassA* be an attribute of type „*ClassA*".

Definition I (*Attribute Application Complexity*):
$$AC_m^{App} = K, \text{ where } K \in IR^+ \text{ is a constant.}$$

Definition II (*Attribute Definition Complexity*):
$$AC_m^{Def} = CC_m^{App} (ClassA)$$

CC_m^{App} is a metric for measuring the class definition complexity, which is defined below. Note that in the definition of CC_m^{App} the metric AC_m^{App} is used thus avoiding any circular definition.

4.2   Operation Metrics

Let $F (A_1:C_1, ..., A_n:C_n) : C_{n+1}$ be a method interface, where F is a method identifier, A_i are attribute identifiers and C_i are class identifiers. Further let A_{n+1} be an (anonymous) attribute of type C_{n+1}, which stands for the return value of the method.

Definition I (*Method Application Complexity*):
$$MC_m^{App} = MIC_m^{App} + MBC_m^{App}, \text{ with}$$

$$MIC_m^{App} = \sum_{i=1}^{n+1} AC_m^{App}(A_i) \quad \text{and} \quad MBC_m^{App} = \sum_{i=1}^{NMLA} AC_m^{App}(A_i) + m$$

NMLA stands for the number of locally defined attributes of a method.

Definition II (*Method Definition Complexity*):
$$MC_m^{Def} = w_{MICm} MIC_m^{Def} + w_{MBCm} MBC_m^{Def}$$

The metrics MIC_m^{Def} und MBC_m^{Def} can be defined analogously to MIC_m^{App} and MBC_m^{App} by replacing AC_m^{App} with AC_m^{Def}.

w_{MICm} and w_{MBCm} are coefficients to be determined by the statistical technique of robust regression (cf. below).

5   Metrics for the Class Layer

Each class is subject to a development cycle consisting of the activities analysis, design, implementation and operational use. According to the project progress along these activities more data become available which can be used for refined effort calculations. Therefore different metrics apply - corresponding to the time of estimation. Note that all given metrics refer to the *total* effort for the class development.

Metric	Name	Metric	Name
Class layer			
CC_m^{App}	Class Application Complexity	$InCC_m$	Inherited Class Complexity (implementation)
CC_m^{Def}	Class Definition Complexity	LC_m	Local Class Complexity (analysis)
CCA_m^{App}	Class Application Complexity during Analysis activity	LCC_m	Local Class Complexity (design)
CCA_m^{Def}	Class Definition Complexity during Analysis activity	$LoCC_m$	Local Class Complexity (implementation)
CCD_m^{App}	Class Application Complexity during Design activity	NDP	Number of Direct Parents
CCD_m^{Def}	Class Definition Complexity during Design activity	NIC	Number of Inherited Classes
CCI_m^{App}	Class Application Complexity during Implementation activity	NLA	Number of Local Attributes
CCI_m^{Def}	Class Definition Complexity during Implementation activity	NLM	Number of Local Methods
CU_m	Class Usability	$NPuCA$	Number of Public Class Attributes
IC_m	Inherited Class Complexity (analysis)	$NPuCM$	Number of Public Class Methods
ICC_m	Inherited Class Complexity (design)		

Fig. 4. Metrics for the class layer

5.1 Analysis Activity

Definition I (Class *Application* Complexity during *Analysis* activity):
$$CCA_m^{App} = NLA + NLM \text{ (number of local attributes and methods)}$$

Definition II (Class *Definition* Complexity during *Analysis* activity):
$$CCA_m^{Def} = LC_m + IC_m, \text{ with}$$
$$LC_m = w_{NLAm} \ NLA + w_{NLMm} \ NLM \qquad \text{and} \qquad IC_m = w_{NICm} \ NIC.$$

w_{NLAm}, w_{NLMm} and w_{NICm} are coefficients for weighting the local and inherited elements, respectively.

5.2   Design Activity

Let A_i, M_i and C_i be the i-th attribute, method or class, resp.. The complexity of a class depends on the complexity of its features, i.e. of its attributes and operation interfaces. For class definitions, the complexity of local features (LCC) and of inherited features (ICC) are considered.

Definition I (Class *Application* Complexity during *Design* activity):
$$CCD_m^{App} = \sum_{i=1}^{NLA} AC_m^{App}(A_i) + \sum_{i=1}^{NLM} MIC_m^{App}(M_i)$$

Definition II (Class Definition Complexity during *Design* activity):
$$CCD_m^{Def} = LCC_m + ICC_m, \text{ with}$$

$$LCC_m = w_{LACm} \sum_{i=1}^{NLA} AC_m^{Def}(A_i) + w_{LMCm} \sum_{i=1}^{NLM} MIC_m^{Def}(M_i)$$

$$ICC_m = w_{ICCm} \sum_{i=1}^{NDP} CCD_m^{App}(C_i) + NIC(C_i)$$

5.3   Implementation Activity

Let A_i, M_i and C_i be the i-th attribute, method or class, resp.. Again, the complexity of a class is derived from the complexity of its features, but now the implementation-specific values and coefficients are taken.

Definition I (Class *Application* Complexity during *Implementation* activity):
$$CCI_m^{App} = \sum_{i=1}^{NLA} AC_m^{App}(A_i) + \sum_{i=1}^{NLM} MC_m^{App}(M_i)$$

Definition II (Class *Definition* Complexity during *Implementation* activity):
$$CCI_m^{Def} = LoCC_m + InCC_m, \text{ with}$$

$$LoCC_m = w_{LoACm} \sum_{i=1}^{NLA} AC_m^{Def}(A_i) + w_{LoMCm} \sum_{i=1}^{NLM} MC_m^{Def}(M_i)$$

$$\text{InCC}_m = w_{\text{InCCm}} \sum_{i=1}^{NDP} CCI_m^{App}(C_i) + NIC(C_i)$$

5.4 Operational Use Activity

Normally, no new calculations are done during operational use. The results of the estimations should be assessed (i.e. compared to the actual values) and documented. The coefficients should be validated and adjusted, if necessary. In case of a repeated development cycle, a new estimation of the next cycle is required (see below).

5.5 Metrics for Reuse

Reuse of classes is not for free but requires some effort, e.g. for understanding and adapting the reused code and documentation. Therefore we define a metric for class usability.

Definition (*Class Usability*): Let A_i and M_i be the i-th attribute / method of a class.

$$CU_m = w_{CU} \left(\sum_{i=1}^{NPuCA} AC_m^{App}(A_i) + \sum_{i=1}^{NPuCM} MC_m^{App}(M_i) \right)$$

With this definition, we can now give a general definition for the complexity of a class CC_m^{Def} (CC_m^{App} can analogously be defined by replacing „Def" with „App").

$$CC_m^{Def}(C) = \begin{cases} \text{constant,} & \text{if } C \text{ is a system-classe} \\ CCA_m^{Def}(C), & \text{if } C \text{ is analysed} \\ CCD_m^{Def}(C), & \text{if } C \text{ is designed} \\ CCI_m^{Def}(C), & \text{if } C \text{ is implemented} \\ CU_m(C), & \text{if } C \text{ is reused} \end{cases}$$

If class C is a specialisation of class S, S plays the role of a reused class and thus $CU_m(S)$ will be assigned to $IC_m(C)$ as the inheritance complexity of C.

5.6 Example: Application of the Metric CCD_m^{Def}

Now we illustrate the application of the CCD_m^{Def} (Class Definition Complexity during Design activity) metric by a brief example.

During the class design activity the static structure of classes and their relationships ismodelled and described by class diagrams. This information can be used to determinate the complexity of classes. As an example, we consider a simplified class diagram for a system managing bank accounts (fig. 5).

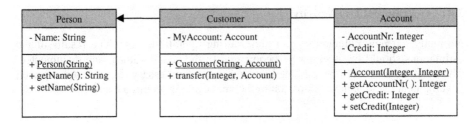

Person	Customer	Account
- Name: String	- MyAccount: Account	- AccountNr: Integer - Credit: Integer
+ Person(String) + getName( ): String + setName(String)	+ Customer(String, Account) + transfer(Integer, Account)	+ Account(Integer, Integer) + getAccountNr( ): Integer + getCredit: Integer + setCredit(Integer)

Fig. 5. A simple class diagram

Now we apply the CCD_m^{Def} metric on the class „Customer". We assign to elementary types (like „Integer" or „String") the complexity value $K = 1$.

$$CCD_m^{Def} \text{ (Customer)} \qquad = LCC_m \text{ (Customer)} + ICC_m \text{ (Customer)}$$

$$
\begin{aligned}
&LCC_m \text{ (Customer)}\\
&= w_{LACm} \, AC_m^{Def}\text{(MyAccount)} + w_{LMCm} \, (MIC_m^{Def} \text{ (Customer)} + MIC_m^{Def} \text{ (transfer)})\\
&= w_{LACm} \, CC_m^{App}\text{(Account)}\\
&\quad + w_{LMCm} \, (AC_m^{Def} \text{ (String)} + AC_m^{Def} \text{ (Account)} + AC_m^{Def} \text{ (Integer)} + AC_m^{Def}\\
&\quad \text{(Account))}\\
&= w_{LACm} * 7 + w_{LMC} *(1 + 7 + 1 + 7) = w_{LACm} * 7 + w_{LMC} * 16
\end{aligned}
$$

Here, for example, AC_m^{Def} (MyAccount) $= CC_m^{App}$ (Account) $= 7$ is calculated by counting the two attributes and the 5 parameters of the methods - all being of elementary type.

$$
\begin{aligned}
&ICC_m \text{ (Customer)}\\
&= w_{ICCm} \, (CCD_m^{App} \text{ (Person)} + NIC \text{ (Person)})\\
&= w_{ICCm} \, (AC_m^{App} \text{ (Name)} + MIC_m^{App} \text{ (Person)} + MIC_m^{App} \text{ (getName)} + MIC_m^{App}\\
&\quad \text{(setName)} + 0)\\
&= w_{ICCm} \, (CC_m^{App} \text{ (String)} + AC_m^{App} \text{ (String)} + AC_m^{App} \text{ (String)}) + AC_m^{App}\\
&\quad \text{(String))}\\
&= w_{ICCm} \, (1 + 1 + 1 + 1) = w_{ICCm} * 4
\end{aligned}
$$

$$CCD_m^{Def} \text{ (Customer)} \qquad = w_{LACm} * 7 + w_{LMCm} * 16 + w_{ICCm} * 4$$

6   Metrics for the Component and System Layer

The following table (fig. 6) summarises the metrics defined in this section.

Metric	Name	Metric	Name
Component layer		**System layer**	
NXC	Number of Component Classes	**NSX**	Number of System Components
XC$_m$	Component Complexity	**SCA$_m$**	System Complexity during Analysis phase
XCA$_m$	Component Complexity during Analysis activity	**SCA$_r$**	System Complexity coarse Analysis
XCA$_r$	Component Complexity coarse Analysis	**SCD$_m$**	System Complexity during Design phase
XCD$_m$	Component Complexity during Design activity	**SCI$_m$**	System Complexity during Implementation phase
XCI$_m$	Component Complexity during Implementation activity		
XU$_m$	Component Usability		

Fig. 6. Metrics for the Component and System layer

6.1   Component Metrics

One of the characteristics of the EOS method is its component-based process architecture. Components are collections of classes and as such have development cycles analogous to those of classes. Since the corresponding metrics have a similar structure, we restrict ourselves to compact definitions.

Let C_i be the i-th class of a component X

Definition (Component Complexity during *Analysis / Design / Implementation* activity):

$$\text{XCY}_{\text{m}} = w_{\text{XYm}} \sum_{i=1}^{NXC} CCY_m^{Def}(C_i) \text{ , where } Y = A(\text{nalysis}), D(\text{esign})$$

or I(mplementation).

Again, particular coefficients w_{XYm} are used for refinement and correction purposes on this level.

If (e.g. in the early stages of a project) only the rough number NXC of classes contained in a component is known, a coarse estimation can be performed using the metric XCA_r.

Definition (Component Complexity *coarse Analysis*): $\text{XCA}_r = w_x \text{ NXC}$

For the operational use of components, similar considerations apply as in the class case.

A reused component is a collection of reused classes   - which leads us the following metric:

Definition (Component Usability): $$\text{XU}_{\text{m}}(X) = w_{\text{XU}} \sum_{i=1}^{NXC} CU_m(C_i)$$

6.2   System Metrics

In a similar way, a system is viewed as a collection of components and its metrics is derived from their ones. Again we give a compact definition which is to be specialised according to the activities of a system development cycle.

Let X_i be the i-th component of a system S.

Definition (System Complexity during *Analysis / Design / Implementation* phase):

$$\text{SCY}_{\text{m}} = w_{\text{SYm}} w_{\text{Quality}} \sum_{i=1}^{NSX} XCY_m(X_i) \text{ , where } Y = A(\text{nalysis}), D(\text{esign})$$

or I(mplementation).

A first coarse estimation can be performed with the metric SCA_r.

Definition: (*System Complexity coarse Analysis*): $\text{SCA}_r = w_s \ w_{\text{Quality}} \text{NSX}$

In addition to the coefficients w_{SYm} and w_s, we consider a quality factor w_{Quality} on this layer. This factor can, for example, be calculated with the help of a quality characteristics table similar to the one adopted by H. Sneed from [8] for his Object Point method [11].

During the operational use of a system, no refinements of the calculations apply but estimation results should be assessed and documented, coefficients should be validated and adjusted, and the effort for a next cycle is to be estimated, if required.

6.3   Determining the Coefficients

In order to keep the CEOS method flexible, we weighted the metrics with coefficients. Different coefficients may be used to reflect the particular work conditions of different companies and institutions. Coefficients are to be determined from earlier projects using the statistical technique of regression analysis. As real data frequently contain outliers, traditional methods, like Gauss's least square technique, would easily distort the results. To avoid this problem, new statistical techniques - called robust techniques - have been developed which provide quite good results even if a certain amount of data is unreliable. For CEOS we chose the LMS (Least Median of Squares) method - one of the best possible methods from a theoretical point of view. In the following we present only the *estimator* for the LMS method.

Least Median of Squares (LMS)

Let n be the number of given data elements and ε_i represent their deviations from corresponding values f_i of a approximation function f. Then f has to be chosen in such a way that the Median of Squares

$$\underset{i=1,\dots,n}{med}\ \varepsilon_i^2$$

adopts a minimum .

Fig. 8. LMS estimator

7   Extending the Model to Multiple Cycles and Partial Estimates

The metrics introduced so far were based on the assumptions of (a) unique and (b) always complete development cycles (cf. end of section 3). Both restrictions can now be dropped in a straightforward way - at least if the required statistical data are available. If an estimation for an incomplete cycle is required (e.g. in case of calculating the rest effort for an already started cycle) particular coefficients may be used which cast the total effort to a particular activity. Such coefficients can be determined from statistical data on the proportion of effort required for each particular activity. Since the size and hierarchy level of a building block essentially influence this proportion, statistical data should be gathered separately for the class, component and systems layers.

If p development cycles are planned for a particular building block (with p > 1), this can be used for calculating proportional efforts for each particular cycle. The simplest way would be to assume a constant factor 1/p for each cycle, but other more sophisticated factors might be derived from statistical data collected during prior projects.

8   Prototype Implementation and Conclusions

In the preceding sections, we have presented an effort calculation and cost estimation method which is based on a component-oriented process model and architecture. A simple prototype has been implemented which explores the user interface and demonstrates some basic functions of the CEOS method. A complete implementation which supports all the presented calculations and which implies the use of statistical techniques will be the next major step in the ongoing CEOS project.

We are aware that applying the CEOS method is not easy since it starts from a rather sophisticated process model and - at least if one expects precise results - it requires encompassing data collections and rather complex calculations. But on the other hand it offers the following advantages:

- It considers development cycles (instead of simple phases) and thus addresses modern software development paradigms like software evolution or component-based development.
- Cost estimations can be done for complete projects or for any of their parts. Parts are the building blocks defined according to the software architecture in form of components, classes or subsystems. Partial estimations can be done and used for time, budget or personnel planning on any level of detail.
- For any building block, the total effort for one development cycle or the partial effort for any particular activity can be calculated as well as the effort for several development cycles concerning the same building block.
- The CEOS method supports particular object-oriented techniques like inheritance or reuse of classes and components.
- Most calculation formulae contain coefficients which allow to tailor all estimations to the particular conditions and requirements of the institution concerned. Coefficients can be adapted to specific influence factors like quality requirements, personnel qualification, customer familiarity or tool support. Continuous adaptation of the coefficients according to the most recent available statistical data make the method a valuable tool for dynamic project management and evolutionary software development.

In a current Ph.D. project, the CEOS method is enhanced and further implemented with the aim to extend an existing UML-oriented development tool ("objectiF" of microTOOL GmbH) by a powerful management tool to be used in software practice.

References

1. Albrecht, A.J.: Measuring Applications Development Productivity. In: Proceedings of IBM Applications Devision Joint SHARE/GUIDE Symposium, Monterey, CA (1979) 83-92
2. Boehm, B.W.: Software Engineering Economics. Prentice Hall (1981)
3. Dumke, R., Abran, A.: Software Measurement / Current Trends in Research an Practice. Wiesbaden: Deutscher Universitätsverlag (1999)
4. van Genuchten, M.: Why is Software Late? An Empirical Study of Reasons For Delay in Software Development, In: IEEE Transaction on Software Engineering 17(1991)6, 582-590
5. Hesse, W.: Life cycle models of object-oriented software development methodologies. Marburg: A. Zendler et al.: Advanced concepts, life cycle models and tools for object-oriented software development. Reihe Softwaretechnik 7, Tectum Verlag Marburg (1997)

6. Hesse, W.: Improving the software process guided by the EOS model. In: Proc. SPI '97 European Conference on Software Process Improvement, Barcelona (1997)
7. Hesse, W.: Wie evolutionär sind die objekt-orientierten Analysemethoden? Ein kritischer Vergleich. In: Informatik-Spektrum 20.1 (1997) 21-28
8. ISO/IEC 9126: Information technology – Software Product Evaluation – Quality Characteristics and Guidelines for Their Use (1991)
9. Nesi, P., Querci, T.: Effort estimation and prediction of object-oriented systems. In: The Journal of Systems and Software 42 (1998) 89-102
10. Rousseeuw, P.J., Van Aelst, S.: Positive-Breakdown Robust Methods in Computer Vision. Department of Mathematics and Computer Science, U.I.A., Belgium (1999)
11. Sneed, H.M.: Schätzung der Entwicklungskosten von objektorientierter Software. In: Informatik Spektrum 19 (1996) 133-140
12. Vaske, H.: Systemhäuser zeigen Schwäche im Support. In: Computerwoche, Nr. 11, März (1999) 9-10
13. Zuse, H.: A Framework of Software Measurement. Berlin/New York: Walter de Gruyter, (1998)

A Measurement Tool for Object Oriented Software and Measurement Experiments with It

Xinke Li, Zongtian Liu, Biao Pan, and Dahong Xing

Institute of Microcomputer Application, Hefei University of Technology,
Hefei 230009, P.R.C, China

Abstract. The research on software metrics has a long history for more than forty years, but the research on object-oriented (OO) software metrics has been going on for a few years only. C&K metrics is one of the most famous researches on OO software metrics. First, this paper analyses the shortcoming of the C&K metrics suite for object-oriented design and provides an improved metrics suite. Then the paper introduces a practical C++ measurement tool, SMTCPP, implemented by the authors based on improved metrics. SMTCPP parses C++ programs by the LL(1) method, extracts a lot of program information, such as classes, members and objects; counts the indications, such as the number of methods per class, the biggest complexity among methods, depth of inheritance tree, the number of children, coupling between object classes, response for class, and relative lack of cohesion in methods. The measure values are very useful to guide the software process. The tool may also put the values into a database to collect sufficient data for building a software quality evaluation model. Last, the paper analyses the experiments for three practical programs. The result shows that SMTCPP is useful.

1 Introduction

Metrics are key components of any engineering discipline, and object-oriented software engineering is no exception. Software metrics refer to a broad range of measurements for computer software. They can be applied to the software process with the intent of improving it on a continuous basis. They can be used in a software project to assist estimation, quality control, productivity assessment, and project control. Finally, software metrics can be used by software engineers to assess the quality of software products and to assist tactical decisions as a project proceeds.

Since metrics were proposed by Rubey and Hurtwick in 1958, software metrics were developed continuously and became an important research area in the field of software engineering. The purpose of software metrics is to evaluate software quality scientifically, to control and to manage the software development process effectively.

Halstead brought up the concept of software science in 1970. Several years later, McCabe set up a software complexity measure method based on the topological program structure. ISO/IEC 9126 and CMM, put forward by Software Engineering Institute of Carnegie Mellon University, have defined a new content of software metrics. Based on the standards of ISO/TC/SC7 and according to the models by McCall and Boeing, the Shanghai Software Center of China has developed a model

R. Dumke and A. Abran (Eds.): IWSM 2000, LNCS 2006, pp. 44-54, 2001.

and a method of a software quality measurement. Beijing University of Aeronautics and Astronautics has developed a C software metrics tool prototype based on Halstead's and McCabe's method.

In the early period of software metrics, procedure-oriented software design methods were established. The purpose of these design methods is to gain a hierarchy of software modules; the traditional software metrics are based mainly on the measurement of models. Then, the researches on software complexity measures went on and this kind of metrics became an important area of software metrics.

Yourdon and Constantine summarized a lot of elements which influence software quality seriously. These are coupling, cohesion, complexity, modeling degree and size of programs. Fory and Zweben used diagrams of the software model structure to extract 21 characteristics that were used as basis of metrics.

As OOP has some new characteristics, such as data abstraction, encapsulation, inheritance, polymorphism, information hiding and reuse, a new theory of and new methods for OOP metrics should be provided.

In 1994, Chidamber and Kemerer [1] developed a suite of six metrics (C&K metrics method) to measure the design quality of object-oriented software. The philosophical insights of these metrics are derived from the ontological primitives provided by Bunge. Brito and Abreu set up an OOD metrics method, MOOD [2], in 1995. A lot of articles have analyzed and evaluated it, such as [3] and [4]. J-Y Chen and J-F Liu introduced a new metrics method for Object-Oriented Design [5]. The method was similar to the C&K metrics method. In this field, Hefei University of Technology has been working for a long time and has developed a Java software metrics tool [6][7].

2   Software Metrics in OOD

In this article, we are going to analyze the characteristics of the C&K method, show its inadequacy and develop an improved C&K metrics method for C++.

2.1   Improved C&K Software Metrics

1) NM (the Number of the Methods) and LCM (the Largest Complexity among the Methods in a class)

According to the definition of Bunge, the complexity of a unit is "the number of the members in the unit". A class includes data members and function members. If the complexity of the data members is neglected, the complexity of a class is equal to the complexity of all function members in the class. So the C&K method introduces weighted methods per Class (WMC) as a metric.

But whether the complexity of each method is computed through the number of its lines or the number of its operators, the relation between the complexity and the number is not linear, so that WMC is not reasonable. We know the psychological 7 ± 2 principle; if the number of methods in a class is more then 7, the complexity of the class will rise rapidly with the number of methods. Similarly, if the number of LOC or the number of operators is more than a certain value, the complexity of the class will rise with the number of lines or operators. In this way, if a class has less than 7 methods and the methods have small or middle complexity, and another class has the same number of methods but the complexity of the methods is worse, thus the WMC of the two classes can be equal. But, it is obviously unreasonable to think, the two classes have the same complexity. In order to reflect the essentiality of a class more objectively, we replace WMC by two metrics, the number of methods (NM) and the largest complexity among the methods (LCM).

2) Depth of Inheritance Tree (DIT)

The C&K method defines DIT as the length of the longest path from the root class to the class that inherits from the root class. This is suitable for pure object-oriented languages, such as SMALLTALK. But for impure object oriented languages, such as C++, there may be more than one root-class in the inheritance tree. Furthermore there are a lot of class libraries in the practical development environment of a language, for example MFC in Visual C++ and OWL in Borland C++. Class libraries form a class hierarchy and the classes written by programmers are usually derived from these libraries. If DIT is defined as the length of the longest path from a root class to a class and the root is one of the class libraries, the DIT is obviously not consistent with the complexity of the class. So we define DIT as the length of the longest path from a class in a library to a class. Thus, the DIT of a class in a library is zero.

3) Number of Children (NOC) in a class

Because of multiple inheritance, it is difficult to calculate the number of children in a class. Since class A can be the first parent class of class B; at the same time, class A can be second parent class of class C, we define that NOC of class A is the sum of NOC(B) and NOC(C).

4) CBO (Coupling Between Objects) in C++

Coupling is one of the most considered inside attributes of products. It has been studied for a long time, including the periods of structured programming and object oriented programming. The C&K method defines coupling between objects (CBO) as the number of other classes coupled to the class. But, there are many kinds of coupling relationships with different effects. So the definition is simple and the counting of CBO is convenient, but the meaning of the metric is fuzzy.

5) Response for Class (RFC)

RFC is the number of methods in a class that could be invoked potentially by messages from other classes. In C++, this is the number of such methods and such operators of a class that can be acted by methods or operators of other classes. There may be two problems. First, because of the polymorphism, a message accepted by a class may come from the parents of the class, but the parents may be provided by the class libraries of the system, so the response for the message could not be discovered from source in C++. Another problem is that a lot of functions may be called by the operating system. So the RFC may be less than the real value.

6) Lack of Cohesion in Methods (LCOM)

LCOM is an inadequate attribute in a class, which should reflect the degree of the resolvability of a class. According to the C&K definition, LCOM correlates with the number of the methods in a class as our experiment proved. The larger the number of methods is, the larger the LCOM. In the example shown in Fig. 1, according to our experience, the cohesion of program C is the worst and that of program B is the best. But, by the formula of the C&K method, LCOM of programs A, B and C is 9, 5 respectively 6. This calculation is different to the intuitive estimate. So we introduce a new metric: Relative Lack of Cohesion in Methods (RLCOM). In a class choose two methods arbitrarily, which are called "method-pair". If there is cohesion between these two methods, we call these two methods a "relative-method-pair". If there is no cohesion between these two methods, we call these two methods "irrelative-method-pair". Here, RLCOM is defined to be the ratio of the number of irrelative-method-pairs to the number of all method-pairs. According to this definition, RLCOM of program A, B and C in the above example is 0.79, 0.67 respectively 1.0. This is consistent with the intuitive estimate. Obviously, a class where RLCOM is zero, presents that cohesion exists in any method-pair of this class. Contrary to this, a class, where RLCOM is 1, presents that cohesion does not exist in any method-pair of this class, and shows that this class is more complex and can be abstracted to a lot of sub-class.

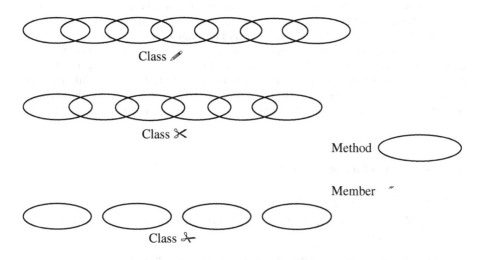

Fig. 1. Contrast to class cohesion

2.2 Other C++ Characteristics that Should be Thought Over

There are some characteristics in C++ that are not included in the C&K metrics suite, reflecting quality or complexity of software. For example:
1) Friends: They include friend classes and friend functions which provide a mechanism to access private members from outside. Their use can enhance the efficiency of a program, but it also destroys the encapsulation of a class.

2) Common and private derivation: The two kinds of derivation produce different effects for the complexity of classes, especially for derived classes of derived classes.

3   The Design Principles and the Implementation Techniques of SMTCPP

3.1   Introduction of the System

We have developed a software metrics tool for C++, SMTCPP, based on the improved C&K theory, running in the environment of Windows 95/98 or Windows NT. The functionality of the system is to scan C++ source code, to determine the improved C&K metrics and to display the class inheritance graph, the methods of a class and the source code. The results of measurements may be stored in a database to discover the relation between quality of the software and its metric values. The results may also be used to guide the maintenance and program tests.

The main window of the system consists of three parts (Fig. 2). The right part displays the source code. The lower part lists metrics results. The left part is a browser to display a file list, a class list or an inheritance tree. With help of the file list users can browse all files in a project. The class list allows users to browse all classes in the project and all members of each class. The inheritance tree shows the inherited relations between classes.

3.2   The Design Idea of SMTCPP

The design ideas of the system are:

1) to make lexical analyses and parsing of a program by scanning the source code of a program;

2) to extract the relations between methods and classes in the program;

3) to store the information in a tree construction by the inherited relations of classes;

4) to count the metrics values by passing the tree.

The work flow chart is shown in Fig. 3.

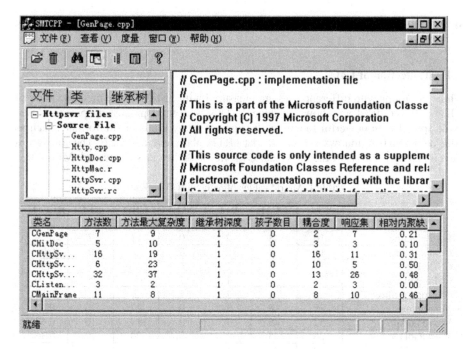

Fig. 2. Main window of SMTCPP

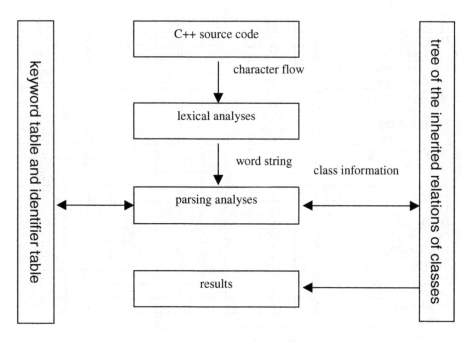

Fig. 3. Work flow chart of SMTCPP

4 The Instances of Software Metrics and Analysis of Metrics Data

4.1 Collection of Data

Three programs with different sizes are measured with SMTCP. The metrics values of Microsoft WordPad are shown in table 1. This is a word processing program used wide-spread with powerful functions. It supports many kinds of file formats, such as MS-WORD 6.0, Windows Writer, standard RTF, plain text, and OLE. The software is developed by Micro Soft Inc. in Visual C++ 4.0, with the class framework MFC 4.0.

Table 1. Metric values of Microsoft WordPad

Class Name	NM	LCM	DIT	NOC	CBO	RFC	RLCOM
CButtonDialog	16	48	2	0	11	7	0.29
CComboRulerItem	11	5	2	0	2	9	0.01
CCSDialog	7	3	1	6	7	7	0.50
CCSPropertyPage	5	2	1	2	2	5	0.50
CCSPropertySheet	5	2	1	1	2	5	0.50
CMainFrame	25	18	1	0	17	20	0.46
CWordPadApp	32	45	1	0	19	10	0.47
CWordPadDoc	26	45	1	0	20	19	0.36
CWordPadView	50	26	1	0	31	42	0.49
CWordPadCntrItem	5	1	1	0	4	3	0.50
CColorMenu	4	31	1	0	10	3	0.50
CDateDialog	7	10	2	0	4	5	0.26
CDocOptPage	5	6	2	1	3	5	0.20
CFileNewDialog	5	10	2	0	4	5	0.30
CLocalComboBox	6	11	1	2	4	2	0.50
CFontComboBox	13	36	2	0	9	5	0.49
CSizeComboBox	7	13	2	0	2	1	0.40
CFormatBar	14	21	1	0	14	10	0.20
CFormatParaDlg	5	16	2	0	4	5	0.01
CFormatTabDlg	19	12	2	0	5	11	0.07
CWordPadResizeBar	1	1	1	0	1	0	0.00
CInPlaceFrame	17	24	1	0	13	13	0.33
CKey	7	12	1	0	0	2	0.02
CListDlg	3	8	1	0	4	1	0.00
CUnit	3	9	1	0	3	2	0.17
CDocOptions	6	11	1	0	4	1	0.30
COptionSheet	4	19	2	0	4	1	0.33
CPageSetupDlg	3	9	2	0	2	3	0.17
CRulerBar	41	58	1	0	16	14	0.31
CRulerItem	20	13	1	2	9	10	0.40
CBigIcon	3	23	1	0	7	2	0.17
CSplashWnd	2	5	1	0	3	1	0.50
CEmbeddedItem	7	27	1	0	7	4	0.45
CUnitsPage	3	3	2	0	1	3	0.17
CFontDesc	1	5	1	0	3	1	0.00
Mean	11.1	16.8	1.34	0.4	7.17	6.77	0.295

The metrics results of the control and management software of a solid depository developed by the Chinese Microsoft Inc. for Shanghai tobacco factory are shown in table 2. The software reads the states of a set of located facilities from serial ports, displays the results in real time, sends control instructions to the located facilities by commendations from a control table and stores relational data into the corresponding database. The software runs on a workstation with Windows NT 4.0, and is developed in Visual C++ 4.0.

Table 2. Metrics results of the solid depository control and management software

Class Name	NM	LCM	DIT	NOC	CBO	RFC	RLOCM
CSRStstus	6	8	1	0	4	4	0.30
PLCSet	15	27	1	0	5	15	0.16
SheetClass	19	21	1	0	3	2	0.34
CBin	13	5	1	0	2	4	0.23
CMain	46	162	1	0	9	2	0.29
CMainFrame	8	40	1	0	5	8	0.50
RSSet	12	45	1	0	4	12	0.00
CSHMainApp	3	9	1	0	6	3	0.50
CSHMainDoc	6	3	1	0	3	6	0.50
CSHMainSet	6	19	1	0	6	6	0.43
CSHMainView	20	8	1	0	12	19	0.47
CMailbox	6	19	1	0	6	6	0.43
CaboutDlg	2	1	1	0	2	2	0.50
Mean	12.5	28.2	1	0	5.2	6.8	0.36

Table 3 presents the metrics results of a simple HTTP server which completes the basic functions of a HTTP server: inspecting the HTTP port of a system and responding the corresponding page by the content of a user's request after the user's request is discovered.

Table 3. Metric results of HTTP server

Class Name	NM	MACM	DIT	NOC	CBO	RFC	RLCOM
CHttpSvrDoc	16	19	1	0	16	11	0.31
CGenpage	7	9	1	0	2	7	0.21
CHttpSvrApp	6	23	1	0	10	5	0.50
CRequest	5	8	1	0	7	2	0.20
CHitDoc	5	10	1	0	3	3	0.10
CListenSocket	3	2	1	0	2	3	0.00
CRequestSocket	39	50	1	0	9	8	0.22
CHttpSvrView	32	37	1	0	13	26	0.48
CMainFrame	11	8	1	0	8	10	0.46
CNamePage	8	13	1	0	5	8	0.29
CNoRootDlg	2	2	1	0	3	2	0.00
CEnvironment	4	9	1	0	2	2	0.00
CBadRootDlg	2	2	1	0	3	2	0.00
CRootPage	8	13	1	0	3	8	0.14
CAboutDlg	2	1	1	0	2	2	0.50
Mean	10	13.7	1	0	5.9	6.6	0.23

4.2 Analysis of the Metrics Data

According to a intuitive analysis, the program difficulty of the second software package is the biggest because it needs to communicate with located facilities and to exchange data with databases. The functions of the other two software packages are much simpler. This can also be seen considering the size of the source code of the three programs. The sizes of the three programs are 281k, 596k, respectively 123k. According to the metrics results, the count of methods in the classes in the first software package is larger than the count in the second program package. The reason is, that the second program deals with a special application; many functions can not be inherited from general class libraries, for that reason most of its parts are developed by non object oriented methods. The two other programs are general applications, so they can inherit a lot of methods from class libraries.

The evaluation of the improved C&K metrics is shown in the following.

1) The number of the methods and the largest complexity of the methods in a class can preferably reflect the complexity of software. The average values of these two metrics measured in the second program are all high, this corresponds with the intuitive analysis. In addition, the largest complexity (the number of lines) of the methods in every class of the three programs is centralized between 5 to 45, this is reasonable for program development and maintenance.

2) The depth of a class in the inheritance tree may reflect the design complexity of the class. In the second and the third example the depth of each class is 1, this means first, that each class directly inherits a class in a library, and second that, either the classes are simple or their design is unreasonable. The depth of each class in the first example is 1 or 2. That means, the classes are a little more complex or their design is reasonable.

3) The number of children of a class can reflect reusability of the class. In the first example, the numbers are 1 to 6, average is 1.2. That means, the construction complexity of the program is reasonable. The reusability of the classes in this program is better than in the other two examples.

4) Overfull coupling between classes is bad for the modular design. But, in what scope should coupling be controlled? It may be a relation with the size and the application area of programs. Considering the metrics results above, the coupling of the first example is the weakest. It indicates that the construction design is more reasonable, the independence of modules is better and the maintenance of the program is more convenient.

5) The average response for class (RFC) in the tree programs is similar indicating that the complexity to respond messages is basically the same. As classes in C++ are polymorphs and they are associated with the environment, the RFC measured is smaller than the real values.

6) Table 2 shows that the counts of the number of methods, the largest complexity of the methods, the coupling, and the relative lack of cohesion in methods of class CMain are evidently larger than the others. That means this class should be emphasized for test and the class may be decomposed into sub-classes.

Otherwise, analyzing the metrics results some shortages of software metrics can be seen:

1) Though the metric results can be used to illuminate characteristics of programs qualitatively, no mapping function from the results to the characteristics has been found.

2) The metric results are quite insufficient to evaluate the quality of a program, so some subjective judgements of experts are needed for the evaluation of the program quality.

3) Since C++ is not a pure object-oriented programming language, and it is not clear how to determine the influence of the non-object-oriented components, the meaning of the metric results can be ambiguous.

4) For programs in different application areas, the metric results can have big differences.

5 Conclusions

In this article, the C&K metrics suite is improved in at least three areas: a) We introduce the new metrics NM and LCM instead of WMC. b) We define DIT as the length of the longest path from a class in a library to the class, to better reflect the complexity of a class. c) We introduce the new metric: Relative Lack of Cohesion in Methods (RLCOM), which is the ratio of the number of irrelative-method-pairs to the number of all method-pairs in the same class.

In this article, a C++ metrics tool SMTCPP with its GUI is introduced. The tool is developed according to the improved C&K metrics suite. The experiments results show the usefulness and suitability of the tool.

We are now in the process of studying how to set up a software metrics architecture based on metrics elements. The research needs to use the knowledge of statistics and neuronal networks. In addition, we are studying how to use the results of software metrics better to guide the software developing process.

References

1. Chidamber, R., Kemerer, F.: A Metrics Suite for Object-Oriented Design. IEEE Trans.software Eng., Vol. 20, No. 6 (1994)
2. Brito, F., Abreu: The MOOD Metric set. Proc. ECOOP'95 Workshop on Metrics (1995)
3. Harrison, R., Nithi, R.: An Evaluation of the MOOD Set of Object-Oriented Software Metrics. IEEE Transactions on Software Engineering, Vol. 24, No. 6, June (1998)
4. Hitz, M., Montazeri, B.; Chidamber and Kemerer's Metrics Suite: A Measurement Theory Perspective. IEEE Transactions on Software Engineering, Vol. 22, No. 4, April (1996)
5. Chen, J.-Y., Liu, J.-F.: A new metrics for Object-Oriented Design. Information and Software Technology, Vol. 35, No. 4 (1993)
6. Dahong, X., Zongtian, L.: The Metrics Theory and methods in Object-Oriented Design. Computer Science, Vol. 1 (1998)

7. Pan Biao: Rearch On C++ Object-Oriented Software Metrics. [Master's degree thesis], Hefei University of Technology (1999)
8. Chidamber, R., Kemerer, F.: Towards a for Metrics Suite Object-Oriented Design. OOPSLA'91 (1991)
9. Gustafson, D.A., Prasad, B.: Properties of software measures. In: Formal Aspects of Measurement. T. Denvir et al., New York, Springer-Verlag (1991)
10. Churcher, N.I., Sheooed, M.J.: Towards a Conceptual Framework for Object Oriented Software Metrics. ACM Softw. Eng.Notes.Vol.20, No.2, April (1995)

Estimating the Cost of Carrying out Tasks Relating to Performance Engineering

Erik Foltin[1] and Andreas Schmietendorf [1,2]

[1] Otto-von-Guericke-Universität Magdeburg, Fakultät Informatik, Institut für Verteilte Systeme, Postfach 4120, D-39016 Magdeburg,
Tel.: +49-391-6712701, Fax: +49-391-6712810,
foltin|schmiete@ivs.cs.uni-magdeburg.de
[2] T-Nova Deutsche Telekom Innovationsgesellschaft mbH, Entwicklungszentrum Berlin, Wittestraße 30N, D-13476 Berlin,
Tel.: +49-30-43577-633, Fax: +49-30-43577-460,
A.Schmietendorf@telekom.de

Abstract. The study presented here analyzes the methods currently used to estimate costs, and how these methods map the tasks related to Performance Engineering (PE) and the costs thereof. To create transparency and acceptance of these extremely important tasks within the context of software development, an approach is pursued which derives the required costs from a corresponding risk analysis and thus examines the business process to be supported, the software development and normal operation. Initial empirical studies are presented which highlight the general trends for possible costs of specific PE methods.

1 Motivation for the Study

The development of information systems which have to meet both functional and qualitative requirements requires the planning of the corresponding human and technical resources needed to carry out the associated tasks. Generally speaking, it is obvious that a system that meets high quality standards requires more development work than one with low quality requirements. However, if one has to look in more detail at the quality aspect of the system's efficiency in terms of time and space (general performance), in line with the concept of quality characteristics specified in ISO 9126, it is much harder to estimate the cost. In practice, general statements are not enough. Here, typically, a measure is needed which allows the higher performance standards to be quantified in detail and to be evaluated in terms of costs.

When developing software systems with more or less restrictive performance requirements, the current procedure generally consists of not examining the performance characteristics until the end of the development as part of the acceptance tests or a pilot operation covering a gradual introduction. The identification of performance bottlenecks at the end of the software development process therefore often calls for time-consuming tuning measures, the expensive redesign of the application, the use of more powerful hardware than had been anticipated or, in extreme cases, the entire information system ceasing to run productively at all. In

R. Dumke and A. Abran (Eds.): IWSM 2000, LNCS 2006, pp. 55-72, 2001.

addition to these generally unforeseen expenses, costs are also incurred in particular by the delayed start-up of the information system, since the planned business process is not supported.

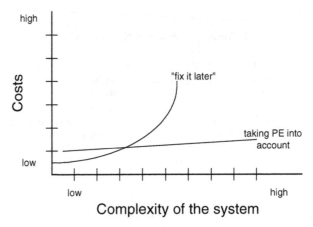

Fig. 1. Relative costs comparison: PE v. "fix it later"

There are various technical, methodic and commercial justifications for this approach. One problem is the insufficient transparency of the costs, which makes it more difficult for project managers to understand the tasks that are required for PE. This topic is to be the object of the present study. [11] compares the costs of performance engineering tasks with those of an insurance company; the necessary "premium" (or expenditure as part of the development) is far lower than the cost of nonperformaning system in normal operations.

Figure 1 shows, in general, the development of costs as a function of the complexity of the system to be developed. Whilst, with simple systems, examining performance at the end of the development (fix it later) can easily be a cheaper alternative, taking the PE tasks into account continuously can have clear cost advantages with complex systems such as distributed web applications. In addition to the complexity, the time when the performance engineering tasks are carried out has a crucial part to play in terms of the expenditure required. [11] talks about an expenditure ratio of 1:100, i.e. getting rid of performance problems after implementation can be up to 100 times more expensive than identifying and removing such problems during the early phases (analysis/design) of development.

The extent to which performance engineering methods are applied within software development phases depends largely on the degree to which these tasks are accepted or supported in the management of the relevant organization. Managers must be convinced, on the basis of cost/benefit analyses, that investments in matters relating to performance engineering help to improve risk management and to avoid the costs caused by inefficient systems. The gradual application of performance engineering methods should be determined by the costs and risks. If the expenditure is minimal or non-existent, the basis for a decision of this type should be a cost/benefit analysis. An explicit identification of the expenditure required for PE should change the fact that it is often not taken into account within software development.

2   Sources of Possible Costs in the Area of PE

The difficulty of determining the costs of performance engineering in monetary terms has already been demonstrated by [11]. The costs depend on the size and complexity of the project and on a number of other factors. In particular, given the constantly increasing costs pressure on software development, performance engineering methods can only be applied if, firstly, the costs involved are made transparent and, secondly, the benefits can be quantified.

The term 'performance engineering' is taken to mean sets of methods to support the performance-oriented development of application systems throughout the entire software development process to guarantee an appropriate, performance-related product quality [8]. Possible costs thus can be detected at an early stage if corresponding performance engineering methods are applied. The following aims to examine a number of selected methods, the application of which can be observed primarily within PE.

In early project phases, information about the costs of an information system is required; such costs will include hardware and software plus operating expenses. In the software development phases (analysis, design, implementation), the requirement is to refine the system concept to the point that information can also be provided on response times and throughput in relation to concrete application functions/interfaces and the related use of resources.

In the first place, it is possible to examine the following methods (the use of which causes the actual costs within PE), which are used to carry out PE tasks:

Rules of thumb are based on a conclusion drawn by making an analogy between the application systems that are already in use and the load and performance characteristics observed in these systems. This method can consequently only be used if suitable experiential values are available, i.e. if there is an empirical background available through the use of corresponding measurement databases. The results relate primarily to cost models for the later information system. On the other hand, concrete information on performance behaviour is not generally possible.

Modelling studies the performance behaviour of real systems through the use of strongly abstracted models, such as queue models or time-based Petri nets which are examined by analysis or simulation to determine their performance behaviour. The essential condition for modelling is the sufficient degree of penetration of the functionality of the information system and the derivation or estimation of model variables. Performance models that are constructed, and the corresponding results, should be subjected to validation using the real systems and be expressed in concrete terms if necessary. The findings obtained in this way should similarly be saved as experiential values.

Measurements   imply a need for an up-and-running system (completed application or system implemented as a prototype) consisting of hardware and software. Typically, these are carried out as part of a benchmarking program or during the ongoing operation of an information system within extensive system management solutions (e.g. Open View Performance Collection Software). One system that is particular interesting for performance engineering is the use of application benchmarks. Using load driver systems, extensive user functions can be simulated, which means that reproducible performance analyses are possible. Through synchronously recording internal and external performance measurements, tuning can be supported, on the one hand, and, on the other, performance behaviour can be estimated from the user's point of view.

One of the most important tasks that performance engineering has to carry out is the **instrumentation** of application functions that are critical for performance. This involves the programmed incorporation of measurement points using standardized interfaces, such as are offered, for example, by ARM-API. In later operation, suitable system management solutions can be used to determine the execution times along the complete interaction chain (from the end-user viewpoint, up to the reaction time of individual object methods).

Basically, irrespective of the method used, the **load model** is required as the input variable for performance studies. Performance-related UseCases (specialist functions) of the application system are to be taken as a basis in terms of the expected load profile (time, quantity and location framework).

In addition, there are other methods that support the tasks listed. Examples of these are using the results of standard benchmarks (e.g. TPC or SPEC) within the scope of rules of thumb, using monitors to record internal performance measurements or also using pilot installations to build up experience with the performance behaviour of a new application.

3   Methods of Estimating Expenditure and Risk

The first methods for estimating expenditure were developed and industrially applied in the 1970s. Whilst early versions of these methods largely failed to consider qualitative aspects. current versions take quality into consideration at least as a factor influencing expenditure for development. Typical examples of this are the **Function Point Method** or the **COCOMO** process. The following intends to analyze how far both methods take the expenditure for performance engineering into consideration. In addition, the study also examines a proposal which tries to deduce expenditure from performance-related risks.

The Function Point Method

The Function Point (FP) method is a process that has been in use (in various forms) for over 20 years for estimating the functional scope of information systems. The approach described here takes into account the current version of the "Function Point Counting Practices Manual" [5]. The approach taken by the Function Point method to determine this scope is to estimate total functionality from the complexity and number of business incidents that the system to be analyzed carries out.

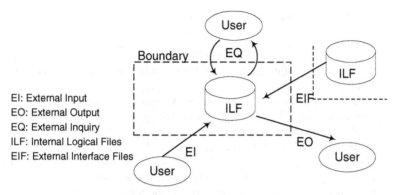

Fig. 2. Elements of the FP method

Figure 2 shows the basic elements for evaluating using the FP method. The boundaries of the system with the outside world are defined. Beyond these boundaries, users communicate with the system, using external inputs to enter new data in the system, which is then stored in the system's internal data (Internal Logical Files). This data is then used to generate outputs (External Outputs) or is output again (unprocessed) in parts through External Inquiries. For the processing logistics, it may be necessary for data files of other systems to be used (External Interface Files).

When carrying out evaluations using the Function Point method, the task is firstly to identify these transactions (inputs, outputs and inquiries) and data files (internal and external files). After this, the individual function types are subjected to a complexity evaluation. It is depicted on an ordinal scale with three complexity levels (low, average and high), which basically depends on the size of the function type in question, shown through the number of data elements and the number of referenced files (in the transactions) or identifiable data groups (with data files). A numerical value (the function point) is then assigned, in turn, to these complexity levels (depending on the function type). The total of all the function points determined is generated, which then forms the evaluation of the total system, expressed n Unadjusted Function Points.

As can already been from the figure and the description, the Function Point method initially does not offer any approach for assessing specifically performance-related aspects of the system. These aspects are then taken into account when the adjusted function points are determined from the unadjusted function points (UFP), with the application of a correction factor (the Value Adjustment Factor, VAF). They are determined using the simple formula:

$$AFP = VAF * UFP \qquad (1)$$

The correction factor VAF is in turn made up of the evaluation of 14 system characteristics. Of these, two in particular are relevant in the context of performance aspects. These are an estimate of the demands that the user makes of performance. As with all system characteristics, the valuation of these aspects is undertaken on an ordinal scale, using the values one to five. These values represent the following characteristics:

Table 1. Characteristic C3 - User requirements for performance

Value	Meaning
0	The user does not have any special requirements in terms of performance.
1	Performance requirements have been listed and rated, but no special action was necessary
2	Response time behaviour is critical in peak load times. No special requirements for CPU load distribution have been listed. The computer result must be available on the following working day.
3	Response time behaviour is critical during the entire system running time. No special requirements for CPU load distribution have been listed. Interfaces to other systems are to be taken into account.
4	In addition, user requirements for performance require a special performance analysis.
5	In addition, the use of performance analysis tools during design, realization and/or implementation were necessary to guarantee that the user's performance requirements are met.

A second system characteristic of the Function Point method which could be affected by performance requirements is the transaction rate:

Table 2. Characteristic C5 – Transaction rate

Value	Meaning
0	No special maximum transaction rate is expected.
1	A maximum transaction rate is expected in certain longer periodic intervals (monthly, quarterly, annually)
2	A maximum transaction rate is expected on a weekly basis.
3	A maximum transaction rate is expected once a day.
4	High transaction rates listed in the requirements or in the Service Level Agreements mean that performance studies must be carried out in the design phase.
5	High transaction rates listed in the requirements or in the Service Level Agreements mean that performance studies must be carried out in the design phase and, in addition, the use of performance analysis tools during design, realization and/or implementation.

The total of 14 influencing factors are totalled to determine the Total Degree of Influence (TDI). This is then used to determine the Value Adjustment Factor for VAF=(TDI * 0.01) + 0.65. From the formula given above for the adjusted function points, it can be seen that 0.65 * UFP <= AFP <= 1.35 * UFP.

On the other hand, if one takes into account only the two performance-specific characteristics given, the resultant range is only 0.95 * UFP <= AFP <= 1.05 * UFP. This means that performance-specific requirements for the information systems only increase the functional scope, determined by the Function Point process by 10 percent. If one continues to assume a linear connection between the determined size of a system in function points and the likely production expenditure, it will be seen that performance requirements require an expenditure that is on average max. 10 percent higher.

The advantage of taking into account performance requirements in the function point method is that these requirements are shown in the functional scope of the system observed. From a pragmatic viewpoint, the assessments of the system characteristics seem to undervalue performance requirements. The value lies primarily in the concept of structuring and adjusting the performance requirements.

COCOMO – Constructive Cost Model

Another expenditure estimating procedure (COCOMO II, see [1]) follows a different approach. Here, performance requirements do not influence the estimate of the scope of the system to be produced; instead they influence the parameters for the expenditure estimate model. Expressed in simplified form, COCOMO uses rule of thumb formula in the following form:

$$PM = A * (SIZE)^B *EM \qquad (2)$$

The value of A is a constant, SIZE is the (estimated) size of the system (in LOC), the exponent B is made up of several scaling factors which are largely determined by the development environment.

The actual performance requirements are reflected in the Effort Multiplier EM. This is (in the detailed Post Architecture Model) the product of 17 factors. Two of these factors relate to "classic" aspects of performance engineering - demands made in terms of memory requirements and execution time.

The requirements for execution time are expressed as the proportion of computer capacity that is expected to be used by the system compared with the total computer capacity available. Depending on the results of this estimate, requirements are classed from "nominal" to "extra high" on an ordinal scale with 4 steps. Nominal means that the system typically uses may. 50% of the computer capacity available, whilst "extra high" is defined as a 95% utilization of the capacity available. The requirements for memory performance are shown in a similar way. In [1] these influencing factors are adjusted as follows, calibrated using a data base of 83 projects:

Table 3. Adjustment of influencing factors in the COCOMO model

	Nominal	High	Very High	Extra High
TIME	1.00	1.11	1.31	1.67
STOR	1.00	1.06	1.21	1.57

If, in the above estimation formula for determining expenditure, these two effort multipliers along are taken into consideration (with all others being set to the nominal value of 1.00), the maximum effort multiplier is 2.62. This means that, according to COCOMO II, it can be assumed that extremely high demands in terms of memory requirements and computer time requirements can increase the expenditure for production of the system by more than a factor of two and a half. This model does not take into account the fact that differently characterized performance requirements will have an effect on the size of the system to be created.

Analysis of Performance-Related Risk

The aim of the procedure proposed by [9] is to derive the costs required for performance engineering tasks from a risk analysis. Firstly, risks are identified within the development which could cause the system to be unproductive, and secondly, risks are determined which could occur at the moment of active operation.

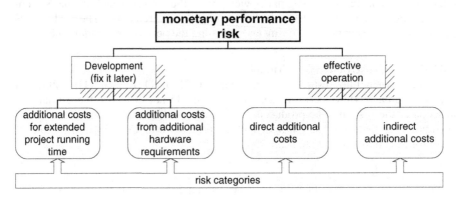

Fig. 3. Classification of cost-related performance risk

A risk analysis should be carried out at the beginning of every new software development project. Firstly, the qualitative risks in accordance with the above-mentioned risk categories should be determined. These must then be assigned a corresponding monetary basic risk, which is derived from experiential values or variables that can be measured. In a further step, the basic risk must be adjusted by means of a factor to reflect its probability of occurrence. In this way, the effective risk can be quantified and the total risk calculated on an summary basis.

– The project running time may be extended through the need for a redesign or extensive tuning measures, because, for example, the performance characteristics of services used (e.g. security) were not explicitly taken into account in the design. A frequent problem is the need for more sophisticated hardware than had originally been anticipated, so that the investments required, and also the costs of normal operation, are higher than had been calculated when planning the total system.

– If performance problems occur within normal operation, these will always have an effect on the performance of the business process. The consequences may be, for example, a reduction in staff productivity, delays in the business process or consequential losses within the entire process chain which can also cause a deterioration in the corporate image.

Overall, the expenditure estimate methods currently used only offer marginal help in estimating special expenditure for performance engineering. These approaches are actually only suitable if a collection of historical data is available for calibration of a productivity model and the appropriate performance requirements can be assigned to this data. Specific aspects of performance engineering, such as expenditure for the use of special test methods, the incorporation of special hardware or tools or the consideration or preparation of effective algorithms are not covered by the current expenditure estimate models. Instead, they try to depict the various factors in an (ordinal) assessment. In addition, expert knowledge is required. The most desirable thing would be a clear delineation of the influencing factors which allow empirically based experiments in the longer term.

4   Empirical Studies

In the literature, the following statements regarding expenditure on performance engineering can be found. [11] compares the costs of SPE[1] with the cost of insurance; the premium required is much smaller than the costs of the possible damage. Her recommendation is that, with a 50 to 100 person project, one person should be made explicitly responsible for SPE tasks. In general, she sees the real expenditure for SPE as usually being less than 1%, although this could be much higher. Capers Jones proposes that 3 % on average of a project budget should be allocated to SPE.

Table 4. Recommendations for PE expenditure

Expenditure estimate methods			Expert reports	
Function Point [5]	Object Point[2] [12]	Cocomo [1]	Smith [11]	Jones [6]
max. 10%	max. 33%	max. 250%	usually below 1%	average 3%

Table 4 compares recommendations for expenditure to be set aside for performance engineering. It is noticeable that there are considerable deviations between the expenditure estimate methods and expert reports. The correlation proven by Barry Boehm in connection with the development of the Cocomo method, which states that the increase in product quality is in a non-linear ratio to expenditure, can also be seen in the area of the performance criteria of the Cocomo model.

The following aims to give some results of empirical studies. Altogether, 21 performance analyses ((17 benchmarks and 4 modellings), carried out within around 4 years, were observed.

The execution period for the benchmarks was at least 2 weeks and at most 6 months. Figure 4 shows the project phases when the benchmarks studied here were carried out. In so far as benchmarks were carried out within software development, they were either used to verify performance characteristics of the complete application before introduction or to evaluate singular techniques, such as middleware, web servers or database management systems.

The four performance modellings carried out required much less effort than the benchmarks. However, it only makes sense to use these if comprehensive empirical performance results are available for the techniques to be mapped in the model. One of these performance modellings is described in [10]. This is the model of a Web-based client/server system with a browser-based client, an Apache web server and an Oracle database which is accessed via the CGI interface. Two different tools (SES-strategizer and BEST/1-predict) were used to create and solve the model. Setting p and running the performance model required an effort of 1 person-month each time, largely irrespective of the tool used.

---

[1] SPE Software Performance Engineering

[2] OP Object Point – the quality requirements for time and space efficiency were taken into account

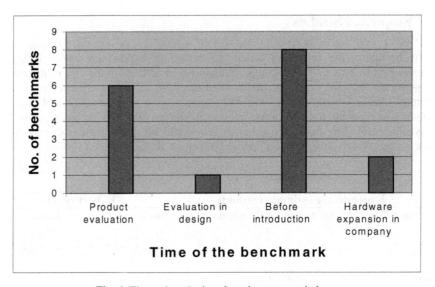

Fig. 4. Time when the benchmarks were carried out

Table 5. Average work required for the use of PE methods

System size	Benchmark	Modelling	Measurement/ Analysis	Estimate
small	3.0 PM	0.5 PM	0.5 PM	0.1 PM
medium	6.0 PM	1.0 PM	1.0 PM	0.2 PM
large	12.0 PM	2.0 PM	2.0 PM	0.5 PM

Classification of Project Size:

- **Large project** – Application has a multi-phase client/server architecture which integrates all sorts of different products. The complex business cases provide corresponding test scenarios. More than 500 users work with the application in parallel.

- **Medium-sized project** – This is a max. 3-phase client/server architecture; max. 3 products are to be incorporated into the performance observations. More than 500 users work with the applications in parallel.

- **Small project** – This is a simple IT architecture with 1-2 protocol interfaces and simple test scenarios. Fewer than 500 users work with the system in parallel. A corresponding test data stock is available.

In addition to the human resources requirements, there are also costs for the necessary hardware infrastructure (computer systems and networks) and for the appropriate software licenses.

In particular, the running of application benchmarks should be offered on a centralized basis, as a service for development projects, because of the considerable costs in large companies (IT department more than 2000 staff). Small development houses should make use of the services of external suppliers. Performance engineering tasks that are integrated into the software development projects should be limited to the use of model-based processes, estimates and instrumentation. If the execution of such benchmarks is justified by the risks identified, staff from the development project and staff from the benchmark service-provider should work together in a team.

5   Identifying Performance-Related Risks

In general, by analogy with [11], the following situations can be determined in which it is absolutely essential to explicitly consider the performance characteristics in order to avoid the risk of a nonperforming system:

- IT systems which fulfil vital functions (e.g. flight computers in airplanes or systems used for medical applications),

- IT systems with which a limited performance have a direct influence on the value creation of the business process supported (e.g. stock exchange systems),

- IT systems that use new technologies which cannot be assessed in terms of their performance-related behaviour,

- IT systems with a high transaction load (e.g. a large number of users working in parallel) or large database stocks.

The idea, developed in [9], of identifying risks along the time course of a project basically with development and normal operation will be expanded in the following. Basically, 3 "affected elements" can be identified where the occurrence of a performance risk will cause losses. Firstly, these are **primary risks** in relation to the business process and **secondary risks** which could occur within the framework of development and normal operation. The aim of the assessment model shown below is to determine the potential risks for the elements concerned.

Ideally, it should be possible to back this assessment model up with objective measured figures. Since, however, the necessary measurement models are not available, or their use would involve unrealistically high financial expenditure, we propose, as the initial assessment model, a catalogue of questions based on the frequently used assessment method.

In the first phase, the questions should be rated on an ordinal scale, whereby one possible scaling could cover values from "0-not true at all" to "5- absolutely true". Both the question of adjusting the individual categories against each other and also adjusting the factors within the category itself are not currently being studied. Our interest focuses more on a **classification** of the individual performance-related risks so that we can carry out a structured investigation.

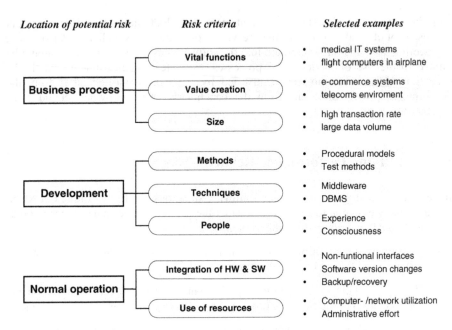

Location of potential risk   *Risk criteria*   *Selected examples*

Fig. 5. Assessment model for performance risks

1   ASSESSING THE PERFORMANCE RISKS OF A BUSINESS PROCESS:

1.1   Vital Functions

1.1.1 Delayed reactions on the part of the system may result in physical or psychological damage to innocent parties.

1.1.2 Delayed reactions on the part of the system may result in physical or psychological damage to users of the system.

1.2   Value creation

1.2.1 The performance of the system is of existential significance for the company using it.

1.2.2 Defective performance can leads to claims for compensation by business partners or other additional costs.

1.2.3 Defective performance leads to a deterioration in the company's image.

1.3   Size

1.3.1 Carrying out the transaction requires a complex integration of products into multiphase client/service architecture.

1.3.2 The data volume to be processed is classified as critical because of its size and the calls made on it.

1.3.3 The number of users working with the system and work carried out by them per time unit are classified as high.

2   *ASSESSMENT OF DEVELOPMENT RISKS*

2.1   Methods

2.1.1 The procedural model contains no explicit measures to record performance-specific requirements.

2.1.2 The procedural models contains no explicit measures to monitor performance-specific requirements during realization.

2.2   Techniques

2.2.1 Because of the techniques used for system analysis and system design, no modelling of performance-related requirements is possible.

2.2.2 The performance characteristics of the middleware solutions used have been insufficiently tested or are not known.

2.2.3 The performance characteristics of the DBMS used have been insufficiently tested or are not known.

2.3   People

2.3.1 The people involved in development have no experience in the implementation of performance-specific requirements.

2.3.2 The significance of performance-specific requirements is not recognized.

3   *ASSESSMENT OF RISK IN NORMAL OPERATION*

3.1   Integration of Hardware and Software

3.1.1 Implementation requires the integration of external products (e.g. server systems) with insufficiently known or tested performance characteristics.

3.1.2 The performance (running time) of necessary backups or the recovery of data in emergencies must be classified as critical.

3.2   Use of Resources

3.2.1 The actual use of resources is unknown or can only be determined using unreliable estimation methods.

3.2.2 A benchmark test under effective operating conditions cannot be carried out; the resource requirements cannot be determined exactly.

3.2.3 Normal operation requires qualified support from human administrators.

This catalogue of questions is not complete; it is merely intended to be an initial approach for a possible model for assessing performance as a quality factor in industrial conditions. We shall not be going into any further detail here, in order to achieve the most generally valid approach possible.

6   Quantifying the Risks Determined

We would like to pursue two approaches to quantify the risks identified in the previous section. Firstly, we will propose a method for providing a monetary context for primary risks which have a direct effect on the business process supported by the IT system.

Typically, the development/ introduction of a new software application requires a demonstration of what benefit (business case) it generates. If the business case of the application is to be fulfilled, the response time t must be in line with the user requirements t_{Ref} and the throughput B must be in line with the user requirements B_{Ref}. In the event of a failure (most extreme case of performance loss), the response time moves towards "infinite", and throughput moves towards "zero", i.e. the entire business case of the application is lost.[3]

Table 6. Performance losses and effects on the business process

		Performance losses			
.	Business Case	X in %	....	Y in %	Loss
Response time	$t <= t_{Ref}$	$t > t_{Ref}$	...	$t >> t_{Ref}$	$t \to \infty$
Throughput	$B \geq B_{Ref}$	$B < B_{Ref}$	...	$B << B_{Ref}$	$B \to 0$

To determine the monetary losses in connection with a nonperforming system, it is necessary to consult the company or internal unit which ordered the IT system. Only this can estimate what the loss will be if, for example, insufficient throughput means that only 100 customers can be served per day instead of the 300 customers that would normally be possible. It is a good idea to look at stepped performance losses in terms of response time and throughput in relation to critical functions of the application, as shown in Table 6. It would be possible, for example, to carry out an analysis for a loss of performance of X=100% (double response time), Y=200% (triple response time) and the failure of the system. The study should take into account not only the specific context of the application itself (direct extra costs), but also possible consequential losses within the process chain. In addition, damage to the company's image should also be considered, although this is hard to quantify.

The following pursues a slightly different approach, in order to provide further information about the secondary risks which could occur at the time of the software development or during normal operation. On the basis of general experience, measured objects (internal measurements) are observed which could have an effect on the performance characteristics (external measurements) of the IT system. No direct statistical connection has been proven yet due to a lack of empirical studies, but it is probable that the selected measured objects will often be listed as the reason for problems in connection with performance-related characteristics.

---

[3] Notations for the response time or throughput are taken from ISO 14756

Table 7. Monetary risk assessment for development and normal operation

	Risk criteria	Measured objects (int. measure-ments)	Empirical assessment (ext. meas-urements)	Basic risk in Euros	Probabi-lity of occurrence in percent	Quantified effective risk in Euros
Develop-ment	Methods	Procedural model without ref. to PE	Extended project running time			
		Test methods without ref. to PE				
		...	Extra costs through increased hardware requirements			
	Tech-niques	Unknown performance behaviour of middleware				
		Unknown performance behaviour of database system	Poorer performance than expected			
		...	...			
	People	No experience with PE methods				
		Low awareness of PE tasks				
		...				
Normal operation	Integratio n of hardware and software	Updating software versions	Delays to the business process			
		Time window for backup and recovery				
		...	Reduced staff productivity			
	Use of resources	Computers (CPU, I/O, memory,...)	Consequentia l losses			
		Network (bandwidth)	within the process chain			
		...				

7   Costs/Time Required and Choice of Methods for PE

On the basis of the assessed primary and secondary risks, the choice of corresponding performance engineering methods can now be made in a further step. It should be noted that the choice of the method to be used to carry out performance engineering tasks depends on the expenditure required, the skills required, the necessary preconditions and the required relevance or precision of the results. The following table gives a rough assessment of the various methods on the basis of the criteria listed:

Table 8: Costs/time required for the use of PE methods

Method	Effort	Skill	Preconditions	Relevance of results
Rules of thumb (e.g. for Web servers, database servers)	Low	Low	• Background of empirical experience • Known application domain • Known performance behaviour of the techniques used	• No exact performance information possible • Typically used for cost models
Modelling (e.g. operational analysis)	Medium	High	• Tools for model solutions • Penetration of application	• Precise for parts of the total system that can be broken down
Measurements (e.g. benchmarks, monitors)	High	Medium to high	• Hardware and software equipment • Load drivers • Runnable application or at least prototype	• With benchmarking of own application, precise results are possible

Whilst rules of thumb and performance models can be used without systems being implemented, runnable applications are at least systems that have been implemented as prototypes are needed to run benchmarks. A considerable amount of work is required to run benchmarks because of the necessary hardware and software (including load driver systems). In addition, there are generally no viable applications that can be used during development.

In general, it can be stated that the higher the total risk determined and the higher the resultant costs, the sooner performance engineering methods should be used in development. As the risk increases, even those PE methods that cause a relatively high expenditure but which provide precise results become more justified. With new technologies in particular, where we have as yet little experience of their performance behaviour, measurements on real systems for running PE are essential.

8   Summary and Outlook

Only 5 to 10 % of software development projects explicitly include performance engineering tasks. This means that no clarity is obtained about performance behaviour (response time, throughput and use of resources) until after the software application has been installed.

The main reasons for this are the insufficient time and money allowed within development projects and the low "awareness" of the additional value that these tasks can provide. One of the most interesting aspects was the analysis of expenditure estimate procedures which at least take account of the tasks as factors influencing total expenditure. The results stating the extent to which PE tasks can play a part in this are, however, as unconvincing as the contradictory information provided by these procedures in general. Basically, a procedure that tries to derive information on the costs of PE on a 'block basis' from the total development expenditure must be treated with scepticism. In terms of development, very "small" systems can also involve major risks in the event of insufficient performance behaviour; one example of this is embedded systems from real-time processing.

The concept presented here of using potential risks as the basis for deriving the time and money required to realize performance engineering tasks offers the advantage, on the one hand, of making risks transparent so that they can be assessed in monetary terms as far as possible. On the basis of the risks assessed, it should be easier for project managers to take account of necessary PE tasks in project plans from both a monetary and a time point of view and to be able to estimate their additional value. In addition, a definite cost framework supports he choice of concrete PE methods. Naturally, efforts should be made to determine general qualitative risks in addition to performance-related risks and to integrate these methods into current expenditure estimating processes such as the function point method. However, it should always be possible to explicitly assign the necessary expenditure to performance engineering so that the extra PE tasks are not regarded as additional expenditure.

In order to carry out performance engineering tasks, efficient service providers are needed who are familiar with both performance engineering methods and software engineering methods. It is a good idea, in terms of cost, to provide complex tasks requiring a high level of skill and extensive hardware and software equipment on a centralized basis.

References

1. Boehm, B.W.: COCOMO II Model Definition Manual. University of Southern California (1997)
2. Dimitrov, E., Schmietendorf, A.: UML-based Performance Engineering. In: Dumke et. al.: Conference Proceedings for the 1st Workshop on Performance Engineering in software development, Darmstadt (2000) 41-52
3. Dumke, R., Foltin, E., Koeppe, R., Winkler, A.: Softwarequalität durch Meßtools (Software quality through measuring tools). Vieweg-Verlag, Braunschweig /Wiesbaden (1996)

4. Dumke, R., Foltin, E., Schmietendorf, A.: Kausalitätsprobleme bei der Aufwandsschätzung in der Softwareentwicklung und –wartung (Causality problems in estimating expenditure in software development   and maintenance). Preprint Nr. 13, Otto-von-Guericke-Universität Magdeburg (1998)
5. IFPUG: Function Point Counting Practices Manual. Atlanta (1994)
6. Jones, C.: Software Quality – Analysis and Guidelines for success. International Thomson Computer Press (1997)
7. Klein, M.H.: Problems in the Practice of Performance Engineering. CMU/SEI-95-TR-020, Software Engineering Institute, Pittsburgh, Pennsylvania – USA (1996)
8. Rautenstrauch, C., Scholz, A.: Vom Performance Tuning zum Software Performance Engineering am Beispiel datenbankbasierter Anwendungssysteme (From performance tuning to software performance engineering using the example of database-based application systems). In: 'Informatik Spektrum', 22(1999)4
9. Schmietendorf, A., Scholz, A.: A risk-driven Performance Engineering Process Approach and its Evaluation with a Performance Engineering Maturity Model. In: Proc. of the 15th UKPEW, Bristol (1999)
10. Schmietendorf, A., Herting, H.: Performance Analyses integrated in the Software Development Phases. VDE-ITG Workshop Non-Funtional Software Requirements, Nürnberg (2000)
11. Smith, C.U.: Performance Engineering of Software Systems – The SEI series in software engineering. Addison-Wesley (1990)
12. Sneed, H.M.: Schätzung der Entwicklungskosten von objektorientierter Software (Estimating the development costs of object-oriented software). SES Software-Engineering Services GmbH, Ottobrunn, München (1995)

Measurement in Software Process Improvement Programmes: An Empirical Study

Tracy Hall[1], Nathan Baddoo[1], and David Wilson[2]

[1]University of Hertfordshire, UK
[2]University of Technology, Sydney, Australia

Abstract. In this paper we report on our empirical study of SPI programmes in thirteen UK software companies. We focus on companies' approaches to SPI and how measurement relates to SPI in those companies. We present quantitative data characterising SPI and measurement in the companies. We discuss how the use of measurement relates to the maturity of software processes and how measurement supports maturing processes.
Our results show that companies are generally enthusiastic about implementing measurement and they believe that SPI is impoverished without measurement. However our data shows that in reality companies have implemented very little substantive measurement. Indeed we suggest that companies find implementing measurement within SPI more difficult than they expect. Furthermore, we report on data from software personnel suggesting that companies are reluctant to implement measurement because it is difficult to justify in terms of quick pay backs. Overall our research suggests that despite companies knowing that measurement is fundamental to SPI, it is rarely implemented effectively.

1   Introduction

The popularity of the Capability Maturity Model (CMM) has contributed to software companies' current appetite for process improvement. Many companies are either formally or informally interested in CMM assessment and many more are interested in SPI generally. Whatever variety of SPI companies have implemented, and regardless of their CMM level, measurement must play a fundamental role in effective SPI programmes.

Although we know of no recent survey that has measured the take-up of measurement in the software industry, anecdotal evidence suggests that the software industry lacks enthusiasm for comprehensively implementing measurement. Many companies have not implemented measurement in any comprehensive sense. Sub-optimal use of measurement can profoundly affect a company's ability to improve its development processes and limit the company's capability to mature. Published work [5], [6] and anecdotal data suggests that a major reason measurement programmes fail is because they are implemented poorly.

In this paper we present data characterising the views developers, project managers and senior managers have towards measurement. Our objective is to identify what the different groups of staff like about measurement and what they dislike about

R. Dumke and A. Abran (Eds.): IWSM 2000, LNCS 2006, pp. 73-82, 2001.

measurement. Our aim is to help companies maximise the best aspects of measurement and minimise the worst and so ensure buy-in to measurement. Our approach is based on the principle that to be effective and successful in the long term, measurements must be useful to, and popular with, all measurement stakeholders. For the purposes of this work we have limited stakeholders to developers, project mangers and senior managers (although clearly other stakeholder groups exist). We offer ways to design measurements for the benefit of all stakeholder groups. We assert that if a measurement process neglects the needs of any one group of stakeholders it is unlikely to be effective and long lasting.

In this paper we discuss how to make the implementation of measurement a clear and easy process that is likely to be successful and enduring. Our findings are based on the analysis of measurement experiences in thirteen different companies. We used the Repertory Grid Technique (RGT) [1] to collect this experiential data. RGT is a social science technique designed to elicit views and attitudes, based on experiences. We used the RGT technique with over 200 staff from software companies to uncover their views, attitudes and experiences of software measurement. We used RGT with three strategic groups of staff in each company to measure attitudes to measurement at grassroots, middle management and strategic management level. Although companies refer to these staff groups using different nomenclature, throughout this paper we refer to these groups as: developers, project managers and senior managers.

In Section Two of this paper we report our study methods. We describe our sample of companies and the people from each that participated. We go on to explain our use of the Repertory Grid Technique in each company. In Section Three we present our detailed results and discuss our analysis of those results. We summarise and conclude in Section Four.

2   Study Methods

In this section we describe the participants in the study and present our study methods. We also give a brief overview of the limitations of the data we have collected.

Appendix One describes the thirteen UK software companies participating in this study. The work forms part of a wider ranging study into software process improvement. The work we present in this paper discusses the data we collected at eleven of the companies.

Between October 1999 and March 2000 we spent between one and three days collecting data at each of the thirteen companies.

We used a group-based Repertory Grid Technique [1] to collect the data. In its pure form RGT is used with individuals in psychological analysis, however we adapted the technique for use in a group setting.

At each company we implemented RGT with groups of between four and six people from three operational levels of the company: developers, project managers and senior managers. Our aim was to measure experiences and perceptions of measurements at each level. We believed that we were more likely to get candid responses from participants if they talked to us within their own peer group.

At each company we implemented at least one group from each strategic level and several groups of developers and project mangers in the biggest companies. In a few companies we were unable to gain access to senior managers. In the 11 companies that we consider in this paper, we discuss data from:

- 13 developer groups
- 12 project manager groups
- 4 senior manager groups

RGT is a simple way of eliciting a rich understanding of the way people think about specific things. It is a basic technique for collecting qualitative people-oriented data. It involves discussing the negative and positive aspects of an entity, with the researcher attempting to 'ladder' responses by asking participants 'why' they think as they do. This should result in a deep understanding of the positive and negative polarity of perceptions that people have about a specific entity.

We audio recorded then transcribed each session. We then performed a simple frequency analysis of the RGT data using a spreadsheet.

3   Perceptions of Measurement

The four tables presented in this section show the positive, negative, best and worst aspects of measurement that emerged from the three types of group sessions (ie developer, project manager and senior manager groups). More issues were cited by groups than we include in the tables, as we present only those issues that were mentioned by more than two groups (consequently the issue labels may not be sequential as we have omitted issues that did not occur in multiple sessions). Data is shown in the tables as a percentage occurrence of an issue in particular types of group, for example, Table 1 shows that issue P1 was cited by 23% of all the developer groups; 25% of project manager groups and 50% of senior manager groups.

3.1   Positive Aspects of Measurement

General. All but one of the positive aspects of measurement cited by groups can be split into the following general characterisation of measurement:

- Assessment (P1, P2, P3)

- Predication (P4, P7)

- Adds substance to arguments (P8)

This is interesting as it reflects the general characterisation of measurement cited in the literature [2].

Table 1. Perceived general positive aspects of software measurement

General benefits of software measurement	Percentage of groups		
	Developers	Project Managers	Senior Managers
P1 Know whether the right things are being done	23	25	50
P2 Finding out what is good and what is bad	23	58	50
P3 Identify problems	8	42	25
P4 Support/improve planning and estimating	38	25	25
P7 Track progress	69	58	50
P8 Makes what you're saying more substantial	15	8	50
P9 Provides feedback to people	8	25	25

Table 2. Favourite aspects of software measurement

Favourite aspects of software measurement	Percentage of groups		
	Developers	Project Managers	Senior Managers
B1 Can target effort into things not doing so well	8	8	25
B4 A check that what you're doing is right	15	17	50
B5 People can't argue with them	8	25	0
B6 The confidence they give	8	17	50

Developers. Although some developers showed amusing irreverence to measurement (for example one said that *collecting data is better than work!*), they were generally positive about measurement and cited many positive features of measurement. Indeed developers cited a similar number of positive issues to project managers. However many of the positive features cited benefited project managers rather than developers. There was also a general feeling given by developers that although they believed measurement could be very positive it was difficult to get right. This is summed up by one developer saying that…

…if any of us came up with a workable approach to metrics we'd become very rich!

Table One shows that the overwhelmingly positive perception of measurement cited by developer groups was that measurement data allows progress to be tracked (69% of developer groups) and improves planning and estimating (38% of developer groups). Furthermore, these two issues were cited by more developer groups than project manager groups. This is interesting as it suggests that developers may suffer from poor planning, estimating and tracking and that they want this to be improved as much as managers. This finding also suggests that the project management benefits of data are highly visible to developers.

Almost a quarter of developer groups also said that they believed measurement data could help assess whether what is being done is good or bad (P1 & P2).

Table Two shows that there was no real agreement amongst developer groups regarding what they consider the best aspects of measurement. An array of specific and individual aspects of measurement were cited.

Project Managers. Project managers generally perceive measurement positively. The following are quotes about measurement from individual project managers…

> *Estimates are just a guess without metrics.*
> *Metrics are a necessary evil.*
> *They may not be perfect, but they're better than nothing.*
> *Best thing since sliced bread!*
> *Data is power!*
> *A great idea if they're implemented properly.*
> *They make me sleep better at night!*
> *They're a sanity check.*

Table One shows that overall project managers have more high scores for each positive issue. The raw data also reveals that they cite a wider range of benefits than developers or senior managers. However we were surprised that although the importance of measurement data to process improvement was mentioned in one group, this did not emerge as a theme of the data.

Table One shows that project managers are keen to use measurement data for assessment purposes (P1, P2 & P7). The most popular perceived benefits project managers cite are: finding out what is good and bad about the way the development processes are currently being operated and to track the progress of projects.

Almost half the project manager groups also believed that measurement was beneficial in identifying specific problem areas (P3).

A quarter of project manager groups also said they believed that measurement allows feedback to be given to people, a theme that did not really emerge from developer groups.

Again, Table Two shows that project managers found it difficult to identify the best aspects of measurement, a quarter of groups thought that the best aspect of measurement data was that people were less likely to argue with it. However there was no real agreement amongst groups about the other best things about measurement.

Senior Managers. Table One shows that senior managers are also very positive about measurement (though the small sample size of four senior manager groups means we must treat this data guardedly). However there is no particular issue that stands out as their most positive aspect of measurement.

Table Two shows that half of the senior manager groups believed that the best aspect of measurement is that it allows them to check that things were being done correctly. Half of the groups also said that they particularly liked the confidence that measurement data gave them that things were as they should be. A quarter of the groups also said that one of the best aspects of measurement data was that it allowed resources to be focussed into areas that were not being done so well.

3.2   Negative Aspects of Measurement

Table 3. Perceived general negative aspects of software measurement

General negative aspects of measurement		Percentage of groups		
		Developers	Project Managers	Senior Managers
N3	Hard to measure what you want to measure	15	25	0
N6	Don't know how, or if, the data is being used	38	8	0
N7	No feedback from the data	38	8	0
N8	Detracts from the main engineering job	8	8	50
N10	Difficult to collect, analyse and use the right measures	23	58	50
N11	Time consuming to collect the data	38	67	25
N12	They must be used for the right reason	15	33	50
N13	There must be integrity in the data	15	17	25
N17	They can be used against people	0	0	25

Table 4. Least favourite aspects of software measurement

Least favourite aspects of software measurement		Percentage of groups		
		Developers	Project Managers	Senior Managers
L1	Extra work	23	8	0
L3	Difficult to compare data across systems or projects	0	25	0
L4	Can be mis-understood	15	8	25
L5	Not used enough	8	17	25
L6	Poorly presented data	23	17	50
L7	Data too abstract to use easily	15	17	0
L8	Poor quality data	15	25	0

General. Most of the negative aspects of measurement can be classified as related to:

- Implementation (N6, N7, N12, N13)
- Time and effort (N8, N11)
- Intrinsic difficulty of measurement (N10)

Developers. Although Table Three shows that there was quite a lot of low level negativity voiced by developer groups, there was no one negative issue that particularly stood out. However three negative perceptions of measurement were cited by 38% of the groups:

- Developers don't know how or if the data collected was used.
- There is no feedback from the data they collect.
- It is time consuming for them to collect data.

The first two of these aspects of measurement are classic problems that the literature warns against [4].

Revealing quotes from individuals in developer groups include:

> *If you've been careless collecting the data then what they tell you is complete rubbish – this happens often.*
> *Metrics can be used to beat people up.*
> *Managers tend to want to only measure things that show we're perfect!*
> *Can become a ticking boxes exercise.*
> *They're for someone else really – meaningless to us.*
> *Never do anything useful – just management by pretty graph!*
> *Data can be manipulated, eg when change requests are being counted there is an incentive not to raise them.*
> *Collecting more data than doing work!*
> *Experience always wins over measurement.*
> *Like reading the telephone directory.*

Table Four shows, again, the difficulty developers had saying what they disliked most about measurement. Although nearly a quarter of groups disliked the extra work measurement involved and a quarter that they disliked poorly presented data, there were no strongly felt issues.

Project Managers. Table Three shows that project managers had a slightly different profile to their concerns about measurement than developers.

There was overwhelming agreement amongst more than two thirds of project manager groups that data was very time consuming to collect and analyse. Furthermore, nearly 60% of project manager groups also said that it was very difficult to identify and collect data for the right measures. Related to this a quarter of groups also said that measures do not always measure what you want them to measure. Project managers' concerns seem highly related to the difficulty of effectively implementing measurement rather than developers concerns which seem to be more related to how measurement works out in practice. Revealing quotes from individual project managers include:

> *Can gather too much data and confuse yourself totally.*
> *Perceived by developers as negative, as they don't get any personal benefit.*
> *Can be manipulated.*
> *Potential benefits rarely realised.*
> *Tempting to measure easy things rather than useful things.*
> *I'm sure people would use metrics if they actually had any value – but they never do.*
> *Depends on how they're used.*

Can be used to show anything.
Can be used for political reasons.
Quality of the data can be dubious.
Can be used just to make glossy presentations
Must be careful not to show customers data as they might draw inappropriate conclusions.

Senior Managers. Table Three shows that senior managers had a slightly different profile of concerns about measurement than the other two types of staff.

Half of the senior manager groups perceived the following negative aspects of measurement:

– collecting data detracts from the main engineering job (which is a slightly different way of commenting on the time and effort involved in measurement, senior managers seem to be focussing on the opportunity cost of measurement, rather than on time and effort).

– Difficult to identify and use the right measures.

– Measurement must be used for the right reason.

Furthermore, a quarter of senior manager groups also commented on the time consuming nature of measurement and that it was important data was not used against people. This is an interesting finding as no other group identified this as a negative issue and we can speculate on a variety of reasons for this: maybe developers and project managers had not experienced measurement being used in this way and so it did not occur to them as a problem. Or that they did not perceive data being used in this way as problematic.

Overall there was much more agreement amongst senior managers about the negative aspects of measurement than there was amongst the other two types of staff group.

Table Four also shows that half of the senior manager groups mentioned poorly presented data as their least favourite aspect of measurement.

4 Conclusions

The most interesting findings we report in this paper include the following:

– Developers do not feel they know how or if measurement data is being used.

– Developers do not feel they get enough feedback from data they have collected.

– The project management benefits of measurement are clear to project managers and developers.

– Despite all type of staff feeling that measurement was very time consuming, automated data collection was not being called for.

– The link between measurement and process improvement was not an explicit issue.

Many of these issues are relatively straight forward for companies to address. We believe that companies addressing these basic implementation issues are likely to generate a more effective and longer term measurement programme.

Acknowledgements

The work we report here form part of a wider ranging study into software process improvement which is supported by the UK's Engineering & Physical Sciences Research Council under grant number EPSRC GR/L91962.

References

1. Fransella, F., Bannister, D.: A Manual of Repertory Grid Technique. Academic Press, London (1977)
2. Fenton, N., Pfleeger, S.L.: Software Metrics: A Rigorous and Practical Approach. Thompson International (1997)
3. Pfleeger, S.L.: Lessons Learned Building a Corporate Metrics Programme. IEEE Software, May (1993)
4. Grady, R., Caswell, D.: Software Metrics: Establishing a Company-wide Programme. Prentice-Hall (1987)
5. Hall, T., Fenton, N.: Implementing effective software metrics programmes. IEEE Software, May (1997)
6. Jeffery, R., Berry, M.: A Framework for Evaluation and Predication of Metrics Programme Success. Procs of the 1ˢᵗ Int. Software Metrics Symposium, Baltimore, Maryland, May (1993)

Appendix One

The companies in the study

Company number	HW/SW Producer	UK or Multi-national?	Size (people)	SE size (people)	Age (yrs)	SW type	CMM Level (self-estimate)
1	HW/SW	MN	>2000	>2000	>50	Real time embedded	1*
2	SW	UK	100-500	100-500	20-50	Business systems	1
3	HW/SW	MN	>2000	500-2000	>50	Real time embedded	1
4	HW/SW	MN	>2000	500-2000	>50	Real time embedded	1
5	SW	MN	>2000	>2000	10-20	Real time	4*
6	SW	MN	>2000	>2000	10-20	Real time	3*
7	SW	MN	>2000	>2000	20-50	Packages	1
8	SW	UK	10-100	10-100	5-10	Business systems	2
9	SW	MN	10-100	10-100	10-20	Real time embedded	3
10	SW	MN	>2000	10-100	10-20	Embedded Systems software	1
11	HW/SW	MN	500-2000	11-25	20-50	Real time embedded	2
12	HW/SW	UK	100-500	<10	20-50	Embedded	1
13	SW	UK	100	40	10-20	Business systems	3

* formal CMM assessment

Improving Validation Activities in a Global Software Development

Christof Ebert[1], Casimiro Hernandez Parro, Roland Suttels, and Harald Kolarczyk

Alcatel, Switching and Routing Division, Antwerp, Belgium / Madrid, Spain / Stuttgart, Germany
[1]Alcatel, SD-97, Fr.-Wellesplein 1, B-2018 Antwerpen, Belgium
Tel.: +32-3-240-4081, Fax: +32-3-240-9935
christof.ebert@alcatel.be

Abstract. Increasingly software projects are handled in a global and distributed project set-up. Global software development however also challenges traditional techniques of software engineering, such as peer reviews or design meetings. Especially validation activities during development, such as inspections need to be adjusted to achieve results, which are both efficient and effective. Effective teamwork and coaching of engineers highly contribute towards successful projects. We will in this article evaluate experiences made in the last 3 years with validation activities in a global setting within Alcatel's Switching and Routing business. We will investigate 3 hypotheses related to effects of collocated inspections, intensive coaching, and feature-oriented development teams on globally distributed projects. As all these activities mean initial investment compared to a standard process with scattered activities, the major validation criteria for the 3 hypotheses is cost reduction due to earlier defect detection and less defects introduced. The data is taken from a sample of over 60 international projects of various sizes from which we collected all type of product and process metrics in the past 4 years.

1   Introduction

Software development involves teamwork and a lot of communication. It looks just rational to put all engineers at one place, share the objectives and let the project run. For many reasons, however, software projects are handled more and more in a global and distributed project set-up. Companies open branches in other continents to be close to the markets. Start-ups merge with competitors in other countries. Outsourcing to a variety of software houses - especially in Asia - allows better access to local resources.

Why developing in distributed sites, while it would be much easier working at one place with much less overhead generated through remote communication and planning? Surely there are advantages of global development, which are pronounced in business journals, such as time-zone effectiveness, availability of skilled engineers, or reduced cost in various countries. There is however heavy trade-off. In fact the business case is surely not a simple accounting of different cost of engineering in different regions. Working in a globally distributed project means overheads for

R. Dumke and A. Abran (Eds.): IWSM 2000, LNCS 2006, pp. 83-93, 2001.

planning and managing people. It means language and cultural barriers. All this impacts especially validation activities such as peer reviews or design meetings and thus ultimately the quality and cost of the delivered product.

We will focus in this case study on impacts of global development on validation results and thus ultimately quality and cost of non-quality. Cost of non-quality is the cost of not reaching the desired quality level at the first run. It is often referred to as "rework". We calculate cost of non-quality by summarizing respective (life cycle phase depending) cost for defect detection and correction across all defects found in the project.

Global software development obviously challenges traditional validation techniques of software engineering and asks for new solutions. We will try in this case study to summarize experiences and to share the best practices from projects of different type and size that involved several locations in different continents and cultures. Especially validation activities during development, such as inspections or unit test need to be adjusted to achieve results, which are both efficient and effective. As a basis we will evaluate experiences made in the past years with validation activities in a global setting within Alcatel's Switching and Routing business. Such complex software systems show the various dimensions of global development and also offer practical solutions as they have been managed since years in a global context. The challenges we were faced and which we will address involve:

- to support of validation in a global product line concept;
- to facilitate early defect detection with an improved validation process;
- to reduce overall cost of non-quality.

Three hypotheses had been set up before that study and were driving the described part of the improvement program as such. These hypotheses reflect three key changes which we gradually implemented in Alcatel over the past three years.

- **Hypothesis 1:** Collocating peer reviews would improve both efficiency and effectiveness of defect detection and thus reduce cost of non-quality.
- **Hypothesis 2:** Providing a certain level of coaching within the project reduces cost of non-quality.
- **Hypothesis 3:** Reengineering the development process towards teamwork and continuous build allows to better managing globally distributed projects, and thus reduces cost of non-quality.

We will analyze these hypotheses in the context of over 60 projects developed in a three-year timeframe. The three hypotheses also reflect the type of changes that we focus on in this case study. This study is unique in that it provides insight in a running software process improvement (SPI) program within a large organization dealing with legacy software in a global context. Around two thirds of the projects had been handled before the changes were implemented, some projects implemented only parts, and several projects implemented all three mentioned changes. This allows comparing impacts directly linked to any of the three factors.

There are few documented results around that quantitatively evaluate the effects of global development. Several recent studies describe experiences gained from distributed projects that are not further described in detail [1,2,7]. They provide a huge set of project management and team management techniques, which we could also apply, but did not give quantitative evidence about the effectiveness. In fact most evaluations of validation techniques happen in classroom settings or collocated projects [11,12,13]. One study describes the problem and a solution how to handle remote inspections in large-scale software development [8]. Experiences are based on a tool that facilitates inspections and annotations of results, even if the checker is located remotely. There are however no concrete results available on efficiency and effectiveness compared to a collocated setting, which is what we were interested in.

The effects of coaching had not been studied in the area of software engineering besides the practical guidelines from change management and technology introduction gained from using the CMM [6,11,2,1]. Most results published so far describe the background of such a program with focus on the assessment and qualitative observations [6,10]. They are in many cases looking on rather small groups of engineers that act like a small- to medium-size company, even when embedded in a big organization [13]. Several qualitative lessons learned have been documented [14], but they are difficult to scale up towards large legacy based development projects. They try to set up a return on investment (ROI) calculation that however typically takes average values across organizations and would not show the lessons learned in sufficient depth within one organization. It has been shown in these studies that the CMM is an effective roadmap for achieving cost-effective solutions. Often these studies seem not to be related to quantitatively specified upfront expectations.

Several current best practices related to continuous build, configuration management, inspections and validations within a product line concept involving legacy software are elaborated in [2,4,5,8]. This involves the impacts of team management based on concrete measurable targets that are followed up [3,10,13] - sometimes even to the extreme when it comes to surviving a project running out of control [2]. Again, what is missing is a timeline study summarizing impacts before and after the introduction of such process.

Within this paper several abbreviations are used that should be briefly explained. CMM is the capability maturity model; SPI is software process improvement; PY is person years and Ph is person hours, r is the correlation coefficient measured in the observed data set. Size is measured in KStmt, which are thousand delivered executable statements of code (incl. declarations). We prefer statement counting compared to lines because the contents of a program are described in statements and should not depend on the editorial style. Failures are deviations from a specified functional behavior. They are caused by defects. Reviews detect defects and need to distinguish between what would cause a failure and what would be editorial or related to nonfunctional behavior.

The paper is organized as follows. Chapter 2 introduces the environment and set-up of the study. Chapter 3 describes some key lessons learned and best practices how to improve validation activities in a global software development. Finally, chapter 4 summarizes results and probes further.

2   Case Study Setting

Alcatel is a globally acting telecommunication supplier with a multitude of development projects, which typically involve different countries. Software development of switching and routing systems involves several thousand of software engineers. This development staff is distributed over the whole world in more than 15 development centers in Europe, the US, Asia (especially India) and Australia. Strong functional and project organizations, which interact in a classic matrix, facilitate both project focus and long-term skill and technology evolution.

The study describes projects within Alcatel's Switching and Routing business. The product spectrum ranges from the proprietary S12 switching system to Corba/Java middleware and frontends. Alcatel is registered for the ISO 9001 standard. The majority of development locations are ranked on CMM L2; few are on CMM L3. In terms of effort or cost, the share of software is increasing continuously and is currently in the range of 90 %. We focus in this study on switching projects as they are developed typically involving at least 2..3 sites, often in several continents. The projects vary in size between few person years and several hundred person years, depending how much new development is involved.

Working in a global context has along tradition for telecommunication suppliers. Main reasons are to be close to local markets, the continuous acquisition of other companies, and cost reduction by going east. To avoid overheads in terms of redundant skills and resource buffers in various locations, engineering is entirely globally managed. Having no option for working local, projects are organized to achieve the best possible efficiency by optimizing the trade-off between temporarily collocating teams, reducing overheads, and having the right skills in due time. The development process focuses on teamwork and continuous build [2,4]. It is further outlined in fig. 1, which distinguishes between upfront Expert Teams for analysis and system design, Development Teams which deliver increments to the continuous build, and the overlapping (sandwich) Test Team doing the regression, feature and system test activities. Some details related to making teamwork more efficient are discussed in the following chapter.

The project data has been collected in a standardized way since years by means of a history database. Data is aggregated from the operational databases (e.g. effort or defect data) towards teams, and finally towards the entire project. Having done that since '96 allows us to study impacts of various process changes and other parameters on project performance. We will use in this study the data of 60 projects, which we combined with some qualitative information to link each project towards the 3 hypotheses. Pilot projects are not included in this study. Only those projects were considered that were linked to a clear customer contract from the beginning.

Having the independent variables closely linked to the over 60 projects in our study, we could extract impacts of each single variable - following the rule that there should be at least 10 samples for each variable. This avoids conclusions of the type described in experimental software engineering as shotgun approach with uncontrolled independent variables or the Hawthorne effect [9]. The subsets of projects used here to explain results are not overlapping. This means that effects attributing to one result would not attribute simultaneously to another and thus hide the real explanation. To avoid long discussion on possible side effects as they could occur if we discuss the entire design process (e.g. tools impacts, skills impact), we narrowed down the design process towards validation activities, especially code reviews. Validation - or not doing it at the right time and with the right process - is a major cost driver and risk factor in almost all software projects.

Normalized cost of non-quality has been calculated based on actual defects detected and actual average cost per defect (incl. detection and correction) per activity where it is detected. Defects detected after handover are accounted with same cost as during test to avoid different types of market-specific opportunistic and penalty cost in the field. Then we calculated the average cost per defect for the entire project and normalized with size. The result is a project-specific average value of Ph/defect.

3   Improving Validation Activities

To improve validation activities in global project settings we have embarked on three separate changes, which we will further discuss. Each change had been linked to a hypothesis (or management expectation) which we evaluated during the projects. Having many projects in parallel and being forced to carefully introduce change to avoid any confusion on which process is applied in a certain project, we had after three years enough data from projects having implemented none or several of mentioned changes. The changes had been piloted first in a small and uncritical environment before starting to roll out the change. This allowed to carefully check results versus initial hypotheses (or assumptions) and to prepare the necessary changes to the management system (e.g. processes, rules, planning guidelines, budgeting guidelines, training materials, tools adaptations, etc.).

The following three hypotheses which we set upfront will be evaluated in the following three subsections:

- **Hypothesis 1:** Collocating peer reviews would improve both efficiency and effectiveness of defect detection and thus reduce cost of non-quality.
- **Hypothesis 2:** Providing a certain level of coaching within the project reduces cost of non-quality.
- **Hypothesis 3:** Reengineering the development process towards teamwork and continuous build allows to better managing globally distributed projects, and thus reduces cost of non-quality.

3.1   Collocating Peer Reviews

Globally distributed software development is highly impacted by work organization and effective work split. Often not all necessary skills to design a complex functionality are available at one location. While some authors recommend building virtual teams [1], we strongly advice to build coherent and collocated teams of fully allocated engineers. Coherence means that the work is split during development according to feature content, which allows assembling a team that can implement a set of related functionality - as opposed to artificial architecture splits. Collocation means that engineers working on such a set of coherent functionality should sit in the same building, if feasible in the same room. Full allocation finally implies that engineers working on a project should not be distracted by different tasks for other projects.

Projects are at their start already split into pieces of coherent functionality that will be delivered in increments to a continuous build. Functional entities are allocated to development teams, which are often based in different locations. Architecture decisions, decision reviews at major milestones, and test are done at one place. Experts from countries with minority contribution will be relocated for the time the team needs to work together. This allows effective project management based on the teams that are fully responsible for quality and delivery accuracy of their functionality.

Collocating a development team to stimulate more interactions is more expensive and might demotivate engineers due to traveling. We based our hypothesis on earlier qualitative studies telling that a team is only efficient when communication of team members happens whenever necessary and without long planning and preparation [7]. To base our decision on experiences within Alcatel, we studied projects where we could distinguish according to the factor of collocation degree.

The hypothesis we tested is that collocating peer reviews would improve both efficiency and effectiveness of defect detection and thus reduce cost of non-quality. Out of 3 recent projects that included several development teams that were globally distributed, we looked into the results of each single code inspection. 87 inspections were randomly selected. We divided 2 data sets, one with collocated development teams and inspections, and one with distributed teams where inspections were conducted remotely. All other variables remained unchanged. The 2 sets showed normal distribution with average values of 25 vs. 13 defects/KStmt and 0,33 vs. 0,08 Ph/defect, respectively. A t-test shows for this data an evidence of more than 98% that indeed the 2 sets can be considered independent. Other impacts such as different knowledge of underlying code or skill level of engineers could not be found as explanation factor in this data, as the involved engineers had experience with the underlying baseline. The hypothesis was thus accepted on a level $\alpha = 0,02$.

Looking into individual team performance we could see that collocated teams achieve an efficiency improvement during inspections of over 50%. This means that with the same amount of defects in design and code, those teams, which sit at the same place, need less than half the time for defect detection. The amount of defects detected shows almost a factor 2 difference in terms of defects per KStmt. Looking towards the low cost of defect detection during inspections compared to subsequent testing activities and the cost contribution of validation towards total cost, we found an impact of >10% on project cost.

3.2   Effective Process Coaching

Continuous technical training and coaching seems natural for any engineering activity. Looking into post mortem studies of finished projects with respect to training activities, we realized that there are big differences in terms of phase-specific training that involves both technical and process aspects. Some project managers focus heavily on providing all necessary technical and process information at respective phase kick-off meetings (e.g. start of detailed design, or start of test), while others just present some rudimentary technical information and do not further bother with ongoing coaching. Often coaching of engineers during the projects is reduced due to assumed negative impacts on total cost and duration. We found however the opposite. Reduced coaching harms overall project performance.

The hypothesis we tested is that providing a certain level of coaching within the project reduces cost of non-quality. Coaching in this study is the amount of on the job support by experienced engineers. Coaching comes on top of regular technical training and happens entirely on the job by means of allocating experienced engineers to teams of less experienced engineers. We analyzed a set of projects that received a coaching effort of ca. 1..2% of total project budget and a second set of projects that received no coaching. We found that coaching intensive projects had an average of 24 Ph/defect, while those with no coaching had an average of 29 Ph/defect. A t-test shows for this data an evidence of more than 90% that indeed the 2 sets can be considered independent. We could not see other impacts such as engineering skills or different stability of baselines. The hypothesis was thus accepted on a level $\alpha = 0,1$.

Intensive coaching (ca. 1..2% of accumulated phase effort) could reduce the cost of non-quality in the project by over 20%. We found that for our own process and defect detection cost a break-even would be reached at ca. 5% coaching effort. Obviously this is much more than what we usually consider necessary. This also means that there are quantifiable limits towards involving too many inexperienced engineers in one project.

3.3 Introducing Teamwork and Continuous Build

A key factor in managing a global project is to create responsibility for results. We faced in the past often a situation where distributed projects were heavily impacted by the functional line organization or even some local legacy organization. However, nobody felt responsible for achieving results. The result was poor productivity and unpredictable delivery accuracy. The effect was that whenever we tried to build the complete product or iteration, huge overhead was necessary to bring the pieces together. These holds as well for individual work products which were not sufficiently validated as for an entire activity, which was not seen as an entity, but only as pieces.

Due to not having a product perspective, work products were handled inefficient. Results were forwarded to the next in the chain, and cost of non-quality as well as delays accumulated. For instance, inspections were considered finished when the respective milestone date appeared, instead of applying reasonable exit criteria, before continuing the defect detection with the next and more expensive activity. Test was conducted with a rather static set of test cases that was not dynamically filtered according to real feature impacts. The root causes were obvious but so much embedded in the culture that a complete process reengineering was necessary to facilitate global development at competitive cost.

The major changes, which we implemented, combine concurrent engineering, continuous build, and teamwork. They are supported by the respective workflow techniques. Concurrent engineering means that we assemble cross-functional teams especially at the beginning of the project. Even before project kick-off a first expert team is assembled to ensure a complete impact analysis which is prerequisite to defining increments. It also means that for instance a tester is also part of the team as experience shows that designers and testers look at the same problem very differently. Testability and reduced cost of test can only be ensured with a focus on test strategy and the potential impacts of design decisions already during the initial phases of the project.

Teamwork was reinforced to the degree that a team has sole responsibility for realizing a set of customer requirements. This means that not anymore a designer would leave the team when her work product is coded, but would stay to test the work products in the context of those changes provided by other team members. Feature-orientation clearly dominates artificial architectural splits [2,4]. The targets of the team are based on project targets and are shared by all team members. The are followed up on the basis of delivered value, i.e. feature content [3]. Periodic reviews of team progress with the project lead are necessary to follow up and help in case of risks that cannot be mitigated inside the team.

The changes we introduced towards achieving real incremental development can be summarized as follows (fig. 1):

- Analyze requirements from the beginning in the view of how they could be clustered to related functionality, which later could be delivered as an increment.
- Analyze context (data structures that are common for all modules) impacts of all increments upfront before start of development. The elaboration phase is critical to make real incremental development and a stable test line feasible. Obviously not all context impacts can be addressed immediately without extending the elaboration phase towards what is unacceptable. It is thus necessary to measure context stability and follow up with root cause analysis why certain context impacts were overseen. As a target the elaboration should not take longer than one third of total elapse time. The reminder of the project duration is related to the development activities.
- Provide a project plan that is based on these sets of clustered customer requirements and allocates development teams to each set. Depending on the impact of the increments, they can be delivered to the test line more or less frequently. For instance, if a context impact is detected too late, a new production cycle is necessary which is taking more effort and lead time, than regular asynchronous increments of additional code within the originally defined context.
- Each increment is developed within one dedicated team, although a team might be assigned to several increments in a row. Increments must be completed until end of unit and feature integration test to avoid that the various components later cannot be accepted to the test line. A key criterion for the quality of increments is that they don't break the build.
- The progress tracking of development and test is primarily based on the integration and testing of single customer requirements. This for the first time gives visibility on real progress because a requirement can only be checked off if it is successfully integrated in the test line. Traceability is improved because each customer requirements links to the related work products.
- Increments are extensively feature tested by the independent test line.
- Increments towards a stable build proved one of the key success factors in global development. We realized that cycle time of projects is heavily impacted by whether continuous build is globally applied or not.

The hypothesis we tested is that reengineering the development process towards teamwork and continuous build allows to better managing globally distributed projects, and thus reduces cost of non-quality. We evaluated the effects of this reengineered process carefully over the past 2 years. As a result we see two effects contributing to the hypothesis. Response time and thus overall cycle time is reduced as defect correction happens in the team (fig. 2). Field defects are reduced due to focus on an optimized test strategy, longer overall test-time and end-to-end responsibility of a development team. Cost of non-quality in the overall project has been reduced significantly due to this earlier defect detection. The hypothesis was tested in a set of 68 projects over the past 4 years (i.e. before and after the change). As a result we can accept with a significance level of >95% in a t-test that the change towards team work and continuous build indeed reduces cost of non-quality.

4 Conclusions

Managing global software development is not easy and has high-risk exposure to lowering overall productivity. Still the positive impacts should not be forgotten. A major positive effect that is boosted by going global is innovation. Engineers with all type of cultural background actively participate to continuously improve the product, to innovate new products, and to make processes more effective. By introducing some changes towards improving the sense of responsibility for end results, we are able to keep certain standards and improve performance - even with this changing work environment.

We had embarked on three specific changes that we first piloted in smaller settings to optimize the underlying process, and then rolled out over the past 3 years. All changes met the expectations in terms of cost versus benefit, although we cannot yet tell that they are fully implemented in all projects. The 3 underlying hypotheses could be validated in this case study covering more than 60 projects over a timeframe of 3 years:

- Collocating peer reviews improves both efficiency and effectiveness of defect detection and thus reduce cost of non-quality.
- Providing a certain level of coaching within the project reduces cost of non-quality.
- Reengineering the development process towards teamwork and continuous build allows to better managing globally distributed projects, and thus reduces cost of non-quality.

We will summarize those best practices related to improve validation activities, which we identified over the past years that clearly support global software development:

- Agreeing and communicating at project start the respective project targets, such as quality, milestones, content, or resource allocation. Similarly, at phase or increment start team targets are adjusted and communicated to facilitate effective internal team management.
- Making teams responsible for their results
- While having one project leader who is fully responsible to achieve project targets, assign her a project management team that represents the major cultures within the project.
- Defining at begin of projects which teams are involved and what they are going to do in which location. This includes a focus on allocation rules, such as scattering or collocation.
- Setting up a project homepage for each project that summarizes project content, progress metrics, planning information, and team-specific information.
- Collocate as much as possible teams to facilitate effective teamwork.
- Provide the necessary coaching on the job and friction-free by mixing different level of expertise.
- Provide the necessary tools and technology to manage workflow and workspaces around the world (e.g. CM, problem management, test environments).

References

1. Karolak, D.W.: Global Software Development. IEEE Computer Society Press, Los Alamitos, USA (1998)
2. McConnell, S.: Software Project Survival Guide. Microsoft Press, Redmont, USA (1998)
3. Royce, W.: Software Project Management. Addison-Wesley, Reading, USA (1998)
4. Karlsson, E.A. et al: Daily Build and Feature Development in Large Distributed Projects. Proc. ICSE 2000, IEEE Comp. Soc. Press, Los Alamitos, USA (2000) 649-658
5. Perry, D.E. et al.: Parallel Changes in large Scale Software Development: An Observational Case Study. Proc. ICSE 1998, IEEE Comp. Soc. Press, Los Alamitos, USA (1998) 251-260.
6. Wigle, G.B.: Practices of a Successful SEPG. European SEPG Conference 1997, Amsterdam, 1997. More in-depth coverage of most of the Boeing results. In: G.G.Schulmeyer and J.I.McManus, Ed.: Handbook of Software Quality Assurance, 3. ed., Int. Thomson Computer Press (1997)
7. DeMarco, T. and T.Lister: Peopleware. 2nd ed. Dorset House, New York (1999)
8. Perpich, J.M., et al.: Anywhere, Anytime Code Inspections: Using the Web to remove Inspection Bottlenecks in Large-Scale Software Development. Proc. Int. Conf. on Software Engineering, IEEE Comp. Soc. Press, (1997) 14-21
9. Fenton, N. E. and S.L. Pfleeger: Software Metrics: A Practical and Rigorous Approach. Chapman & Hall, London (1997)
10. Grady, R.B.: Successful Software Process Improvement. Prentice Hall, Upper Saddle River (1997)
11. Jones, C.: Software Quality. Analysis and Guidelines for Success. Thomson, Boston, USA (1997)
12. Tagaki, Y. et al.: Analysis of Review's Effectiveness Based on Software Metrics. Proc. Int. Symp. on Software Reliability Engineering '95. IEEE Comp. Soc. Press, Los Alamitos, Ca, USA (1995) 34-39
13. Humphrey, W.S.: Introduction to the Personal Software Process. Addison-Wesley, Reading, USA (1997)
14. McGarry, F. et al: Measuring Impacts Individual Process Maturity Attributes Have on Software Products. Proc. 5. Int. Software Metrics Symposium, IEEE Comp. Soc. Press (1998) 52-60

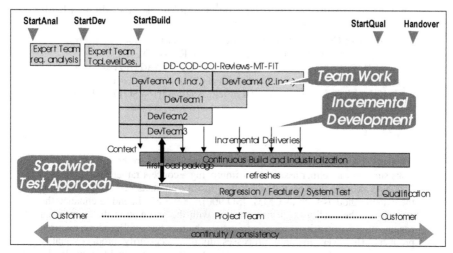

Fig. 1. Process Overview Building upon Feature-Oriented Teams and Continuous Build

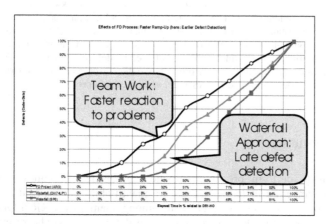

Fig. 2. Effective Team Management Scales Directly up to Faster Reaction Time

A Generic Model for Assessing Process Quality

Manoranjan Satpathy[1], Rachel Harrison[1], Colin Snook[2], and Michael Butler[2]

[1]School of Computer Science, Cybernetics and Electronic Engineering
University of Reading, Reading RG6 6AY, UK
{M.Satpathy, Rachel.Harrison}@reading.ac.uk
[2]Department of Electronics and Computer Science
University of Southampton, Highfield, Southampton SO17 1BJ, UK
{cfs98r, mjb}@ecs.soton.ac.uk

Abstract. Process assessment and process improvement are both very difficult tasks since we are either assessing or improving a concept rather than an object. A quality process is expected to produce quality products efficiently. Most of the existing models such as CMM, ISO 9001/9000-3 etc. intend to enhance the maturity or the quality of an organization with the assumption that a matured organization will put its processes in place which in turn will produce matured products. However, matured processes do not necessarily produce quality products [21, 6]. The primary reasons are: (i) In the process quality models, the relationship between the process quality and product quality is far from clear, and (ii) many of the process models take a monolithic view of the whole life-cycle process, and as a result, the idiosyncrasies of the individual processes do not receive proper attention.
In this paper, we first define an internal process model in a formal manner. Next, we define a generic quality model whose scope covers all the development processes and most of the supporting processes associated with the development phase. The generic quality model is a parametric template and could be instantiated in a systematic manner to produce the quality model for any individual process. We then show such a customization for the formal specification process and use this customized model to formulate a GQM-based measurement plan for the same process. We then discuss how the generic model would be useful in process assessment and process improvement.

1 Introduction

Our aim is to perform process assessment by using techniques from Empirical Software Engineering including the use of quantifiable metrics. Many methods exist for the selection of metrics; prominent among them is the Goal-Question-metric (GQM) method [1]. Under this approach, we define some goals, refine those goals into a set of questions, and the questions are further refined into metrics. Of course it is important, in relation to a certain objective, to neither measure too much nor too little. The measured values are then interpreted to answer the goals that we started with. The question that then arises is: from where should we choose the goals whose refinement will give us the metrics? The usual approach is to choose a quality model, and keeping both the model as well as the application domain of the process in mind, the goals are derived through extended consultation [17, 6]. Among the models

R. Dumke and A. Abran (Eds.): IWSM 2000, LNCS 2006, pp. 94-110, 2001.
© Springer-Verlag Berlin Heidelberg 2001

available for process assessment, the most influential ones include: the Capability Maturity Model (CMM) [12], ISO/IEC 12207 [15], ISO 9001/9000-3 [14], the BOOTSTRAP model [3], and the SPICE model [7]. These process models are not specific enough to cater to the needs of each of the individual processes. The reasons are: (i) the nature of processes vary widely (ii) most of the models are more oriented towards enhancing the maturity of the organization and take a monolithic view of the overall development process, and finally (iii) the process models, while emphasizing on the process activities, often put too little importance on the products which are the results of the process activities. In this context, there are certain process aspects (including the duality of process attributes which we discuss later) which are not addressed by any of the existing models. In order to alleviate these problems, we define a generic process quality model that incorporates the merits of all the existing models, and takes care of their deficiencies. The generic model could be instantiated to be the customized model of any individual process.

The organization of the paper is as follows. Section 2 describes related work. Section 3 presents an internal process model. Section 4 discusses the generic model and its instantiation of individual processes. Section 5 discusses a GQM-based measurement plan. Section 6 discusses the role of the generic model as regards to process assessment and improvement, and finally, section 7 concludes the paper.

2   Related Work

ISO/IEC 9126 [13] describes a generic model for specifying and evaluating the quality of software products. The model isolates six factors, called Functionality, Usability, Reliability, Efficiency, Maintainability and Portability; and the quality of a product is defined in terms of the quality of the above factors. Each factor may in turn be defined by a set of subfactors. The FURPS+ model used by HP [10] is quite similar to ISO/IEC 9126. Focusing on product quality alone may not guarantee that an organization will deliver products of good quality. Products are created by processes. So, based on an orthogonal view that improving the quality of a process will deliver products of good quality [9], many models have been developed. Prominent among them are the CMM [12] and ISO 90001 [14]. Models like Bootstrap [3] and SPICE [7] are variants of the CMM. ISO/IEC 12207 [15] does a classification of all processes associated with the software development and offers general guidelines which can be used by software practitioners to manage and engineer software. The scope of most of these standards cover an entire organization.

The CMM deals with the capability of a software organization to consistently and predictably produce high quality products [12]. The model defines five maturity levels: from Level 1 to Level 5. A maturity questionnaire assesses the following three areas of the organization: (i) organization and resource management, (ii) software engineering process and its management and (iii) the tools and technology; and based on the assessment the model certifies that the organization is at certain maturity level. The model also identifies the weak areas and prescribes a set of guidelines; following those guidelines, an organization can attain the next higher maturity level. Measurement, quantitative feedback from the processes and continuous process improvement are some of the highlights of the model. However, it has been suggested [21] that increasing the maturity level of an organization may not necessarily lead to improvements in the quality of processes. Further, there is no evidence of a link between a high CMM rating and products that are of high quality [6].

ISO 9001/9000-3 is a model for quality assurance in the development, supply, and maintenance of software. The key strength of ISO 9001 is in its quality system processes. Most of the basic practices of the 9001 translate to level 2 practices of CMM and some translate to level 3 practices [5]. The continuous improvement paradigm has not also been adequately addressed by the standard.

The GQM method [1, 20] proposes a measurement plan for assessing the quality of entities like products, processes or people. It starts with a set of business goals and the goals are progressively refined through questions till we obtain some metrics for measurement. The measured values are then interpreted in order to answer the goals. Existing approaches choose a quality model from those that exist so as to generate the business (or the primary) goals of the GQM formulation for any individual product or process. Application of Metrics in Industry (ami) [Pul 95] combines CMM and the GQM method, and the result is that it provides a complete framework for process improvement. The ami approach is: iterative, goal-oriented, quantitative, involves everyone in the organization and integrates necessary management commitment. It covers the whole of the process improvement cycle. CMM or other standards like Bootstrap, SPICE, ISO 9001 *etc.* is used to identify weak areas in the development process. This information along with the business and environment specific objectives is used to define some software process goals. The goals are validated and next, using the principle of GQM, they are refined into subgoals. The subgoals are further refined into metrics and a measurement plan is made to collect data. The data are then analysed and related to the original goal. Based on the data collected an action plan may be made to improve the development process. New goals are then defined and the cycle is repeated.

Focusing on either process quality or product quality alone is not sufficient. In a European-wide awareness survey 65% of the respondents agreed that certification against ISO 9000 is not enough to guarantee the quality of software products [2]. 40% of the respondents agreed that a combined certification of products and processes is necessary, and almost all of the models fail to make the relationship between process quality models and product quality clear. We will make such a relationship clear by taking the dual nature of process attributes into account. Also note that the models cannot compare lateral processes; for example, they cannot address a question like: is formal specification more suitable than informal specification for a particular organization? Two development processes following one of the approaches may have similar ratings under a process model and hence such a model cannot do such a comparative study.

The PROFES (product-focused) improvement methodology [18] follows an orthogonal approach to process improvement. It first uses ISO 9126 to identify the subfactors in relation to product quality which need to be improved. Following a PPD (Product-Process Dependency) model, it identifies the process attributes which need to be improved for achieving the desired product quality. Then an action plan is made following an ISO 15504 compliant method and the plan is executed. So far as improvement of product quality is concerned, our objective is similar to that of the PROFES methodology. However, in addition, we also address some process specific issues like process faults, process understandability and process reliability.

3   An Internal Process Model

In this paper, unless otherwise stated, by a process we will mean *any software activity associated with the development and maintenance of software*: from requirement analysis through to maintenance. A product is an entity, which a process (e.g. any software activity) produces as output. Examples are requirement documents, specifications, end-products *etc.* Products may also be fed to processes as inputs – specification is an input to design, implementation is as input to testing and so on. Each of the products has a type in the sense that it belongs to a set. Table 1 enumerates some of the products and their types. For a uniform treatment, we will assume that a requirement that exists in a user's mind is also a product. The set of pre-elicitation requirements (the requirements in the user's mind) is well-defined in the sense that an analyst is capable of extracting it in order to produce a requirements document. The set of product definitions above are not exhaustive; based on the application context, a process designer may add or modify the above sets. But once they are defined, they should be adhered to by the process executers.

We will now define our process model which will elucidate the internal structure of a process. A process is any software activity which takes product(s) as input and produces product(s) as output. Formally, it could be defined as a relation from a set of products to another set of products; the set of relations from m input products to n output products could be denoted by:

$$IP_1 \bullet IP_2 \bullet ... \bullet IP_m < - > \quad OP_1 \bullet OP_2 \bullet ... \bullet OP_n$$

where IP_i and OP_j are the types of the i-th input product and the j-th output product respectively. Software processes can be classified into two categories:

(i) **Constructing processes:** These processes take a set of products and apply some transformations over them to generate a new set of products; e.g. formal specification, implementation, maintenance etc.

(ii) **Verifying processes:** Such processes take a set of products and do some verification or validation over them to determine whether they hold or do not hold certain properties. They are more like functions. They do not apply any transformations on the input products. The result is usually a Boolean condition, and some other information such as defect data, certain inferences from verification and/or other documentation. Examples of such processes are: formal verification, validation, code inspection, testing etc.

Our definitions of constructing processes and the verifying processes mostly correspond to the development processes and some of the supporting processes of ISO/IEC 12207 [15]. Some examples of processes are shown in Table 2.

The above definitions are not absolute but should be adapted by the designer of a process who will choose the input product set and the output product set keeping the application context in mind. For instance, the validation of formal specification may output a set of features which are found invalid; the code inspection process in addition to indicating whether code is good, bad or of moderate quality may output a set of suggestions for code improvement. But a prior definition of a process on the above lines by its designer establishes a standard, which, if adhered to by the process executers, will make the process execution more disciplined. Usually the output product of a process is fed as input to another process. So giving a type to such a product helps in better communication between the process executers of both the processes.

Table 1. Some products with their types

req:	*PRE-ELICIT-REQ*	// Set of pre elicitation requirements
rd:	*RD*	// Set of requirement documents.
spc:	*SPEC*	// Set of Specifications
fs:	*FML-SPEC*	// Set of formal specifications
des:	*DESIGN*	// Set of designs
mod:	*MODULES*	// Set of set of program modules
fd:	*FDESIGN*	// Set of formal designs
impl:	*IMPL*	// Set of implementations
testdata:	*TESTDATA*	// Set of test data
defectdata:	*DEF-DATA*	// Set of defect data
doc:	*DOC*	// Set of documentations
insp-flag:	*FLAGSET*	// Set of flags to indicate quality of code
form-proof:	*FML-PROOF*	// Set of formal proofs
safety-cases:	*SAFETY-CASES*	// Set of safety cases

Table 2. Some processes with their types

Requirement analysis:	*PRE-ELICIT-REQ* $<->$ *RD*
Formal specification:	*RD* $<->$ *FS*
Formal design:	*RD • FS* $<->$ *FD*
Maintenance:	*RD•SPEC •DES • IMPL • DOC* $<->$ *RD •SPEC•DES • IMPL • DOC*
Validation of formal spec.:	*RD • FS* $<->$ *Bool*
Verification of formal design:	*FS • FD* $<->$ *Bool*
Code inspection:	*IMPL* $<->$ *FLAGSET*

To show that a process may have many type definitions, let us take the example of the formal specification process (FS process). Table 2 defines the type of the FS Process as: *RD* $<->$ *FS*. A process designer may design this process so that the specifier not only consults the RD, but also interviews the users to complete the specification. Then the type of the FS process would be:

$$PRE\text{-}ELICIT\text{-}REQ•RD \ <-> \ FS$$

Thus a process, depending on its design, may have many types; but an organization, in relation to a specific project and for a specific set of processes, will usually stick to one type definition. However, any type definition of a process will uniquely identify a process. For instance, both the preceding type definitions correspond to the FS process.

The proof follows from the construction of process definitions, and we will not elaborate it here.

The question may arise as to whether our simplistic type definitions given to processes do really correspond to the complex nature of processes. To illustrate this point, consider a type definition of the design process as: $SPEC < -> DESIGN$. Some requirements may arise quite late, i.e., during the design process. The given type definition then cannot handle such a situation. As mentioned earlier, the type definition of a process is not unique, but an organization should follow one type definition which suits its best. To accommodate the fact that requirements may arise during the design phase, an organization can have the type definition:

$$PRE\_ELICIT\_REQ \ X \ SPEC \ < -> DESIGN$$

Further, the arrival of such requirements may demand that the specification be changed accordingly. Such a situation could be handled by the type definition:

$$PRE\_ELICIT\_REQ \ X \ RD \ < -> \ SPEC$$

A process may be composed of subprocesses. For example, consider the testing process and let it consist of unit testing and integration testing (we will ignore system testing and acceptance testing for the time being). Both are subprocesses of the testing process. A subprocess is also a process in the sense that it takes a product set as input and gives out a product set as output. Unit testing also consists of subprocesses like black-box testing and white-box testing. Whether a process should be decomposed into subprocesses or not is decided by the process designer. For instance, the designer may decide not to decompose further the processes like the black-box testing and the white-box testing. We refer to such processes as *atomic* processes. When considered from a process point of view, the inputs and outputs of subprocesses are called intermediate product sets. Usually, the output of a process becomes the input of another process (see Figure 1). Note that the subprocesses within the scope of a process need not be homogeneous; for instance, in Figure 1, in between unit testing and integration testing, there may be an integration subprocess which is not strictly a part of the testing process. An atomic process is in turn defined as a set of steps, like the steps of an algorithm. But unlike the case of an algorithm, the steps usually do not have rigorous definitions: a process executer usually has degrees of flexibility; for instance, during the code inspection process, an inspector may pass a piece of code as OK, while another inspector may find it complex and suggest simplification. During structured design, a designer has flexibility when deciding which group of nodes in a structured chart would be put inside a module. Thus, process executers often have to use their artistic skills rather than sticking to some strict and rigorous definitions.

There are three aspects to the steps of an atomic process: *what are its process steps, who will execute those process steps* and *how they will be done*? A process is defined in terms of process steps and each process step is in turn defined by a set of flexible guidelines. Further, some resources like supporting tools may be needed to execute the process steps. All of these contribute to the 'how' part of the questions. Each atomic process, in addition to its input and output product sets, will have its starting and ending conditions. They correspond to the 'what' part of the questions. The 'who' part will be taken care of by a person or some automatic tool. ISO/IEC 12207 follows a similar (though less formal) approach to process modeling.

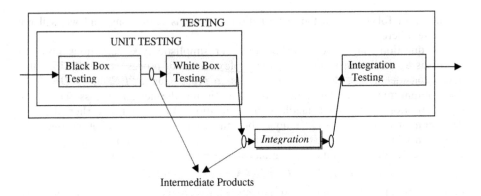

Fig. 1. Intermediate products in the testing process

Our process model is useful in many ways. The type structure offers a general view; depending on specific needs, restrictions can be imposed upon them. Consider an organization which formally verifies its code; and in order to facilitate this process, code is written in SPARK [16]. In such a case, a constraint can be imposed upon the coding process that code must be written in SPARK. Further, our process architecture takes a modular view of the process in the sense that the type of every process or subprocess is made clear at the definition level. The well-defined type structure of our process model makes the larger context of a task or activity or process step clearer.

There are three ways of looking at a process for assessment (i.e. evaluation of a process through measurable attributes). The first one is the black-box view. Under this scheme, we do not look at the internals of a process (that it may consist of subprocesses or process steps), but rather view it as a black box and try to observe its effects by analysing its input and output product sets. Under the white-box assessment scheme, we analyse the internal behaviour of the process; this may include analyzing the subprocesses that the process consists of. By subprocess analysis, we mean that we observe the intermediate products corresponding to an input product set of the main process. There are certain product independent attributes such as process cycle time, process cost, total process effort *etc.* are also very important observation entities. Process failures also need to be considered. Examples of process failures are: a supporting tool (say a testing tool in the testing process) crashing or a verifying tool failing to verify *etc.* To summarize, for assessing a process we need to have (i) its black-box view (ii) white box view and (iii) the study of the product-independent attributes discussed above.

Unlike product assessment, process assessment is non-trivial for the following reasons.

• For assessing a process, we in turn look at the input, output and the intermediate products. So assessment is *mostly* indirect in nature. (Although, products are usually assessed in this way as well, it is possible to assess software directly through code reviews, static analysis, formal verification etc., which is not the case for processes.) Further, we need to assess a number of input and output product sets and their intermediate products in order to find out something concrete about the process. In a sense, the process behaviour is the average of the observations of a large number of input and output products and their intermediate products.

- Most of the process attributes have a dual perspective. Consider, for instance, the understandability attribute. The two perspectives are (i) the concepts of the process should itself be understandable to the process executer and further (ii) the process should make its output product sets understandable. When we consider the formal specification process, the method of creating the formal specification and the formal specification language itself must be understandable to the specifier, and further the specification process must make the formal specification understandable to its users. In conclusion, any process assessment must consider a dual perspective. Of course since we are looking at product attributes from the process quality point of view, we may miss out some important product factors which are not directly addressed by process quality factors. In order to alleviate this problem, we use major product quality models (see Section 4) as references while defining our generic process quality model.

- If a process introduces a defect in its output, then at a later period it may be discovered and the source of the defect could be traced back to the process. So, it is not only the case that time span of process assessment is long but also it may include time periods when the process is not active.

4   Our Generic Quality Model

In the last section, our process model has been described at a much higher level. In order to make it a generic quality model, its internal details need to be filled in. To do this, we take as reference the ISO 9001/9000-3 model, the ISO/IEC 12207 model, the CMM, the ISO/IEC 9126 model and the FURPS+ model. We have included the last two product quality models because while dealing with process quality we also want to put emphasis on the product aspects. Table 3 illustrates our generic model in which each factor is defined by a set of subfactors. Appendix A presents the definitions of the subfactors of the generic model. This generic model (Gmodel) could be seen as a template with three parameters:

$$Gmodel(\textbf{\textit{inp-prod-set-type, out-prod-set-type, application-domain}})$$

where by application domain we mean whether it is a safety-critical application, a real-time application, a business application *etc.*

The customization proceeds in two steps: (i) the substitution step and (ii) the refinement step. In the substitution step, we substitute the parameters with their actual bindings. Let us take the example of the FS process and let its type be **RD** $<->$ **FS**. The substitution is illustrated by the expression:

$$Gmodel\ [\ \underline{RD}\ /\ \textbf{inp-prod-set-type}\ ]\ [\ \underline{FS}\ /\ \textbf{out-prod-set-type}\ ]$$

Table 3. Factors and their Subfactors in the Generic Process Quality Model

Functionality	Compliance Completeness Consistency Generality Suitability Inter-operability Security
Usability	Understandability Learnability Operability
Efficiency **&** **Estimation**	Cost/ Effort estimation Cycle Time Complexity estimation Resource Usage Schedule/ Priority estimation Process maturity
Visibility and Control	Automatic checks and feedback Progress Monitoring Improvement Measures
Reliability	Failure Frequency Fault Tolerance Recoverability
Safety	Risk avoidance
Scalability	Scalability
Maintainability	Analysability Modifiability Stability Testability Defect Trend Formal Verifiability Informal Verifiability Reusability Portability

Note that if a particular process has input product set type IP and output product set type OP, then the process takes a member of IP as input and produces a member of type OP as output. So the above expression signifies that, all occurrences of the input product set in the definitions of the factors and the subfactors in the generic model are substituted by RD (requirement document). Similarly, all occurrences of output product set are substituted by FS (formal specification). Thus, at the end of the substitution step, we have a crude definition of each of the subfactors of the process concerned.

With these assumptions, since we already know the type of the process, we also know the process name (refer to Section 2). For the *application-domain parameter*, assume that it is a safety critical application. Now, with the knowledge that we are dealing with a FS process in a safety critical application, the refinement step refines the crude definitions that we have obtained after the substitution step. The result then will be the customized quality model for the FS process. As an illustration, the definitions of some of the subfactors of the FS process are given in Appendix B. For example, consider the first part of the subfactor 'completeness'. After the substitution step, we obtain the following definition: *the degree to which the process transforms all of the functionalities of the RD into the FS*. In the refinement step we know that it is the FS process and the application domain is the 'safety critical application'. Further FS process achieves transformation through specification; and at the RD level, a functionality is understood by a 'feature'. So the refined definition is: *the degree to which the FS process specifies all of the features (including the safety critical features) of the RD in the FS*.

5   The Measurement Plan through the GQM Paradigm

The GQM-based measurement plan starts with the specification of some goals concerning the project. Then a set of questions are formulated whose answers would in turn provide an answer to this main goal. Then one should determine what metrics should be measured so that each of the questions could be answered. Let us start with a goal such as: *assess the Functionality of the FS process*. From the quality model for FS, the functionality of the FS process is defined in terms a set of subfactors. Now the definition of these subfactors will give rise to questions in the GQM formulation, and the questions when considered in the context of formal specification, will help to formulate the metrics. Table 4 elaborates the measurement plan.

6   Benefits of the Generic Model

- The fact that certain individual processes need special attention is more or less ignored by the existing process quality models. Our generic model provides an answer to this. During the course of instantiation, the generic model takes the application-domain as a parameter. This parameter, in combination with the other parameters of a process, emphasizes those individual process attributes which need special attention. Further, we offer a systematic approach to the instantiation of the customized model.
- The relationship between the process quality model and product quality is never well-defined in existing process models. ISO 12207 suggests following ISO 9126 to ensure product quality and ISO 9001 for quality assurance [19]. Our dual perspective of process attributes makes this relationship between process quality and product quality more visible. So, our model can be used as a companion to the ISO 12207 standard.
- **The Generic Model and Process Assessment/Improvement:** the ami method [Pul 95] classifies primary goals into two categories: knowledge goals and change goals. Knowledge goals are for assessment purposes and the change goals are for improvement purposes. Under the ami approach, primary goals are transformed into a goal tree. Building the goal tree is always an art. For the refinement of a goal (or a subgoal) we must identify the products, the processes associated with the goal and also the participants who are responsible for each of

such products or processes, and further what resource the participants use or can use [Pul 95]. We claim that our quality model will help in building such a goal tree in a systematic manner. Because of the duality of the subfactors, their definitions themselves cover both the process as well as the product aspects of the goal. The context of the process easily identifies the participants associated with the subgoal. Further, the definitions of the subfactors provide enough information for identifying the associated quantitative metrics.

Table 4. A GQM based measurement plan

Goal:	*Object of Study:*	FS Process
	Purpose:	To assess
	Focus:	Functionality
	Points-of-view:	Manager/Maintainer/Specifier
Q1.	Underlying specification language? *Metric:* Note the language	
Q2.	Specification process complying with the syntax and semantics of the formal language? *Metric:* No. of deviations	
Q3.	Specification of functions matching the RD/User needs? *Metric:* Trend of incorrectly specified features.	
Q4.	Specification process uncovering all contradictions in RD? Process introducing contradictions during specification? *Metric:* No. of contradictions found in RD No. of contradictions discovered in FS	
Q5.	(i) Process specifying all features of a RD? (ii) Process failing in specifying a RD? *Metric:* (i) No. of missing features in a FS (ii) History of failures in specifying RDs	
Q6.	Process over-specifying the features of a RD? *Metric:* No. of over-specified features in a FS (subjective assessment by the Specifier)	
Q7.	Process addressing all security features in FS? *Metric:* No. of security lapses in implementation/end-product linked to FS process.	
Q8.	Process addressing all inter-operability features in RD? *Metric:* No. of inter-operability problems in implementation/ end-product linked to FS process.	

7   Conclusions and Future Work

In this paper we have presented a new process model which assigns types to the processes and the products associated with them. We have then defined a generic quality model which could be instantiated to be the quality model for any particular process, and shown how such a customization could be done in a systematic manner. One important highlight of our generic model is that it makes the relationship between product quality and process quality much clearer. This relationship is handled in an ad-hoc manner by existing models.

Like the PROFES improvement methodology, our generic model can be used to achieve better product quality. However, the PROFES methodology depends on previous experience to address process-specific issues, which can lead to neglect of issues like process defects, process scalability, process understandability etc. A detailed comparison between PROFES methodology and our generic model is a part of our future work.

The processes that we have handled in our model have the same type structure: they are relations between an input product set and an output product set. However, there are processes with complicated type structures. One such example is the *quality improvement process (QIP)* which takes a quality model and a process (say a development process), and returns a process (which should be improved). Part of our future work will be to extend our model to cover the whole spectrum of processes. We also intend to validate our generic model using industrial platforms.

Acknowledgements:

The authors wish to acknowledge the support of UK EPSRC, which has funded EMPAF (ER/L87347) and a Ph.D. studentship for this work.

References

1. Basili, V.R., Caldiera, G., Rombach, H.D.: The Goal Question Metric Approach. The Encyclopedia of Software Engineering, John Wiley (1994)
2. Bazzana, G. et al.: ISO 9000 and ISO 9126: Friends or Foes? Proc. of IEEE Software Engineering Standards Symposium, Brighton, Sept (1993)
3. Bootstrap Team, Bootstrap: Europes's Assessment Method. IEEE S/W, Sept (1993)
4. Chaudron, M. et al.: Lessons from the Application of Formal Methods to the Design of a Storm Surge Barrier Control System. Proc. of FM'99, LNCS No. 1709, Springer (999)
5. Coallier, F.: How ISO 9001 fits into the Software's World. IEEE S/W, January (1994)
6. Debou, C.: Goal-Based Software Process Improvement Planning in Better Software Practice and Business Benefit (Eds. R. Messnarz and C. Tully). IEEE Computer Society (1999)
7. Dorling, A.: SPICE: Software Process Improvement and Capability Determination. Software Quality Journal, Vol. (2) (1993)
8. Fenton, N.E., Pfleeger, S.L.: Software Metrics: A Rigorous & Practical Approach. International Thomson Computer Press (1996)

9. Grady, R.B., Caswell, D.L.: Software Metrics: Establishing a Company-wide Program. Printice Hall, New Jersey (1987)
10. Grady, R.B.: Practical Software Metrics for Project Management and Process Improvement. Printice Hall, New Jersey (1992)
11. Haase, V. et al.: Bootstrap: Fine-Tuning Process Assessment. IEEE S/W, July (1994)
12. Humphrey, W.S.: Introduction to Software Process Improvement. SEI Report CMU/SEI-92-TR-7 (1992)
13. International Standard: ISO/IEC 9126, ISO, Geneva (1991)
14. ISO 9001, Quality Systems – Model for Quality Assurance in Design, Development, Production, Installation and Servicing. 2nd Ed., ISO (1994)
15. ISO/IEC 12207, Software Life Cycle Processes. 1st Ed., Aug (1995)
16. King, S., Hammond, J., Chapman, R., Pryor, A.: The value of verification: Positive experience of Industrial Proof. FM'99, LNCS No. 1709, Springer (1999)
17. Pulford, K., Kuntzmann-Combelles, A., Shirlaw, S.: A Quantitative Approach to Software management: The AMI Handbook. Addison Wesley (1996)
18. The PROFES Methodology. website http://www.profes.org
19. Singh, R.: International Standard ISO/IEC 12207 Software Life Cycle Processes, Software Process – Improvement and Practice. 2(1996) 35-50
20. Solingen, R.v., Berghout, E.: The Goal/Question/Metric Method: A Practical Guide for Quality Improvement of Software Development. Mc Graw Hill (1999)
21. Voas, J.: Can Clean Pipes Produce Dirty Water. IEEE Software, Jul/ Aug. (1999)

Appendix A: Definitions of the Subfactors of the Generic Model

(a) Subfactors of Functionality

Compliance:

(i) The degree to which the process conforms to prescribed (IEEE, ISO or company-specific) standards.

(ii) The degree to which the process conforms to its own model (i.e. it consists of a set of subprocesses and the subprocesses in turn consisting of subprocesses or sets of steps).

Consistency:

(i) The degree to which the process uncovers contradictions in the input product set.

(ii) The degree to which the process does not introduce contradictions in the output product set.

Completeness:

(i) The degree to which the process transforms all of the functionalities of the input product set into the output product set.

(ii) The degree to which the process handles all inputs with valid types.

Generality (*robustness*): The ability of the process to address by over-specifying/ over-implementing conditions which are not covered by the input product specification but are relevant to its context.

Suitability (also known as *correctness*):

(i) The degree to which the process makes the functionalities of the output product set match accurately those in the input product set.

(ii) The degree to which the implementation of the process accurately matches its own specification (any gap between what the process does and what it is supposed to do?)

Security: The degree to which the process addresses the security issues of the final product against hostile environments (too important for network applications involving critical activities such as e-commerce)

Inter-operability: The degree to which the process contributes to the inter-operability (the ability of the product to interact with specified systems) of the final product.

(b) Subfactors of Usability

Understandability:
(i) The effort with which a typical process executer (any of Analyst/ Specifier/ Developer/ Programmer/ Maintainer) understands the logical concepts of the process.
(ii) The degree to which the process contributes to the understandability of its output product set and that of the end-product.

Learnability:
(i) The effort required for a typical process executer to learn to use the process.
(ii) The degree to which the process makes the output product set/ the end-product easy to use (through informative help messages, good user interface etc.)

Operability:
(i) The effort required for a typical process executer to execute the process with a level of confidence (this could be inferred from the learning curve of the process executer).
(ii) The degree to which a process contributes to the operability of the output product set and the end-product (through informative help messages, guidelines).

(c) Subfactors of Efficiency & Estimation

Cost/ Effort Estimation: The degree to which the cost/ effort of process execution remain within a specified range and the ability of the process to support their estimations.

Cycle Time estimation: The degree to which a process meets its expected cycle time and the ability of the process to support its estimation.

Complexity estimation: The ability of the process to support the prior estimation of various forms of complexity (Computational Complexity, Communication Complexity, Structural Complexity, Cognitive Complexity etc [8, 9]), and the degree to which the estimates are accurate.

Schedule/ Priority estimation: The priority of various stages in the process and the ability of the process to support their estimations and scheduling.

Resource Estimation: The degree to which a process keeps its resource usage in a specified range, and its ability to support their estimations.

Process Maturity: The CMM maturity level and/or any ISO certification of the organization.

(d) Subfactors of Visibility & Control

Progress Monitoring: The ability of the process to facilitate monitoring of its progress at any point of time during the process execution to show that progress so far has been correct and effective. (e.g. work product analysis [10], PERT charts etc.)

Automatic Feedback: The ability of the process to provide (or support in providing) feedback data and to support corrective actions if necessary (e.g. Automatic work product analysis tools [10]).

Improvement Measures: The ability of the process to support the analysis of the feedback data in combination with the data of previous runs and improve itself, or result in the improvement of a sibling process, continuously (e.g. FS process improving the testing process [4]).

(e) Subfactors of Reliability
> (i)The degree to which the process prevents failures in the final product (a process relying on unsafe unsafe features of C may lead to failures).
> (ii)The degree to which the process is reliable itself. In that case, we will have the sub-factors:
> > - **Failure Frequency:** The number of (and the interval between) failures encountered during the execution of the process. The failures are due to defects in the design/ implementation of the process itself. (e.g. an automatic tool crashing or taking too much time)
> > - **Fault Tolerance:** Whether the process can still continue in presence of faults/ failures in the process itself (e.g. use of redundant tools).
> > - **Recoverability:** Whether the process can attain its level of operation after a process failure has been addressed.

(f) Subfactors of Scalability
> (i) The degree to which a process makes its output or the end-product perform in an expected way (in terms of time and resource usage) in face of a large problem context (e.g. A robust and complete design of a database system can make it handle a large problem).
> (ii) The degree to which the process maintains its efficiency level in terms of time, cost and resource usage in handling a problem of larger dimension.

(f) Subfactors of Safety
> (i) Depending on the underlying application, the input product set may define safety conditions which could take the form of (a) liveness (b) degraded performance and (c) limiting damage from failures. The degree to which the process addresses them (say, through introduction of fault-tolerance).
> (ii) The process must not introduce unsafe features that may result in hazards occurring (a compiler, for optimization purposes converting static memory to dynamic memory [16]).

(g) Subfactors of Maintainability
Analysability: The effort with which a typical process maintainer can analyse the cause of a fault, process failure or unexpected feedback data. A fault could be one of the following categories.
> (i) the fault is discovered during the process execution and the fault may be with the process itself, or it may be with the input product set.
> (ii) the fault is discovered at a later point in time, and the cause of the fault is linked to the process.

Modifiability: The effort with which a Maintainer addresses failures, detection of faults and unexpected feedback data during the process execution; or faults discovered at a later time but linked to the process.

Stability:
> (i) The degree to which addressing a process fault adversely affects the process itself (say, process efficiency or properties like process consistency).
> (ii) The frequency of changes done to the process (less the number of changes, more is the stability).

Formal Verifiability: Effort with which properties like consistency, correctness and invariant conditions of the transformed product could be formally verified during process execution.

Informal Verifiability: Effort with which properties like completeness, generality etc. of the product under transformation could be informally verified during process execution.

Testability:
- (i) The degree to which the process could be validated itself (success history of its output products).
- (ii) The degree to which the process contributes to the testability of its output or the final product (say, for generating an adequate test suite).

Defect Trend:
- (i) The trend of defects that are observed in the process itself (defects linked to the process – during or after process execution).
- (ii) The degree to which the process detects the defects or deficiencies in the product set under transformation so that defects in the output product set and the final product are minimal.

Reusability:
- (i) The degree to which the process contributes to the reusability of its output product .
- (ii) The degree to which components of the process could be reused in a different context (testing process of one organization could be reused in another organization).

Portability: The degree to which the process contributes to the portability of the end-product; i.e., the process should facilitate the migration of the product to a different environment.

Appendix B: Some Sufactors of the FS Process

Completeness:
- (i) The degree to which the FS process specifies all of the features (including safety critical) of the RD.
- (ii) To what extent the specification process can handle all RDs with valid types.

Consistency:
- (i) The degree to which the FS process uncovers contradictions in the RD.
- (ii) The degree to which the FS process does not introduce contradictions in the FS.

Security: The degree to which the FS process specifies the security issues (unauthorized access to program and data) of the final product against hostile environments (too important for network applications involving critical activities such as e-commerce, e-banking etc.)

Understandability:
- (i) The degree to which the syntax and the semantics of the specification language, and the logical concepts of Specifying are understandable to the Analyst, Specifier, Developer, and the Maintainer.

(ii) The degree to which the FS process contributes to the understandability of the FS (say, through comments).

Cost/ Effort Estimation: The degree to which the cost/ effort of the FS process are kept within allowable limits, and the ability of the FS process to support their estimations.

Maturity Evaluation of the Performance Engineering Process

Andreas Schmietendorf and André Scholz

University of Magdeburg, Faculty of Computer Science, Germany
schmiete@ivs.cs.uni-magdeburg.de,
ascholz@iti.cs.uni-magdeburg.de

Abstract. This contribution presents a model for process improvement in the area of performance engineering, which is called performance engineering maturity model. The use of this model allows the evaluation of the level of integration and application of performance engineering. It leans against the well-established capability maturity model from the software engineering institute. The model is based on a questionnaire catalog, which was transferred into a web based evaluation form. The results of this anonymous evaluation are analyzed in this contribution.

1   Introduction

In practice, software engineering most time only considers functional specifications. But meanwhile companies pay more and more attention to non-functional requirements. Therefore, processes are adapted in order to develop high quality software and quality assurance systems are installed.

One of the most critical non-functional quality factor is the performance characteristic of a software system. Performance can be defined as the capability of a system to process a given amount of tasks in a determined time interval. Thereby, performance of software systems stands in direct relationship with the speed of accompanying business processes. This relationship appears especially important in the context of the current market 'Electronic Commerce by using internet technologies'. The performance characteristic of this kind of applications is one of the major success factors with regard to the acceptance of the user. Gartner Group evaluated this market as the most important expansion market for the next years [1]. A special attention must be paid on the right integration of customer's, subcontractor's and service provider's business processes with regard to performance aspects.

A lot of software engineering projects as well as productive systems fail because of insufficient performance characteristics. Up to now, performance characteristics are often only considered at the end of the software development process. If performance bottlenecks are only recognized at the end of the software development, extensive tuning activities, design modifications of the application or complete rejectings of entire software systems will be necessary.

That is why, a performance oriented software development method, like performance engineering (PE), should be integrated within the engineering process [2]. PE considers the response time as a design target throughout the whole software

R. Dumke and A. Abran (Eds.): IWSM 2000, LNCS 2006, pp. 111-124, 2001.

development process. Response time targets and analyses of the respective design structures are continuously compared. In early stages response time metrics can be quantified using estimation formulas, analytical models, simulation models and prototypes. Deviations lead to an immediate change in the software design. Thus, PE guarantees an adequate response time behavior of the productive system. PE of software systems needs an entire approach, considering the complete software development process. For this purpose, practical models of integration are already available [3].

The efficiency of the PE application depends decisively on the maturity of the PE integration and application. The higher the integration of PE processes and methods, the lower the PE costs and the performance-entailed development risks. The need for an evaluation technique of the PE integration and application was already pointed out at the "First International Workshop on Software and Performance in 1998". For that reason, we now propose a Performance Engineering Maturity Model (PEMM), which leans against the capability maturity model (CMM) to determine the grade of maturity of the PE process within the software development.

After an introduction of the basic framework of the CMM, the PEMM and it's practical application is explained. In addition, it is shown how the model was transferred into a web based evaluation form and evaluation results are discussed.

2   The Capability Maturity Model

The quality of software systems depends decisively on the quality of the corresponding software engineering processes. That is why, a software buyer is interested in getting to know the grade of maturity of the vendors software engineering process to draw conclusions on the software system's quality.

The Software Engineering Institute (SEI) of Carnegie Mellon University developed a framework for evaluating the maturity of a company's software engineering process in 1987 by order of the US Department of Defense. This framework, which is known as the capability maturity model (CMM), distinguishes five different maturity levels. With the help of an evaluation catalog, the maturity of a company's software engineering process can be assigned to one of these levels. The levels are based on each other, which means that if an engineering process fulfills the requirements of a level, it also fulfills all requirements of all levels below. With an increase of the CMM level the development risk can be reduced and the productivity of development as well as the quality of the product can be increased. The individual levels and evaluation catalog can be borrowed from the relevant literature [4][5].

The CMM focuses on the software engineering process only. Additional accompaniment concepts of software engineering, like performance engineering, are hard to consider within this model. Among others the SEI also recognized the need of linking the basic CMM with performance engineering processes on some way[6]. In principle, there are two possibilities for considering performance engineering processes. On the one side the CMM could be extended or on the other side a new model could be created. We propose to create a new maturity model for performance engineering, because some companies still don't use performance engineering concepts, because they even develop performance uncritical systems.

3   The Performance Engineering Maturity Model

It is the aim of the PEMM to evaluate PE processes as well as the process integration [7]. The proposed evaluation model can be used for evaluation as well as for developing processes further. Furthermore, the PEMM level can become a selection criteria for choosing a software system provider for critical or semi-critical products. Thereby, a PEMM level states to what extent a concrete process is in the position to carry out a performance oriented software development. Thus, a system provider is in the position to stand out against the market. The model refers to classical business information systems like financial application systems. The inclusion of special systems with a real time behavior is not recommended at this time, because the development of such kinds of systems is based on very specific engineering processes and methods.

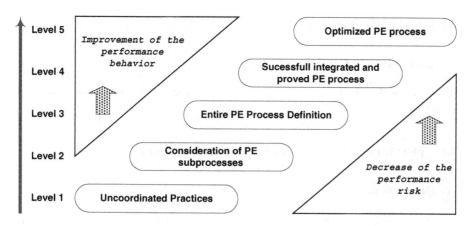

Fig. 1. Maturity Levels of Performance Engineering Processes

In the following, every individual level of the PEMM (see Figure 1) is described by its most important characteristics in three sections. First, a description determines the general contents of the level. Similar to the CMM, PEMM key criteria, which are the elementary basis of each level, were defined for every maturity level. Several aspects are assigned to every key criteria, which show which tasks have to be done for the fulfillment of the key criteria. Leaning against the Goal Question Metric Method (GQM) wise questions and metrics need to be derived from these aspects. Suitable questions have to be selected and then necessary ordinal measures (at present only 'Yes' or 'No') need to be determined for a quantified answer of these questions [8]. In this contribution, selected questions of the perspectives organization, project management, process management and technology are listed in a questionnaire catalog. However, by considering all facets of the aspects the whole questionnaire catalog would be much more complex. Because of the respective scope, the presentation of the whole catalog is not possible in this contribution.

Similar to the CMM, all levels are based on each other. A respective level implies the description and process maturity of all subordinate levels.

3.1   PEMM Level 1 - Uncoordinated Practices

(a) Description:

- The use of PE depends on the personal engagement of individual developers.
- The organizational structure does not support the PE process explicitly.
- Accordingly, individual methods are only used unstructured.

(b) Key Criteria: do not exist

(c) Examples for a Catalogue of Questions:

PEMM Level 1 is the initial stage of all processes. Therefore, it is not useful to define questions to determine this level.

3.2   PEMM Level 2 - Consideration of PE Subprocesses

(a) Description:

- Parts of the whole PE process are already considered.
- Individual PE service provider exist.
- However, a complete process description is not yet available.

(b) Key Criteria:

- **Performance Requirement Management:** Performance characteristics of essential system functions are defined, which are required from the customer.
- **Performance Tracking:** The performance characteristics are verified throughout the whole software life cycle.
- **Personal Identification:** All engineers, which are involved in the development and in maintaining the software, are obliged to the quality factor performance.

(c) Examples for a Catalog of Questions:

Table 1. Level 2 - Examples of Questions

Perspective	Questions		yes	no
Organization	•	Is there a fundamental management-agreement, that performance should be considered within the development process?		
	•	Is there a performance-related communication channel?		
Project Management	•	Are there enough resources (personnel, infrastructure) to do PE?		
	•	Do the staff have the necessary skills to do PE?		
	•	Does the project manager know elementary concepts of PE?		
	•	Are performance-related tasks delegated within the project?		
Process Management	•	Are single PE procedures completely defined in written?		
	•	Is a PE plan for each project created?		
Technology	•	Are single tools used for PE tasks?		
	•	Are there already performance experiences with technologies in use?		

3.3   PEMM Level 3 - Entire PE Process Definition

(a) Description:

- The PE process is considered within the entire software development process. All available PE methods and tools are used comprehensively with regard to the existing performance risk.
- Performance-relevant product and resource metrics are selected and standardized within the company. These metrics and their quantifications are stored and managed in appropriate database systems to guarantee a continuous reflux of experiences.
- The performance requirements of customer, which are defined in the system analyze phase, are used as success criteria at the final inspection test. Furthermore, they are arranged in service level agreements (SLA) with the provider of the software system.
- Furthermore, an initial organizational structure for the entire PE process is defined and introduced step by step in level 3.

(b) Key Criteria:

- **Definition of PE Processes:** There is an entire definition of all processes, which are necessary for PE. Different levels of abstraction have been considered.
- **Performance Problem Prevention:** Performance related problems as well as PE related costs are recognized very early.
- **Performance Goal Management:** Engineering tasks are focussed on performance goals, having an equal position as functional requirements.

- **Performance Engineering Management:** PE tasks are assigned to organizational structures. A management coordinates the whole process.

(c) **Examples for a Catalog of Questions:**

Table 2. Level 3 - Examples of Questions

Perspective	Questions	yes	no
Organization	• Is there an instance, which is responsible for improving and adapting the PE process? • Is the training of project members in PE methods fixed by an organizational instance? • Is there an independent instance, which controls the correspondence of performance analyses and determined standards?		
Project Management	• Do wrong performance characteristics lead to an immediate consideration within the software engineering? • Are there coordination mechanism, adjusting and scheduling single activities?		
Process Management	• Is the whole PE process defined and documented? • Is the integrated PE process the standard process within the software development?		
Technology	• Is there an extensive tool support for all PE methods within the whole life cycle? • Is there a policy to use standardized PE tools only?		

3.4   PEMM Level 4 - Successful integrated and proved PE Process

(a) **Description:**

- The PE tasks are a firm part of the software development. Thus, they are integrated in respective process models. Process, product and resource metrics, which are introduced in level 3, lead to extensive empirical experiences.
- All employees of the software developer and the service provider, which are involved in PE processes, have access to performance relevant metrics and experience data under the consideration of different security and view properties.
- Metrics are used for estimations of characteristics (rules of thumb), for performance models or for statistical evaluations. Furthermore, it should be possible to estimate the costs of PE.
- By the gradual increase of experience and a decrease of performance problems while implementing software systems, the surplus value of PE can be understood directly.
- Furthermore, domain specific instances of PE are defined, e.g., for software systems, graphical tools and technical applications.
- The organizational structure develops itself further in accordance with the experiences.

(b) Key Criteria:

- **Coordination of the Reflux Circle:** Information flows are established between the developer and the service provider to exchange performance-relevant experiences and metrics. This reflux circle is supported on this level by repositories or metric databases.
- **Metrics based PE Controlling:** The surplus value of PE can be proved on the basis of saved costs.
- **Performance Transparency:** All used components in different layers of the software system have a sufficient description of their performance characteristics and resource consumption.
- **Quality Control:** The product to develop as well as all necessary components are subject to a continuos quality control. Thus, customer requirements with regard to performance can be fulfilled.

(c) Examples for a Catalog of Questions:

Table 3. Level 4 - Examples of Questions

Perspective	Questions	yes	no
Organization	• Are organizational structures assigned to the comprehensive PE process?		
Project Management	• Is there a cost-benefit analysis to determine the surplus value of PE?		
Process Management	• Can the PE process immediately be adapted to new technologies and new fields of application? • Are metrics used to compare and evaluate performance characteristics?		
Technology	• Does the technology infrastructure support the rapid customization of the process? • Are performance metrics stored in a database, which is available within the whole development and maintenance process?		

3.5   PEMM Level 5 - Optimized PE Process

(a) Description:

- The maximum degree of process maturity is achieved.
- PE can be applied to all fields of application.
- PE can also absorb technological modifications within the software development like the use of a new middleware.

(b) Key Criteria:

- **Innovation Management:** The PE process is adaptable. Experiences from new application domains as well as new research results with regard to methods and tools flow continuously in the optimization of the process. The process can be adapted to new requirements. User and customer requirements in still unknown domains and technologies can be realized with determined performance characteristic.

(c) Examples for a Catalog of Questions:

Table 4. Level 5 - Examples of Questions

Perspective	Questions	yes	no
Organization	• Is there a continuous PE improving process system?		
Project Management	• Are new and promising methods automatically tested and integrated?		
Process Management	• Do improved engineering techniques lead to a revision of the software engineering process?		
Technology	• Are there tools, which can be used in all kinds of PE applications?		

4   Practical Aspects of Application

4.1   The Maturity Level – A Strategic Target

For a practical application of the PEMM, it is useful to restrict the initial application of the model to a manageable time frame. The model, which is shown in Figure 2, only consistent of the core of the evaluation model with four levels. Level four should be achieved in five years. From our point of view, this is a typical time frame for a strategic plan, which also can be presented to the management. Respectively, the temporal sequence when which step is reached can be understood as a master plan with corresponding mile stones.

Not only statements of the temporal horizon of the achievement of a maturity level, but also cost based statements are necessary for the introduction of the evaluation model:

- **ROI „Return on Investment":** This critical measure is the decision basis for the management of a respective company. It indicates them, if PE concepts should be initiated or improved.
- **Infrastructure based Costs:** These costs comprise the costs for the creation and maintaining of the measuring and modeling instruments, e.g., the creation of a benchmarking laboratory or the implementation of databases for storing performance metrics.

- **Personnel Costs:** The complex tasks of PE require high-specialized employees. Costs are induced by continuos training as well as by project tasks.
- **Performance based Development Risk:** The performance based development risk should reduce in the same degree as the PE maturity level increases.

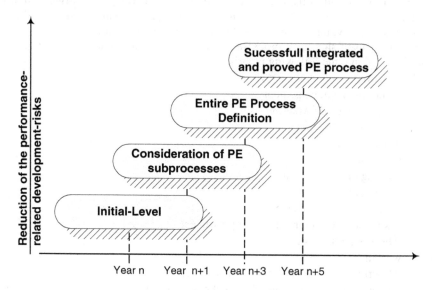

Fig. 2. Introducing the Performance Engineering Maturity Model

4.2   Cooperative Exchange of Performance Related Experiences

Performance engineering relates software development and maintaining. Often two different companies are involved in these both phases, working independently together. The information flow between maintaining and development, which is necessary for performance engineering, should be regulated within a contract. Thus, the operator of the IT system is charged with costs for providing this information. An intercompany initiative, collecting respective data and providing them to all participants, could be an alternative. This kind of experience database was already tested in the field of expense estimation. But still, only a loose cycle can be set up, so that experiences flow back late to the development.

In our point of view, companies, unifying the development and maintaining of software systems, are in a better position for realizing a successful performance engineering.

The problem addressed is not covered by the PEMM explicitly in this first version. But it should be considered within the practical application.

4.3   The Evaluation Process

Obviously, expenditures for determining the maturity level should be minimized. This can be ensured by a tool based process evaluation or by an integration of the evaluation process within the evaluation process of the CMM, if the organization is intending to determine its CMM level, too. By that, questionnaire catalogues should be designed in a way, that organizational units are only polled once.

The polling itself should be processed in a predefined and standardized procedure. It can be parted into the following phases:

- Preparation:
  - Order by the management
  - Collection of information
  - Training
  - Enabling trust
- Realization:
  - Polling different groups
  - Evaluation
  - Strengths weaknesses profile
  - Explication of potentials for improvement
  - Discussing the results
- Reworking:
  - Description of the present and rated situation
  - Description of the strengths weaknesses profile on different topics, e.g., phase or technology based

5   Web-Based Evaluation Form

The questionnaire catalog was transferred into a web based evaluation form (see Figure 3). The form is provided on the web page: http://www-wi.cs.uni-magdeburg.de/~ascholz/PEMM. Beside the evaluation questions, basic questions concerning the classification of the company were integrated into the form. Thus, the kind of business, the sales volume and the number of software projects a year could cluster evaluations. Furthermore, the catalog includes questions to get to know if the companies still have introduced the CMM and subscribed to the ISO 9000 standard. In total 34 questions have to be answered including a commentary field.

The input is forwarded to a CGI script. The script stores the results in a relational database, calculates the results and creates a user feedback page.

With the help of the answers, the PEMM level is calculated. To reach a specific level, all questions of the perspectives organization, process management, project management and technology, which are assigned to that level, have to be answered with "Yes".

Furthermore, to allow a deeper analysis of the results, the maturity levels of these individual perspectives are also calculated (see Figure 4). With it, the evaluation page provides five maturity levels in total.

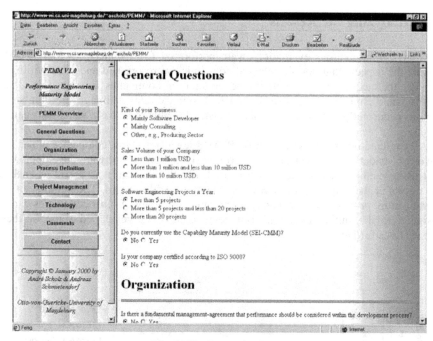

Fig. 3. The Evaluation Form

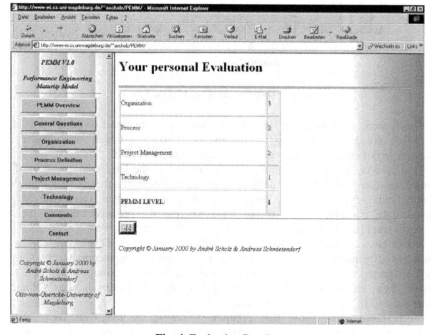

Fig. 4. Evaluation Results

6   Analyzing the Results

Totality, 26 anonymous evaluations were performed from January to March 2000. Beside the aspects that not all potential companies were reached and were willing to provide the necessary information, the amount of companies interested in doing performance engineering is also limited to a small circle. Although the number of records is currently to low for intensive statistical evaluations, basic statements can be made.

All evaluated companies are still on PEMM level one. Most companies either still haven't considered performance engineering tasks within the software development or still using methods and models unstructured. For that reason, it is useful to analyze the results of the single perspectives (see Figure 5 and Figure 6). The maturity of the organization, process, project management and technology of most companies can be assigned to the initial level one. But some companies developed some of these perspectives further.

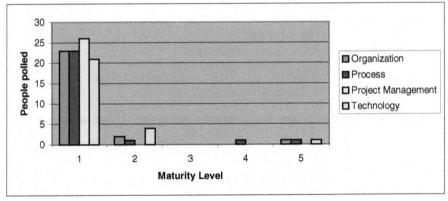

Fig. 5. Distribution of the PEMM Level

In detail, some of them could reach the maturity level two and some of them reach level five already. It is from special interest to get to know which companies are the pioneers in developing their performance engineering processes.

That is why, the data was analyzed with regard to the basic classification of the companies (see Table 5). The development steps were divided into an initial and a matured category, which give a more clustered view on the data. The initial category includes the maturity level two and three whereas the matured category includes maturity level four and five.

It can be seen that in opposite to consulting companies, developing companies show partially initial developments of their performance engineering technology as well as partly matured performance engineering process management. The same development tendencies could be realized at companies having a sales volume of more than 10 million Euro / US-$ a year.

Furthermore, data show that companies managing less than five software engineering projects a year have a partial developed initial performance engineering technology and organization. Maybe this kind of companies is focussed on developing a small amount of high quality software.

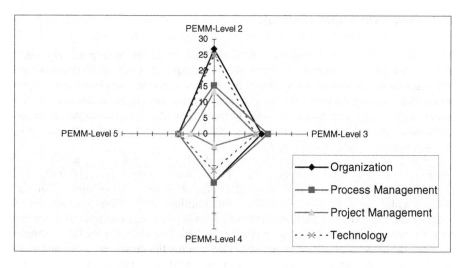

Fig. 6. Kivat Diagram of the Maturity Distribution (in %)

Table 5. Further Influences and Relationships

		Organization		Process		Project Management		Technology	
		initial	matured	initial	matured	initial	matured	initial	matured
Kind	Development				partial			partial	
of	Consulting								
Business	Other								
Sales	< 1 Mill.								
	> 10 Mill.				partial			partial	
Number	< 5	partial						partial	
of	> 5 and < 20								
Projects	> 20								
CMM	Not subscribed							partial	
	subsribed								
ISO 9000	Not subscribed	partial						partial	
	subsribed				partial				

Further on, it was interesting in getting to know if companies using the CMM or subscribing to the ISO 9000 standard can be assigned to a higher maturity level. Data show that such a relationship could not be determined. It can be concluded that performance engineering is still not be focussed in the course of the introduction of the CMM and ISO standards.

The study has shown that all companies have to be rated with the PEMM level one. Some of them show further developments in the perspectives organization, process management and technology. The project management is the least considered.

7   Conclusions and Outlook

We propose a performance engineering maturity model for evaluating the application and integration of PE processes. Thus, the IT management has an instrument for a continuos comparison and improving of these specific processes. The model supplies systematics and guidelines for a process improvement and identifies existing weaknesses. These advantages become more important when it becomes clear that processes have a higher potential for improvement with regard to the whole development task than methods and tools.

For that reason we have the vision, that the PEMM can reach a comparable field of application as the CMM already has. IT software system projects with strict performance requirements, especially electronic commerce applications, software systems within the telecommunication or within military applications, are now able to consider the PEMM level within a contract. With it some developing companies will be not longer in the position to take part on invitations to bid, if they don't improve their performance engineering processes. This assures the customer, that companies, which come in range, develop a solution with the necessary performance requirements at a given duration of time and a fixed price.

But unfortunately some aspects still remain problematic while using the PEMM. The structure and the extension of the questionnaires are very sensitive. Empirical evaluations, if the PEMM levels are sufficiently refined by the questionnaires despite the binary set of answers, are still missing up to now.

References

1. GartnerGroup: Tagungsband. Symposium/ITexpo99, Cannes, Frankreich, Nov. (1999)
2. Scholz, A., Schmietendorf, A.: Zu den Aufgaben und Inhalten des Performance Engineerings. In: HMD – Praxis der Wirtschaftsinformatik (2000)
3. Scholz, A., Rautenstrauch, C.: Vom Performance Tuning zum Software Performance Engineering am Beispiel datenbankbasierter Anwendungssysteme. In: Informatik Spektrum, 22(1999)4
4. Balzert, H.: Lehrbuch der Software-Technik. Software-Management. Software-Qualitäts-sicherung. Unternehmensmodellierung, Heidelberg, Berlin (1998)
5. Chrissis, M., Curtis, B., Paulk, M.: Capability Maturity Model for Software. Version 1.1, Software Engineering Institute, Technical Report-24, Feb. (1993)
6. Klein, M.: State of the Practice Report. Problems in the Practice of Performance Engineering. Technical Report, No. SEI-95-TR-020, Software Engineering Institute, Pittsburgh (1995)
7. Scholz, A., Schmietendorf, A.: A risk-driven Performance Engineering Process Approach and its Evaluation with a Performance Engineering Maturity Model. In: Proceedings of the 15th Annual UK Performance Engineering Workshop, Bristol, UK, July 22-23 (1999)
8. Dumke, R., Foltin, E., Koeppe R., Winkler, A.: Softwarequalität durch Meßtools. Vieweg-Verlag, Wiesbaden (1996)
9. IEEE Standard for a Software Quality Metrics Methodology. IEEE Std. 1061-1992, New York (1993)

COSMIC FFP and the World-Wide Field Trials Strategy

Alain Abran[1], S. Oligny[1], and Charles R. Symons[2]

[1]Software Engineering Management Research Laboratory
Université du Québec à Montréal
C.P. 8888, Succ. Centre-Ville
Montréal, Québec, Canada
Tel: +1 (514) 987-3000 (8900), Fax: +1 (514) 987-8477
abran.alain@uqam.ca
[2]Software Measurement Service Ltd., St. Clare's, Mill Hill
Edenbridge, Kent TN8 5DQ, UK
Tel: +44 (0) 1732 863 760, Fax: +44 (0) 1732 864 996
charles_symons@compuserve.com

Abstract. Building on the strengths of previous work in the field of software functional size measurement, the Common Software Measurement International Consortium (COSMIC) proposed a set of principles in 1998 onto which a new generation of functional size measurement methods could be built. The COSMIC group then published version 2.0 of COSMIC-FFP, in 1999, as an example of a functional size measurement method built on those principles. Key concepts of its design and of the structure of its measurement process are presented, as well as the strategy of its world-wide field trials.

1   Origin of Software Functional Size Measurement

Measuring the functional size of software was originally proposed in 1979 by Albrecht in a communication [1] describing the results of an effort started in the mid-seventies in one IBM business unit. The overall goal of the work described in Albrecht's original paper was to measure the productivity of software development, as viewed from an economic perspective. His method, Function Points Analysis, was proposed as a specific measure of the "output" of the development process allowing a comparison of projects where software was developed using different programming languages.

The overall approach described in Albrecht's paper to achieve that goal was to select a specific subset of 22 software projects, mostly MIS software, completed within this one organization. The measurement of the functional size of the software delivered by these projects consisted of a weighted sum of "inputs", "outputs", "inquiries" and "master files". The weights assigned to these items "were determined by debate and trial" [1]. Some extra adjustments (+/- 25%) were provided for "extra complicated" [1] items. In this communication [1], Albrecht also offered a set of forms and rules to aid in calculating "function points". Many of the rules proposed originally were based on some aspects of the physical implementation of software.

R. Dumke and A. Abran (Eds.): IWSM 2000, LNCS 2006, pp. 125-134, 2001.
© Springer-Verlag Berlin Heidelberg 2001

In 1986, the International Function Point Users Group (IFPUG) was formed to foster and promote the evolution of the function point method. The group used Albrecht's revised version of the original method, using a fifth function type ("interface files") and a set of weight tables. Much work went into the subsequent releases of the method to include rules allowing an interpretation of functionality increasingly independent of the particular physical implementation of software. The contribution of IFPUG to the field of functional size measurement has been the documentation of the measurement procedure, which enabled a certain level of uniformity in the application of the method. The basic concepts and implicit model of software, though, remained unchanged from what was proposed by Albrecht in 1984. However, it can not be postulated that the sample of software used by Albrecht in 1984, which were developed between 1974 and early 1979, is representative of all software developed in the '80s, '90s and '00s.

2   A New Generation of Functional Size Measure

A group of experienced software measurers gathered, in 1998, to form the Common Software Measurement International Consortium (COSMIC). This group aimed at designing and bringing to market a new generation of software measurement methods. With the support of industrial partners and tapping on the strengths of IFPUG, MarkII [9], NESMA [10] and version 1.0 of Full Function Point [2,3,4,5,6,7,8] methods, the group proposed some basic principles on which a new generation of software functional size measurement method could be based [11,12,13]. In November of 1999, the group published version 2.0 of COSMIC-FFP, a measurement method implementing these principles. Overall, close to 40 people from 8 countries participated in the design of this measurement method. Key aspects of the COSMIC-FFP measurement method are now highlighted.

2.1   Allocation of Functional User Requirements

From the perspective proposed by COSMIC, software is part of a product or service designed to satisfy functional user requirements. From this high-level perspective, functional user requirements can be allocated to hardware, to software or to a combination of both. The functional user requirements allocated to software are not necessarily allocated to a single unit of software. Often these requirements are allocated to pieces of software operating at different levels of abstraction and cooperating to supply the required functionality to the product or service in which they are included.

In the context of the COSMIC-FFP measurement method, which is aimed at measuring the functional size of software, only those functional user requirements allocated to software are considered. (The method may be applicable to size functional requirements for information processing which are allocated to hardware, but this needs further research.) For instance, as illustrated in Figure 1, the functional user requirements in this example are allocated to three distinct pieces, each exchanging data with another through a specific organization: one piece of the software lies at the application level and exchanges data with the software's users and with a second piece lying at the operating system level. In turn, this second piece of the software exchanges data with a third piece lying at the device driver level. This last piece then exchanges data directly with the hardware. The COSMIC-FFP measurement method associates the functional user requirements for each piece with a specific layer. Each layer possesses an intrinsic boundary for which specific users are identified.

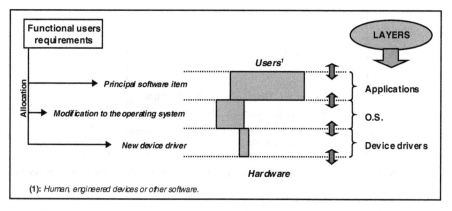

Fig. 1. Example of functional user requirement allocation to different layers [14]

2.2   Representation of Functional User Requirements in Software

The functional user requirements allocated to one or more pieces of software are decomposed into and represented by functional processes. In turn, each functional process is represented by sub-processes. A sub-process can either be a data movement type or a data transform type. Version 2.0 of the COSMIC-FFP measurement method recognizes only data movement type sub-processes. Further research is deemed necessary to incorporate data transform sub-process types in the measurement method. In the meantime, an approximating assumption is made that each data movement has an associated (small) amount of data transformation. This assumption, which should be valid for most MIS, real-time and operating system software is being tested in the field trials (see section 3 below), but will clearly not be valid for algorithm-intensive software as used in e.g. scientific or engineering domains. The approach is illustrated in Figure 2.

Given the approximating assumption, a COSMIC FFP functional process is defined as 'a unique and ordered set of data movements which is triggered by an event outside the software being measured, and which, when complete, leaves the software in a coherent state with respect to the external event.

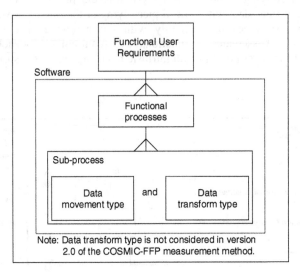

Fig. 2. COSMIC representation of functional user requirements within a piece of software [11]

2.3   COSMIC-FFP Software Model

The COSMIC-FFP measurement method defines an explicit model of software functionality, derived from the functional user requirements. Based on this explicit model of functionality, relevant functional attributes of software are identified. Their extent and limits are defined and their generic interactions are described. Taken as a whole, these functional attributes form a generic model for any type of software which is not 'algorithm-rich'. The model is illustrated in Figure 4.

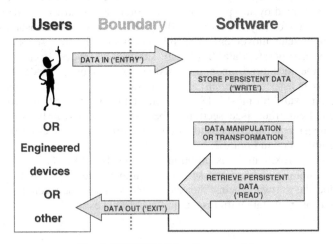

Fig. 4. COSMIC-FFP software model

Four types of data movement are defined within this model. They form the basis for defining the standard unit of functional size. The four types of data movement are presented in Table 1 below.

Table 1. Definition of COSMIC-FFP data movements [16]

Data Movement Type	Definition
ENTRY	An ENTRY (E) is a movement of the data attributes found in one data group from the user side of the software boundary to the inside of the software boundary. An ENTRY (E) does not update the data it moves. Functionally, an ENTRY sub-process brings data lying on the user's side of the software boundary within reach of the functional process to which it belongs. Note also that in COSMIC FFP an entry is considered to include certain associated data manipulation (validation) sub-processes (see [30] for further details).
EXIT	An EXIT (X) is a movement of the data attributes found in one data group from inside the software boundary to the user side of the software boundary. An EXIT (X) does not read the data it moves. Functionally, an EXIT sub-process sends data lying inside the functional process to which it belongs (implicitly inside the software boundary) within reach of the user side of the boundary. Note also that in COSMIC FFP an exit is considered to include certain associated data manipulation sub-processes.
READ	A READ (R) refers to data attributes found in one data group. Functionally, a READ sub-process brings data from storage, within reach of the functional process to which it belongs. Note also that in COSMIC FFP a READ is considered to include certain associated data manipulation sub-processes.
WRITE	A WRITE (W) refers to data attributes found in one data group. Functionally, a WRITE sub-process sends data lying inside the functional process to which it belongs to storage. Note also that in COSMIC FFP a WRITE is considered to include certain associated data manipulation sub-processes.

Version 2.0 of the COSMIC-FFP measurement method uses only four base functional components: entry, exit, read and write. Data manipulation sub-processes are not used as base functional components. The method assumes, as an acceptable approximation for many types of software, that the functionality of this type of sub-process is represented among the four types of sub-process defined earlier.

In COSMIC-FFP, the standard unit of measurement, that is, 1 *Cfsu*, is defined by convention as equivalent to one single data movement at the sub-process level. Another alternative, initially considered by the COSMIC group, was to define the standard unit of measurement based on the number of data element types moved by a data movement type sub-process. The study of such an alternative was one of the field trial aims.

3   Industrial Field Trials

3.1   Context

Another key aspect in the development of the COSMIC-FFP measurement method is the conduct of a formal field trial period designed to demonstrate that it can withstand being scaled up to industrial software from multiple and varied contexts. The Field Trial aims were the following:

1. to test for a common, repeatable interpretation of the version 2.0 Measurement Manual under widely-varying conditions: organizations, domains, development methods and so forth,
2. to establish a detailed measurement procedure, where necessary to ensure repeatable interpretation,
3. to test that the measures properly represent functionality ,
4. to test that the measurement results correlate with development effort ,
5. to enable a full transfer of technology to the trial 'Partners'.

Starting at the end of 1999, a 9 months period has been allocated for conducting formal and organized field trials of the COSMIC-FFP measurement method in a significant number of organizations around the world. The data collection was completed in a formal context in a number of organizations: a European aerospace manufacturer , a UK Bank with MIS applications, two European tele-communications manufacturers and an Australian defence software contractor. Additional data were also received from Australia (a defence contractor, a real-time software house, an aerospace manufacturer) and from Canada (a small software house, a defence contractor and a public utility organization).

During this period, each participating organization received formal training on the application of the method. Furthermore, multiple items of software were selected from each organization's portfolio and their functional size was measured. These results, along with some key data on effort and schedule involved in delivering each software were registered and centralized for analysis. Once analysed, a specific report was prepared for each participating organization, offering: a) guidelines for applying the method based on the organization's software engineering standards, and b) some preliminary benchmarking information allowing the organization to leverage its investment in the new data and put it to use immediately. Consolidated highlights from the field trials are reported next, at a high level. Further work is required to formally document such observations.

3.2   Preliminary Results Highlights

The high-level preliminary results highlights are reported here using the structure of the field trials aims.

Common, Repeatable Interpretation. As can be observed in the number and origin of the field trial participants, COSMIC-FFP was used under widely-varying conditions: organizations, domains and development methods. To ensure common implementation of the COSMIC-FFP method at the trial partners sites, training material was developed centrally at UQAM and reviewed by COSMIC team, 'train the trainers ' sessions were organized in three countries to ensure common training. The trainers then delivered the same training material to all trial partners. This training included repeatability exercises during the practical sessions.

Establishing detailed procedures, where necessary to ensure repeatable interpretation. This was performed by each organization participating in the trials, sometimes with the help of the training and support staff. Some organizations already having significant experience in measurement did not have to ask support.

Test that the measures properly represent functionality. The following three questions were of interest:

A. Can the method be applied equally to MIS and real-time software? Observations and feedback from the field trials indicated that it is easy to interpret the model in both domains. Where some parallel measurement were conducted with the IFPUG method, participants from the domain of real-time software reported significant difficulties at classifying Functional Processes in only one of the three IFPUG transaction types (Inputs, Outputs or Inquiries).

B. Are the four Data Movements types of equal 'size'? On very preliminary evidence, using one data set, the answer is "yes"; of course such results still have to be formally documented and reported.

C. The trials also included a participants' questionnaire to collect their feedback on their assessment of the ability of COSMIC-FFP to adequately represent the size of the functionality of their software, reported on a Likert scale. Again, the preliminary analysis confirmed a significant alignment of the measurement results with participants' intuitive assessment of software size.

Correlation of the measurement results with development effort. The field trial participants, both from the formal and informal contexts, provided two sets of projects: development projects and maintenance projects. The Development projects included 18 projects from 5 organizations (16 New Developments & 2 Enhancements). They were developed on multiple platforms (7 PC, 4 DEC, 2 HP, 2 IBM mainframe and 1 Compaq), and completed between March 1999 and May 2000 with a duration: from 5 to 75 months.

The other set of Maintenance requests provided 21 small functional enhancements completed in a single organization.

For both sets of data, the correlations with effort were significant. Again, these results still have to be consolidated, formally documented and reported.

Full transfer of technology to the trial 'Partners'. The general feedback is very positive and the project teams were able to grasp the elements of the method easily and were enthusiastic about the method. It was also reported that the documentation and effort needed is similar to that for applying the IFPUG method, though there is an extra step to identify layers. Also one of the participating organizations decided early on to continue CFFP measurements for all new projects and decided to implement this measurement technique as a standard procedure in their development process (a European participant). Other participants are either preparing or pursuing the deployment of this method within their respective organizations.

From the perspective of the participants in the field trials, the benefit of this approach lies in the availability, at the end of the field trial period, of a database of historical data useful for jump-starting the implementation of the measurement method within their own organizations whilst respecting the confidentiality of the sources. The benefit to the software engineering community will be the availability of the first functional size measurement method to be developed by an international group of experts and to be subjected to industrial field trials before finalization.

4   Summary and Conclusions

Albrecht proposed the Function Point method, more than 20 years ago, as a new way to measure the size of software. In the past 15 years, although the method continues to give useful results for much MIS application software, many practitioners have found that Albrecht's measurement method cannot be applied satisfactorily to non-MIS software.

In 1998, building on the strengths of previous methods, the COSMIC group identified the principles on which the next generation of functional size measurement methods were to be built, offering applicability to MIS, real-time and operating system software. A year later, the group published COSMIC-FFP, a functional size measurement method implementing these principles. Key aspects of this method were presented in this paper and industrial field trials are underway to demonstrate that it can withstand being scaled up to industrial software environments in multiple and varied contexts.

COSMIC FFP method has achieved a number of 'firsts': it is the first Functional Sizing method to:

- be designed by an international group of experts on a sound theoretical basis;
- draw on the practical experience of all the main existing FP methods;
- be designed to conform to ISO 14143 Part 1;
- be designed to work across MIS and real-time domains, for software in any layer or peer item;
- be widely tested in field trials before being finalised.

Significant progress has been made and the acceptance from those who have tried the method is good in both MIS and real-time environments. There is strong international interest: the COSMIC-FFP measurement manual is already available in three languages (English, French and Spanish) and the translation into three additional languages is progressing well (Italian, Japanese and German). The Measurement Manual has been down-loaded to date from over 30 countries.

And, planning further ahead, the COSMIC-FFP method was proposed in early 2000 to ISO/IEC/JTC1 SC7 (Software Engineering sub-committee) for a New Work Item to introduce the COSMIC FFP method through the ISO standardisation process. In the July 2000 vote, it received an approval rate of over 90%.

In addition, research activities have been initiated to address the following themes:

- Convertibility studies with previous methods such as: FFP V1,Mark II and IFPUG;
- Estimation of functional size with COSMIC-FFP, much earlier in the development cycle;
- Mapping of measurement rules in UML-based specifications domain;
- Measurement of Functional Reuse using COSMIC-FFP;
- Development of requirements identification and measurement with Computer Based Reasoning - CBR approach.
- Web-site (standards & publications): www.lrgl.uqam.ca/ffp
- Web-site (generic information) : www.cosmicon.com

Acknowledgements

The authors of this paper wish to acknowledge the specific contributions of Jean-Marc Desharnais, Denis St-Pierre, Pam Morris, Roberto Meli, Grant Rule and Peter Fagg in the elaboration of the COSMIC-FFP measurement method, the support of Risto Nevalainen and of Jolijn Onvlee, and the thoughtful and generous comments from all the reviewers of the COSMIC-FFP Measurement Manual [16].

References

1. Albrecht, A.J.: Measuring Application Development Productivity. presented at IBM Applications Development Symposium, Monterey, CA (1979)
2. Abran, A., Maya, M., Desharnais, J.M., St-Pierre, D.: Adapting Function Points to real-time software. American Programmer, Vol. 10, No. 11, November (1997) 32-43
3. St-Pierre, D., Maya, M., Abran, A., Desharnais, J.M., Bourque, P.: Full Function Points: Function Points Extension for Real-Time Software - Counting Practices Manual. Technical Report no. 1997-04, Software Engineering Management Research Laboratory, Université du Québec à Montréal, Montreal, Canada, Downloadable at http://www.lrgl.uqam.ca/ffp.html, September (1997)
4. Oligny, S., Abran, A., Desharnais, J.M., Morris, P.: Functional Size of Real-Time Software: Overview of Field Tests. Proceedings of the 13th International Forum on COCOMO and Software Cost Modeling, Los Angeles, USA, October (1998)
5. Kececi, N., Li, M., Smidts, C.: Function Point Analysis: An application to a nuclear reactor protection system. Proceedings of the Probabilistic Safety Assessment - PSA' 99 conference, Washington DC, USA, August (1999)
6. Bootsma, F.: Applying Full Function Points To Drive Strategic Business Improvement Within the Real-Time Software Environment. Proceedings of the 1999 Annual IFPUG Conference, New Orleans, USA, October (1999)

7. Schmietendorf, A., Dumke, R., Foltin, E.: Applicability of Full Function Points for Siemens AT. Proceedings of IWSM '99, Proceedings are downloadable at http://www.lrgl.uqam.ca/iwsm99/index2.html, September (1999)
8. Büren, G., Koll, I.: Process improvement by introduction of an effort estimation process. Proceedings of the 12th International Conference on Software and System Engineering and their Applications (ICSSEA), Paris, France, December (1999)
9. Symons, C.R.: Software sizing and estimating – MkII FPA (function point analysis). John Wiley & sons, Chichester, UK (1991)
10. The Netherlands Software Metrics Users Association (NESMA): Definitions and counting guidelines for the application of function point analysis. version 2.0 (1997)
11. Symons, C.R., Rule, P.G.: One size fits all – COSMIC aims, design principles and progress. Proceedings of ESCOM '99 April (1999) 197-207
12. Abran, A.: FFP Release 2.0: An Implementation of COSMIC Functional Size Measurement Concepts. Proceedings of FESMA '99, Amsterdam, Oct. (1999)
13. Symons, C.R.: COSMIC aims, design principles and progress. Proceedings of IWSM '99, Proceedings are downloadable at http://www.lrgl.uqam.ca/iwsm99/index2.html, September (1999) 161-172
14. Oligny, S., Abran, A., St-Pierre, D.: Improving Software Functional Size Measurement. Proceedings of 14th International Forum on COCOMO and Software Cost Modeling, Los Angeles, USA, October (1999)
15. International Organization for Standardization (ISO): ISO/IEC 14143-1:1997 – Information technology – Software measurement – Functional size measurement – Definition of concepts. October (1997)
16. Abran, A., Desharnais, J.M., Oligny, S., St-Pierre, D., Symons, C.R.: COSMIC-FFP Measurement Manual. version 2.0, Ed. S. Oligny, Software Engineering Management Research Laboratory, Université du Québec à Montréal, Montreal, Canada, Downloadable at http://www.lrgl.uqam.ca/ffp.html, Oct. (1999)
17. International Organization for Standardization (ISO): International Vocabulary of Basic and General Terms in Metrology. Switzerland, 2nd edition, ISBN 92-67-01075-1 (1993)

Extraction of Function-Points from Source-Code

Harry M. Sneed (MPA)

CaseConsult, Wiesbaden
Software Data Service, Vienna
Software Engineering Service, Budapest
Harry.Sneed@T-online.de

Abstract. In spite of the efforts of the IFPUG group to standardise the counting of Function-Points, there is still a lot of room left for interpretation. This is especially true when it comes to counting Function-Points in modern client server or web-based applications. There is no standard means of identifying inputs and outputs in such systems. The author proposes here a tool supported method for extracting Function-Point counts from C++ and Java Source-Code. This method has been applied and calibrated to the GEOS Stock Brokerage system under development in Vienna, where the author is currently engaged.

1 Original Function-Point Counting

The Function-Point is a measure of software system size which can be used for estimating development and maintenance effort, but also for comparing the functionality of alternative systems. Originally, Function-Points were intended to be extracted from the design documentation of software systems prior to their implementation. At the time the notion of "Function-Point" was invented by Alan Albrecht from IBM, the prevailing method for documenting system design propagated by the IBM was the HIPO - Hierarchical /Input /Processing /Output - method [1]. This method proposed the top-down, decomposition of a system in a hierarchy of functions. Then, it was possible to describe each function node in the hierarchy by means of an input/processing/output table, with a box on the left for the inputs, a box on the right for the outputs, a box at the bottom for master files or databases, and a box in the middle for processing steps (see Figure 1).

In light of this diagramming technique, it is easy to see how Albrecht came to his method of counting Function-Points. He simply took the top level of function nodes - the basic business processes - and weighted their inputs, outputs and master files. The inputs were weighted from 3 to 6, the outputs from 4 to 7 and the master files from 7 to 15, depending on their complexity. Inputs were at this time 3270 panels, card decks, paper tapes and transaction files from a disc or magnetic tape. Outputs were 3270 panels, printouts or transaction files. If the transaction files were also interfaces to a foreign system, Albrecht assigned them a weight of 5 to 10. Master files were at this time either VSAM indexed files, random access files or databases such as IMS or IDMS.[2] From the viewpoint of the time at which it originated, this early method of counting Function-Points was perfectly logical and consistent with the existing development environment (see Figure 2).

R. Dumke and A. Abran (Eds.): IWSM 2000, LNCS 2006, pp. 135-146, 2001.
© Springer-Verlag Berlin Heidelberg 2001

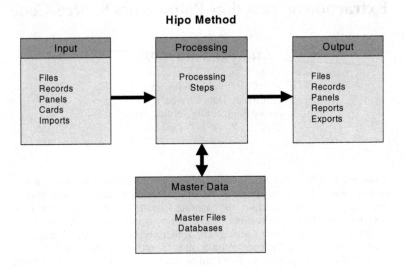

Fig. 1. Original HIPO Method

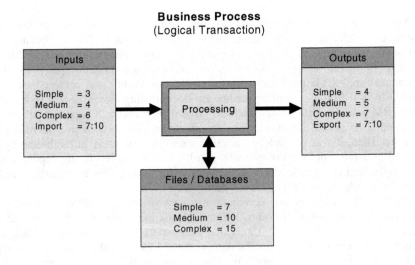

Fig. 2. Original Function-Point Method

In order to account for project and product specific conditions, Albrect introduced 14 influence factors which enabled him to adjust the raw Function-Point count by 35 % more or less, depending on the weight of the influence factors on a scale of 0 to 5. To compensate for great differences in complexity Albrecht allowed one factor - the complexity factor - to range from 0 to 50, a rather dubious deviation which caused concern to later generations of Function-Point counters and puzzled statistical analysts [3].

2 Evolved Function-Point Counting

Since the advent of the Function-Point method in the late 1970's software development technology has evolved from the structured top-down functional decomposition advocated by IBM to the data flow oriented approach - structured analysis - introduced by Ed Yourdon [4], Tom De Marco [5] and others (see Figure 3), to the entity-relationship data modelling approach propagated by Chen [6], Orr [7] and Jackson [8], to the object-oriented modelling approach of the 1990-s introduced by Coad and Yourdon [9], Shlaer and Mellor [10] as well as by Rumbaugh [11], Odell [12], Jacobson [13] and all the other pioneers of object-oriented analysis. Currently we have the Unified Modelling Language - UML - as a standard to structure our design documentation [14].

Yet the Function-Point method has persevered and survived all of these paradigm changes without departing from its original counting scheme. There are still inputs weighing from 3 to 6, outputs weighing from 4 to 7, and databases weighing from 7 to 15. The International Function-Point User Group - IFPUG - has worked up a set of conventions for deciding the degree of complexity and has changed the meaning of system interface files to data exchange formats. It has also revised the factors of influence somewhat, although this is still a point of dispute. Nevertheless, the basic measurements remain unchanged [15].

This is all the more astonishing when one considers the effects of relational databases, graphical user interfaces, client server architectures, object-oriented reuse and networks of interacting components, all of which makes the definition of inputs and outputs very obscure, to say the least. Charles Symons introduced in the late 1980`s a radically different method of counting Function-Points known as Mark-II [16]. This method counts individual input and output variables instead of data streams and entity references instead of physical databases. The outcome is quite different than with the original Albrecht method, yet it is still retains the name Function-Points, causing a certain amount of confusion among Function-Point advocates. This author has proposed two different alternatives to the Function-Point - the Data-Point in 1988 [17] and the Object-Point in 1995 [18]. The Data-Point is a measure of system size based on the data model. Data-Points are weighted counts of entities, relationships, attributes and views. This method has proved to be very effective in sizing 4GL projects. Object-Points are a size measure based on the object model. Object-Points are weighted counts of classes, methods, attributes, interfaces, parameters and use cases. This method has proved to be effective in sizing object-oriented projects.

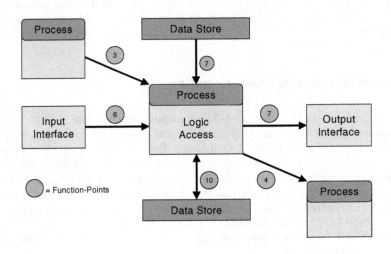

Fig. 3. Structured Analysis

3   Problems with the Function-Point Method

The problem with all of these methods is that they rely on design documentation as a source of information. This is frustrating for practitioners from two points of view. For those who are trying to estimate the size of new systems, it is frustrating because the design documentation does not exist, and if it does, only in an incomplete and inconsistent form. For those who are trying to estimate the size of existing systems for maintenance, migration or evolution projects, it is frustrating because the design documentation is usually obsolete. The only basis they have for their estimation is the source code. Even for those who are estimating new products, it is more likely that they will have the source code of a prototype or a predecessor system than any design documentation worthy of building an estimation on.

It is, therefore, the contention of this author that Function-Points, or for that matter Data-Points, Object-Points or Component-Points, must be extractable from code if they are to be of any practical value in cost estimation. It has been pointed out many times before that the only true description of a program is the program itself. The program specification, whether function model, data model or object model will always be just an approximation of the final solution. In practice it is more often a very rough approximation. This being the case, the only complete and consistent description of a software system is the source code.

4   Using Source Code as a Basis for Counting Function-Points

Lines of code and statements have been used in several models such as COCOMO [19] and SLIM [20] as a means of sizing software. They are either taken from the source itself or estimated based on comparable systems. There is no reason why the same cannot be done with Function-Points. Function-Points are weighted counts of inputs, outputs and databases. Therefore, it only remains to identity these entities within the source. The author has developed a series of code-auditors especially for this purpose. The auditor scans the code looking for certain language specific statements which indicate where data is being received such as the *COBOL ACCEPT* or the *CICS RECEIVE* command. On the other hand it looks for statements where data is being sent such as the *COBOL DISPLAY* or the *CICS SEND*. It also looks for commands which assign a master file or connect to a database such as *OPEN* or *CONNECT*. Finally, it identifies which maps and reports are opened. If a file, map, report or database is referenced to more than once, it is still only counted once, since the auditor maintains a table of current entities for each online transaction or batch process [21].

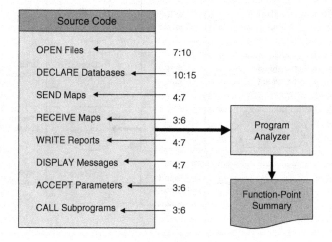

Fig. 4. Program Analysis

In counting Function-Points in conventional languages such as PL/I, COBOL or Natural, the task of identifying inputs, outputs and databases is simplified by the use of standard keywords and a standard syntax. The only problem comes up in weighting these measures. Determining whether an individual input or output is complex or not is often impossible within the context of the source. As an alternative one can either assign a standard complexity level set by the user or derive the complexity of all inputs, outputs and databases of a given program from the overall complexity metric of that program. The latter alternative was selected by the author for the conventional languages.

In the course of the last ten years, the author has conducted numerous software audits for major European enterprises counting among other things - lines of code, statements, Data-Points, Object-Points and Function-Points [22]. The technique for counting Function-Points has concentrated on the files opened by, the databases connected to, the maps or panels used by and the reports produced by each program. Files are picked up from the OPEN statements, databases from the *SQL Declare* or *IMS-PCB* or *IDMS-Schema*, maps from the *CICS SEND* and *RECEIVE* or from the *IMS-Get Unique* or *INSERT* from an *IO-PCB*, and the reports from the print file opens, put edits or *DISPLAY* statements (see Figure 4). The recognition of inputs and outputs as well as of master files is, in any case, highly language dependent, but there are standard language constructs in conventional languages which allow them to be recognised (see Figure 5).

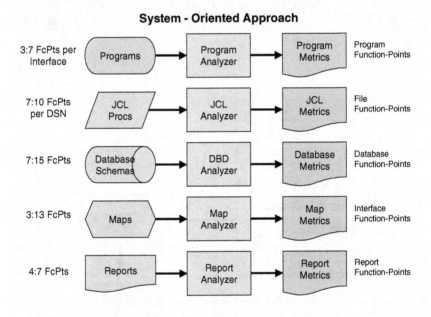

Fig. 5. Source Analysis

Determining the level of complexity has always been more problematic. In dealing with source code it is practically impossible to apply the criteria proposed by the IFPUG standard. Therefore, one must either assign a standard level or one devises another set of criteria. This author uses the overall complexity of the program as a median value of data usage complexity, data flow complexity, data access complexity, interface complexity, control flow complexity, decisional complexity, branching complexity and language usage complexity to determine the complexity level of the inputs, outputs and files. In the audits performed so far, this was acceptable to the users [23].

5   Counting Function-Points in Object-Oriented Languages

In the case of object-oriented languages such as C++ and Java there are no longer standard commands for assigning inputs, outputs and files. There are instead functions, some of which are standard such as *cin* or *cout* in C++ and *InputStream* or *ShowDocument* in Java. In addition there are standard classes such as *InputStream*, *Scrollbar*, *List* and *Print* in Java. The majority of classes and functions are, however, user defined. The user may inherit and override standard functions with his own. He may also create completely new functions of his own or to design special classes for user interface event handling or database accessing. This of course gives the developer much more flexibility, but it makes it much harder to recognise inputs, outputs and database assignments and to count Function-Points [24].

Inheritance compounds the problem. It could be argued that a base class *"Panel"* which creates and manipulates a user interface should only be counted once. If, however, this class is inherited by several other classes which are all processing user interfaces, then it is in the spirit of the Function-Point method to count this as an input and an output everywhere it is reused. The same applies to database access classes with standard SQL, ODBC or JDBC functions which are inherited by all classes accessing databases. The clue here is that each database table should only be counted once, so only the *OPEN* functions are regarded and even here it must be assured that if a database is opened more than once, it is only counted once.

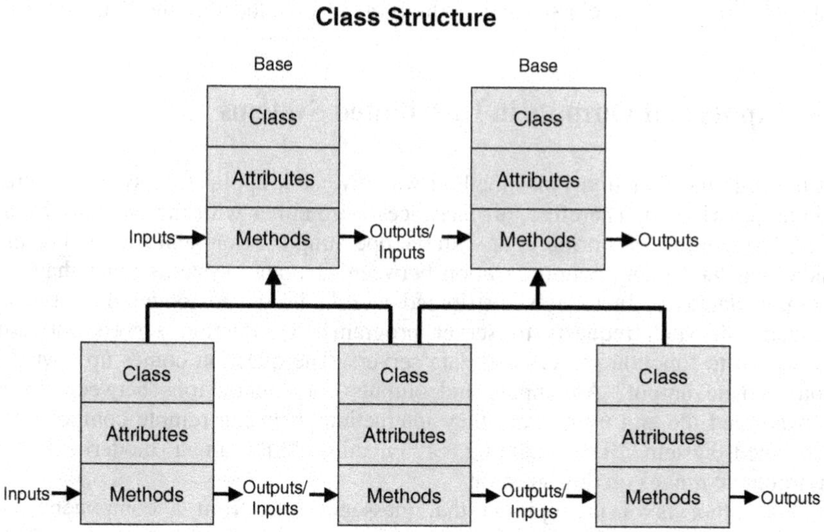

Class Structure

Fig. 6. Function-Points in OO-Software

To solve the function recognition problem, the author has designed a function table to be filled out for each application. In the table there are two types of entries - classes and functions. In the class entry there is the name of a base class and the number of Function-Points assigned to it. In the function entry there is the name of the method and the number of Function-Points it represents. The Function-Points of the base classes are added to every subclass that inherits them. The Function-Points of the methods are added to every class which invokes or inherits that particular method. In this way, the user can determine how many Function-Points an input, output or database is worth. If he wants he can follow the IFPUG recommendations or he can create his own criteria. Important is that he remains within the bounds of 3 to 6 for inputs, 4 to 7 for outputs and 7 to 15 for databases.

Element_Type	Interface_Type	Fcpt_Pt Count	Name	Signature
Class	Mask	7	Panel	Panel ()
Class	File	10	File	File ()
Method	Input	3	GetEvent	GetEvent()
Method	Output	4	PutMsg	PutMsg()

When parsing the C++ or Java code, each class inherited is checked against the Function-Table. If it is found, its Function-Points are added. Each Function invoked is also checked against the Function-Table. If it is found and it is not a member of a class also contained in the table, then its Function-Points are added. The parser keeps a table of all classes inherited and all foreign methods invoked, so it is possible to validate which of these classes and methods are also included in the Function-Table.

6   Inputs and Outputs in Distributed Systems

At the time the Function-Point method was invented, application systems were as a rule not distributed. Therefore, all interfaces were either with the end user by means of a 3270 terminal or a printout or with the operating environment files and databases. There was hardly any communication between separated systems other than via the common database. In today's distributed world, this is no longer the case. Client programs dispatch requests to server programs. Transaction servers forward the request on to function servers and data servers. The question comes up - what is an input and an output? Are inputs and outputs only interactions between the client software and the end user or are they interactions between remote components of a distributed system? The counting of Function-Points in a modern distributed environment hinges on this question.

This author is of the opinion that messages sent from a component on one computer or in one address space to a component on another computer or in another address space constitutes an output for the sending component and an input to the receiving component. In assuming this stand-point, it means that there are many more inputs and outputs in a distributed system than in a monolithic one. Web-based applications with clients, servers and middleware may have Function-Point counts up to three times greater than the conventional host based transaction processing applications, because of the high rate of interaction among distributed components (see Figure 7). Such is the case with the GEOS system in Vienna.

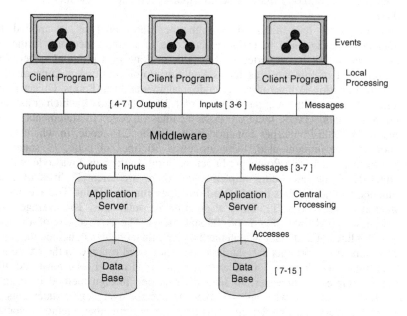

Fig. 7. Function-Points in Distributed Systems

Some traditional advocates of the Function-Point method may argue against this approach, but the author is convinced that it is tune with the original intentions of Albrecht. The functionality of distributed systems cannot be judged solely on what the end user sees, as he only sees the peak of an iceberg. The size of distributed systems can only be measured accurately, if the interfaces between remote interactive components are recognised and counted. If Function-Points are to be used for estimating effort, then the effort required for the internal interfaces must also be considered. That is why, in counting Function-Points for object-oriented distributed systems remote method invocations and CORBA calls are also treated as inputs and/or outputs, depending on the parameters and return values.

7   Experience with Counting Function-Points at the SDS in Vienna

Software Data Service is a software house in Vienna dedicated to the development of distributed stock brokerage systems and investment fond management systems for banks. The author is engaged there as a consultant in quality assurance and product management. Quality assurance encompasses testing support, technical documentation and concept as well as source analysis. Source analysis of the now more than

6.682.313 source lines of C/C++ and Java code takes place every three months, as does the analysis of the requirement specifications consisting of 290.000 lines of internal text and 800.000 lines of semiformal specification statements in more than 8.000 documents.

The numerical data acquired through the static analysis is applied to the maintenance management to estimate the costs of maintenance and further development. The author has reported on how this is done in a previous paper.[25] The interesting part of this work as far as Function-Point counting is concerned, is the relation of Function-Points to lines of code, statements, Data-Points, Object-Points. In the macro C code, with an expansion rate of 1:3 for standard C, which constitutes the function and data servers, there are circa 42 lines of code, 15 statements, 3 Object-Points and 6 Data-Points per Function-Point. In the C++ code, in which the client components are implemented, there are circa 30 lines of code, 11 statements, 4 Object-Points and 4 Data-Points per Function-Point. In the new Java code, with which the internet clients are being implemented, there are circa 27 lines of code, 10 statements, 5 Object-Points and 4 Data-Points per Function-Point. The average size of a function in macro C is 115 lines of code or 50 statements. The average size of a module in C is 954 lines of code or 408 statements. The average size of a function in C++ is 385 lines of code or 184 statements. From this, one can conclude that the more object-oriented the systems are, the less code they need relative to their functionality and the higher the degree of modularity they have. However, one must add, that the interface complexity increases. In Java there is one foreign method invocation for every three statements, whereas in C there is one for every eight statements and in C++ one for every six. The density of foreign, i.e. non member, method invocation is a good indicator of interface complexity. On the other hand, the control flow complexity, measured by the number of edges and nodes in the control graph, decreases from a high of one decision node per five statements in C to one decision node per eight statements in Java. Thus, decisional, data and cyclomatic complexity decreases while interface and language complexity increases.

The productivity data of the last four years at the SDS differs from product to product ranging from a low of 1.38 person days per Function-point for the oldest, largest and most complex product to a high of 0.62 person days per Function-point for the youngest and smallest product. This goes to show that the ratio of Function-Points to effort is not as linear as some would have us believe. There are many other factors to be considered including total system size, complexity, quality, age, technology basis and organisational environment. Younger teams tend to out perform older teams and personnel fluctuation has a significant impact. It should also be noted, that the oldest system has the greatest proportion of C code and the oldest programmers, with an average age of 37. The youngest product has the greatest proportion of Java code and the youngest programmers, with an average age of 28. From this one might assume that a C Function-Point produced by older programmers, is twice as expensive to produce than a Java Function-Point produced by younger programmers, or from another point of view, Function-Points in one environment are not equal to Function-Points in another environment, making it difficult to form a basis of comparison.

8   Need for New and Better Sizing Methods

This author has taken issue with the Function-Point method of measuring functionality in the past and will continue to do so in the future, even while struggling to interpret it. As one manager put it "Function-Point is something like the Dow Jones of IT". Capers Jones and others have done much to establish the Function-Point as the great common denominator according to which everything from Assembler to Visual Basic can be compared [26]. However, the method, like every religion, has always been subject to multiple interpretations and requires a good deal of localisation to be usable at all in a specific environment. On top of that, it is now becoming obsolete. We have come a long way from the days of Albrecht and the HIPO method out of which the Function-Point method evolved. We now live in a development environment where the integration and testing of components costs more than their design and coding. What is needed are new measurement methods for sizing distributed, object-oriented, network systems which do justice to the complexities of such systems, especially to testing them. In light of the rapidly changing technology. It is high time to take a new look at the role of software and to redefine it's functionality in terms of information and communication theory [27] as well as in terms of economic value [28].

References

1. IBM: HIPO – Hierarchy plus Input-Processing-output. IBM Form SR-20-9413, Poughkeepsie, N.Y. (1974)
2. Albrecht, A.: Measuring application development productivity. Proc. of IBM Applications Development Joint SHARE/GUIDE symposium, Moterey, CA (1979) 83-92
3. Albrecht, A., Gaffney, J.: Software function, source lines of code and development prediction. IEEE Trans. on S.E., 9(1983)6, 639-649
4. Yourdon, E.: Techniques of Program Structure and Design. Prentice-Hall, Englewood Cliffs (1975)
5. DeMarco, T. : Structured Analysis and System Specification. Yourdon Press, Englewood Cliffs (1978)
6. Chen, P.: The Entity-relationship Model – Toward a Unified View of Data. ACM Trans. on Database systems, Vol. 1, No. 1, March (1976) 9-36
7. Orr, K.: Structured Requirement Definition. Ken Orr & Associates Press, Topeka (1981)
8. Jackson, M.: System Development. Prentice-Hall Int., London (1983)
9. Coad, P., Yourdon, E.: Object-Oriented Analysis. Yourdon Press, Englewood Cliffs (1990)
10. Shlaer, S., Mellor, P.: Object-Oriented systems Analysis. Yourdon Press, Enlewood Cliffs (1988)
11. Rumbaugh, J., Blaha, M., Premberlani, W.: Object-Oriented Modelling and Design. Prentice-Hall, Englewood Cliffs (1991)
12. Martin, J., Odell, J.: Object-Oriented Analysis and Design. Prentice-Hall, Englewood Cliffs (1992)
13. Jacobson, I. et al.: Object-Oriented Software Engineering. Addison-Wesley, Wokingham, G.B. (1992)
14. Eriksson, H.-E., Penker, M.: Business Modeling with UML. John Wiley & Sons, New York (2000)
15. IFPUG: Function Point counting Practices Manual. Relaese 4.1, Int. Function-Point User Group, Westerville, Ohio (1999)

16. Symons, C.: Function-Point Analysis – difficulties and improvements. IEEE Trans. on S.E., 14(1988)1, 2-11

17. Sneed, H.: Die Data-Point Methode in Online-Zeitschrift für Datenverarbeitung. Rudolf Müller Verlag, 5(1990) 42-49

18. Sneed, H.: Estimating the development costs of object-oriented Software. Proc. of 7th European Control and Metrics Conf., Wilmslow, U.K., 135-152

19. Boehm, B.: Software Engineering Economics. IEEE Trans. on S.E., 10(1984)1, 4-22

20. Putnam, L., Fitzsimmons, A.: Estimating Software Costs, Datamation. Nov. (1976) 137-150

21. Abran, A., Robillard, P.: Function-Point Analysis – An Empirical Study of is Measurement Processes. IEEE Trans. on S.E., 22(1996)12, 899-910

22. Sneed, H.: Understanding Software through Numbers. Journal of Software Maint., 7(1995)6, 405-420

23. Sneed, H.: Experience with the Measurement and Assessment of Application Software. SES-Report 98-3, Munich, March (1993)

24. Larajeira, L.: Software Size Estimation of object-oriented Systems. IEEE Trans. on S.E., 16(1990)5, 510-522

25. Sneed, H.: Projektaufwandsschätzung durch die Hochrechnungsmethode. Proc. of 3. Fachtagung Management und Controlling vin IV Projekte, GI Fachgruppe 5.2.1, Glashütten, March (1999) 71-80

26. Jones, C.: Backfiring – Converting lines of code to Function-points. IEEE Computer, Nov. (1995) 87-88

27. Shannon, C.: Recent Developments in Communication Theory. Electronics, No. 23, April (1950) 80-84

28. Baetzer, H.: Software as Capital – An Economic Perspective on Software Engineering. IEEE Press, Los Alamitos, CA. (1997)

Early & Quick COSMIC-FFP Analysis Using Analytic Hierarchy Process

Luca Santillo

Data Processing Organisation, 00196 Roma, v. Flaminia, 217, Italy
Tel.: +39-06-3226887, Fax: +39-06-3233628
luca.santillo@iol.it

Abstract. COSMIC-FFP is a rigorous measurement method that makes possible to measure the functional size of the software, based on identifiable functional user requirements allocated onto different layers, corresponding to different levels of abstraction. The key concepts of COSMIC-FFP are software layers, functional processes and four types of data movement (sub-processes). A precise COSMIC-FFP measure can then be obtained only after the functional specification phase, while for forecasting reasons the Early & Quick COSMIC-FFP technique has been subsequently provided, for using just after the feasibility study phase.

This paper shows how the Analytic Hierarchy Process, a quantification technique of subjective judgements, can be applied to this estimation technique in order to improve significantly its self-consistency and robustness. The AHP technique, based on pair-wise comparisons of all (or some of) the items of the functional hierarchical structure of the software provided by E&Q COSMIC-FFP, provides the determination of a ratio scale of relative values between the items, through a mathematical normalization. Consequently, it is not necessary either to evaluate the numerical value of each item, or to use statistical calibration values, since the true values of only one or few components are propagated in the ratio scale of relative values, providing the consistent values for the rest of the hierarchy.

This merging of E&Q COSMIC-FFP with AHP results in a more precise estimation method which is robust to errors in the pair-wise comparisons, and self-consistent because of the redundancy and the normalization process of the comparisons.

1   COSMIC Full Function Point Overview

The COSMIC-FFP measurement method consists of the application of a set of rules and procedures to a given piece of software in order to measure its functional size. Two distinct and related phases are necessary to perform the measurement: mapping the functional user requirements (FURs) for the software to be measured onto the *COSMIC-FFP software model* and then measuring the specific elements of this software model (Figure 1).

R. Dumke and A. Abran (Eds.): IWSM 2000, LNCS 2006, pp. 147-160, 2001.
© Springer-Verlag Berlin Heidelberg 2001

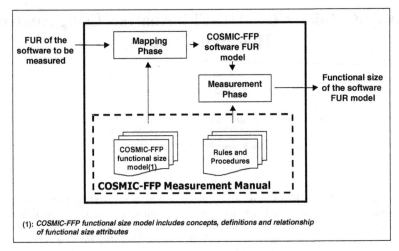

Fig. 1. COSMIC-FFP measurement process model [1]

The COSMIC-FFP software model captures the concepts, definitions and relationships (functional structure) required for a functional size measurement exercise. Depending on how the FURs are allocated, the resulting software might be implemented in a number of pieces. While all the pieces exchange data, they will not necessarily operate at the same level of abstraction. The COSMIC-FFP method introduces the concept of the software layer to help differentiate levels of abstraction of the FURs.

The functionality of each layer may be composed of a number of functional processes. A functional process is defined as a "unique and ordered set of data movements (Entry, eXit, Read, Write) implementing a cohesive set of FURs." The COSMIC-FFP software model distinguishes four types of data movement sub-process: in the "front end" direction, two types of movement (Entry and eXit) allow the exchange of data attributes with the users (or other layers); in the "back end" direction, two types of movement (Read and Write) allow the exchange of data attributes with the storage hardware (Figure 2). These data movements are also referred to as BFC's (Base Functional Components).

The COSMIC-FFP measurement rules and procedures are then applied to the software model in order to produce a numerical figure representing the functional size of the software, layer by layer. The unit of measurement is 1 data movement, referred to as 1 COSMIC Functional Size Unit, e.g. 1 C_{FSU}. Theoretically, functional processes can be assigned any size expressed in C_{FSU} (from 1 to no theoretical limit - they are not bounded, but in practice they're expected to have some sort of "natural" upper boundary, or *cut-off*).

Conceptually, the mapping phase of the COSMIC-FFP method can be considered as a process of "viewing" a software from different levels of functional detail. First, the software is viewed at the highest level as composed of software layers, if applicable. Then, each software layer is viewed at a lower level of detail, i.e. functional processes. Finally, each functional process is in turn viewed at the lowest level of detail of interest for measurement with COSMIC-FFP, that is, sub-processes (data movement types, or BFC's).

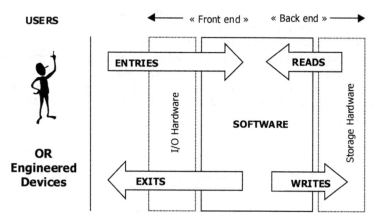

Fig. 2. COSMIC-FFP software model and data movement types [1]

2 Early & Quick COSMIC-FFP Overview

Functional size of software to be developed can be measured precisely after functional specification stage. However, functional specification is often completed relatively late in the development process and a significant portion of the budget has already been spent. If we need the functional size earlier, we must accept a lower level of precision since it can only be obtained from less precise information.

The Early & Quick COSMIC-FFP method (E&QCFFP, [2]) has been designed to provide practitioners with an *early* and *quick* forecast of the functional size, based on the hierarchical system representation cited in the previous section, which can be used for preliminary technical and managerial decisions at early stages of the development cycle. Of course, a precise standard measure must always be carried out in the later phases to confirm the validity of decisions already taken. Here, "Early" means that we may obtain this value before having committed a significant amount of resources to a project; "Quick" means that we may also use the technique when the software is an existing asset and some constraints (such as costs and time) prevent a precise measurement.

The starting point for an E&QCFFP estimation is the acknowledgement of the hierarchical structure in the functional requirements for the software to be estimated: when we document a software structure, we usually name the root as the application level and then we go down to defining single nodes, each one with a name that is logically correlated to the functions included; we reach the leaf level when we don't think it is useful to proceed to a further decomposition. In the COSMIC-FFP model, the leaves are the functional processes.

On the one hand, in the early stages it is not possible to distinguish the single data movements, or BFC's, because the information is not available at this level of detail. On the other hand, however, the preliminary hierarchical structure of the software shows as leaves what are actually nodes in the detailed version. What is required early on in the life cycle is, then, to assign forecasts of average process size, in C_{FSU}, at the intermediate and top levels in such a way that the final result will be obtained by the aggregation of the intermediate results.

The E&QCFFP technique is based on the capability of the estimator to "recognize" a software item as belonging to a particular functional class; an appropriate table, then, allows the estimator to assign a C_{FSU} average value for that item (this is applied for each identified layer separately). Each functions can be classified, in order of increasing magnitude, as Functional Process, General Process, or Macro-Process (Figure 3):

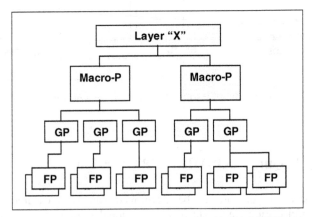

Fig. 3. Hierarchical process decomposition in E&QCFFP

a) A Functional Process (FP) is the smallest process, performed with the aid of the software system, with autonomy and significance characteristics. It allows the user to attain a unitary business or logical objective at the operational level. It is not possible, from the user's point of view, to proceed to further useful decomposition of a Functional Process without violating the principles of significance, autonomy and consistency of the system. A Functional Process can be Small, Medium or Large, depending on its estimated number of BFC's (E,X,R,W).

b) A General Process (GP) is a set of medium Functional Processes and may be likened to an operational sub-system of the application. A GP can be Small, Medium or Large, based on its estimated number of Functional Processes.

c) A Macro-Process (MP) is a set of medium General Processes and may be likened to a relevant sub-system of the overall Information System of the user's organisation. A MP can be Small, Medium or Large, based on its estimated number of General Processes.

Note that each level is built up on the basis of the previous one. There is a 4th type of process, the Typical Process (TP), which is off-line from the hierarchical structure outlined: it's just the set of the four frequently used Functional Processes, which are: Create, Retrieve, Update and Delete (CRUD) information in a relevant data group.

Each E&QCFFP element is associated with three values in terms of C_{FSU} (minimum, most likely and maximum). These numerical assignments are not reported, since they are currently subject to definition and trial on the basis of the data collection activity and statistical analysis for actual projects in the Field Trial Phase of the COSMIC-FFP method. Next Table 1 reports the ranges to help in classify the items of the estimation (the quantities n_1, n_2, n_3 are to be found out empirically during the Field Trial Phase).

Table 1. Scale ranges and numerical EFP assignments

Small Functional Process	n_1 (C_{FSU})
Medium Functional Process	n_2 (C_{FSU})
Large Functional Process	n_3 (C_{FSU})
Small General Process	6-12 FP's
Medium General Process	13-19 FP's
Large General Process	20-25 FP's
Small Macro-Process	2-3 GP's
Medium Macro-Process	4-7 GP's
Large Macro-Process	8-12 GP's

One advantage of this technique is that estimates can be based on different and non homogeneous levels of detail in the knowledge of the software structure. If a part of the software is known at a detail level, this knowledge may be used to estimate it at the Functional Process level, and, if another part is only superficially known, then a higher level of classification may be used. The overall global uncertainty in the estimate will then be the weighted sum of the individual components' uncertainties. This property is better known as multi-level estimation.

Another characteristic of the E&QCFFP technique is that it mixes both an analytical approach (use of the composition table, Table 1) and an analogy-based approach (the analogy can be used with respect to an abstract model or to a concrete set of software objects actually collected and classified, helping to classify the unknown items).

3   The Analytic Hierarchy Process (AHP)

The Analytic Hierarchy Process ([4]) provides a means of making decisions or choices among alternatives, particularly where a number of objectives have to be satisfied (*multiple criteria* or *multi-attribute* decision making) (Figure 4).

Let's assume that n items are being considered with the goal of providing and quantifying *judgements* on the *relative weight* (*importance*) of each item with respect to all the other items. The first step (*design phase*) set the problem as a hierarchy, where the topmost node is the overall objective of the decision, while subsequent nodes at lower levels consist of the criteria used in arriving at this decision. The bottom level of the hierarchy consists of the *alternatives* from which the choice is to be made, i.e., the n items we wish to compare.

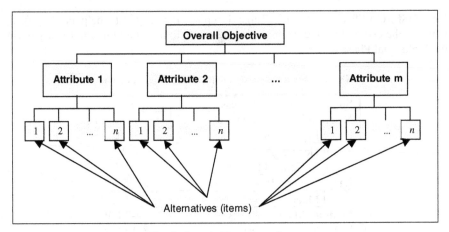

Fig. 4. Generic hierarchy scheme

The second step (*evaluation phase*) requires pair-wise comparisons to be made between each two items (of the given level of the hierarchy), with respect to their contribution towards the factor from the level immediately above them. The comparisons are made by posing the question 'Of two elements i and j, which is *more important (larger)* with respect to the given factor and how much more?'. The strength of preference is usually expressed on a ratio scale of 1-9. A preference of 1 indicates *equality* between two items while a preference of 9 (*absolute importance*) indicates that one item is 9 times larger or more important than the one to which is being compared. This scale was originally chosen, because in this way comparisons are being made within a limited range where perception is sensitive enough to make a distinction [4].

These pair-wise comparisons result in a *reciprocal n-by-n matrix A*, where $a_{ii} = 1$ (i.e., on the diagonal) and $a_{ji} = 1/a_{ij}$ (*reciprocity property*, i.e., assuming that if element i is "x-times" more important than item j, then necessarily item j is "$1/x$-times" more important, or equally "x-times" less important than item i).

Suppose firstly that we provide only the first column of the matrix A, i.e., the relative importance of items 2, 3, .., n, with respect to item 1. If our judgements were completely *consistent*, the remaining columns of the matrix would then be completely determined, because of the transitivity of the relative importance of the items. However we do not assume consistency other than by setting $a_{ji} = 1/a_{ij}$. Therefore we repeat the process of comparison for each column of the matrix, making independent judgements over each pair. Suppose that at the end of the comparisons, we have filled the matrix A with the exact relative weights; if we multiply the matrix with the vector of weights $w = (w_1, w_2, \ldots, w_n)$, we obtain:

$$Aw = \begin{bmatrix} a_{11} & a_{12} & \cdots & a_{1n} \\ a_{21} & a_{22} & \cdots & a_{2n} \\ \vdots & \vdots & & \vdots \\ a_{n1} & a_{n2} & \cdots & a_{nn} \end{bmatrix} \begin{pmatrix} w_1 \\ w_2 \\ \vdots \\ w_n \end{pmatrix} = \begin{bmatrix} w_1/w_1 & w_1/w_2 & \cdots & w_1/w_n \\ w_2/w_1 & w_2/w_2 & \cdots & w_2/w_n \\ \vdots & \vdots & & \vdots \\ w_n/w_1 & w_n/w_2 & \cdots & w_n/w_n \end{bmatrix} \begin{bmatrix} w_1 \\ w_2 \\ \vdots \\ w_n \end{bmatrix} = n \begin{pmatrix} w_1 \\ w_2 \\ \vdots \\ w_n \end{pmatrix}$$

So, to recover the (overall) scale from the matrix of ratios, we must solve the problem:

$$Aw = nw, \text{ or } (A-nI)w = 0,$$

that is a system of homogenous linear equations (I is the unitary matrix). This system has a nontrivial solution if and only if the determinant of $(A-nI)$ vanishes, i.e., n is an *eigenvalue* of A. Notice that A has *unit rank* since every row is a constant multiple of the first row and thus all its eigenvalues except one are zero. The sum of the eigenvalues of a matrix is equal to its *trace* and in this case, the trace of A is equal to n. Thus n is an eigenvalue of A and we have a nontrivial solution, unique to within a multiplicative constant, with all positive entries. Usually the normalized vector is taken, obtained by dividing all the entries w_i by their sum.

Thus given the comparison matrix we can recover the scale. In this *exact* case the solution is any column of A normalized. Note also that in the *exact* case A is consistent, i.e., its entries satisfy the condition $a_{jk} = a_{ji}/a_{ki}$ (*transitivity property*). However in real cases we cannot give the precise values of w/w_j but estimates of them, the *judgements*, which in general are different from the actual weights' ratios. From matrix theory we know that small perturbation of the coefficients implies small perturbation of the eigenvalues. Therefore, we still expect to find an eigenvalue, with value near to n: this will be the *largest eigenvalue* (λ_{max}), since due to the (small) errors in the judgement, also other eigenvalues are different from zero, but still the trace of matrix (n) is equal to the sum of eigenvalues (some of which can be complex).

The solution of the largest eigenvalue problem, i.e., the weight eigenvector w corresponding to λ_{max}, when normalized, gives a unique estimate of the underlying ratio scale between the elements of the studied case. Moreover, the matrix whose entries are w/w_j is still a consistent matrix, and is a consistent estimate of the "actual" matrix A. A itself need not be consistent (for example the judgements could have stated that item 1 is more important than item 2, 2 is more important than 3, but 3 is more important than 1!). It turns out that A is consistent if and only if $\lambda_{max} = n$ and that we always have $\lambda_{max} \geq n$. That's why we take as a "consistency index" (*CI*) the (negative) average of the remaining eigenvalues, which is exactly the difference between λ_{max} and n, divided by the normalizing factor ($n-1$):

$$CI \equiv \frac{-\sum_{i=2}^{n} \lambda_i}{n-1} = \frac{\lambda_{max} - n}{n-1}, \quad \lambda_{max} = \lambda_1$$

To measure the error due to inconsistency, we can compare the *CI* of the studied case with the average *CI* obtained from corresponding random matrices with order n and maximum ratio scale r. Table 2 shows the random average consistency indexes $Ci_{n,r}$ for various n and r. Revisions in the pair-wise comparisons are recommended if the consistency ratio (*CR*) between the studied *CI* and the corresponding $CI_{n,r}$ is considerably higher than 10%.

Table 2. Consistency indexes ($Ci_{n,r}$)

n	\multicolumn{9}{c}{R}								
	2	**3**	**4**	**5**	**6**	**7**	**8**	**9**	**10**
5	0,07	0,13	0,20	0,26	0,31	0,37	0,41	0,48	0,51
6	0,07	0,14	0,21	0,27	0,34	0,39	0,46	0,50	0,57
7	0,07	0,15	0,22	0,29	0,35	0,42	0,48	0,53	0,60
8	0,07	0,15	0,23	0,30	0,37	0,43	0,49	0,57	0,62
9	0,08	0,15	0,23	0,31	0,38	0,44	0,50	0,57	0,64
10	0,08	0,16	0,23	0,31	0,38	0,45	0,52	0,59	0,65
11	0,08	0,16	0,24	0,31	0,39	0,46	0,53	0,60	0,66
12	0,08	0,16	0,24	0,32	0,39	0,47	0,54	0,61	0,67

This consistency ratio CR simply reflects the consistency of the pair-wise judgements and shows the degree to which various sets of importance relativities can be reconciled into a single set of weights. In the above example, (1 larger than 2, 2 larger than 3, and 3 larger than 1) the consistency score would be poor, and would be considered a violation of the axiom of transitivity. AHP tolerates inconsistency through the amount of redundancy of judgements. For a matrix of dimension n only $(n-1)$ comparisons are required to establish weights for the n items. The actual number of comparisons that can be performed in AHP is $n(n-1)/2$. This redundancy is conceptually analogous to estimating a number by calculating the average of repeated observations: the resulting set of weights is less sensitive to errors of judgement.

A quick way to find the weight eigenvector, if one cannot solve exactly the largest eigenvalue problem, is that of normalizing each column in A, and then average the values across the rows: this "average column" is the normalized vector of weights (or priorities) w. We then obtain an estimate of λ_{max} dividing each component of Aw (= $\lambda_{max}w$) by the corresponding component of w, and averaging. Finally, we can compute CI (and the corresponding CR) from this estimate of λ_{max} in order to verify the goodness of the judgements.

So far, we have illustrated the process for only one level in the hierarchy: when the model consists of more than one level then hierarchical composition is used to weight the eigenvectors by the weights of the criteria. The sum is taken over all weighted eigenvector entries corresponding to those in the lower level, and so on, resulting in a global priority vector for the lowest level of the hierarchy. The global priorities are essentially the result of distributing, or propagating, the weights of the hierarchy from one level to the next level below it. For the purpose of applying AHP to E&QCFFP estimation, this multi-level weighting is not required, as shown in the following section.

4   Merging E&QCFFP and AHP

The analogy between the hierarchical functional decomposition of E&QCFFP and the intrinsic hierarchy of AHP can be quite confusing; we must recall that the nodes in different levels in a AHP hierarchy carry very different meaning (going from the objective level, to the attribute level, to the alternative level), while in the E&QCFFP

approach the decomposition is made only in order to separate different ranges (or groups) of functions. This means that the elements of a E&QCFFP hierarchy are indeed all homogenous with respect to the attribute to be estimated, i.e., the functional size. So there is no strict correspondence between the hierarchical structures in the two techniques, but still a strong tie can be found. Although AHP was developed as a mathematical method for prioritizing the alternatives, we can recognize that what we called *importance* is just an extensive property as many others, as software functional *size* is expected to be, too.

When estimating the software functional size (number of C_{FSU}), the only criteria is the size itself. Consequently, we can consider a simple AHP hierarchy, with only one level (and the objective "estimated size" above it); the nodes of this level are the n items listed by the estimator, eventually prior to the functional decomposition (this list could even include all from possible functional processes to macro-processes).

In order to review the possible ways to merge E&QCFFP and AHP, let's recall the intrinsic characteristics of both: AHP makes the subjective comparisons consistent through a mathematical step (the largest eigenvalue solution) and provides the *CR* to evaluate the self-consistency of the estimation, while the E&QCFFP alone provides a estimation together with an uncertainty range (minimum, most likely, and maximum values), permitting to assign a class to each item based on analogy (eventually with respect to known cases); note that the uncertainty range in the E&QCFFP can be quite large when using mostly the macro-process level.

We could gain better forecasts by combining the two techniques; the possible ways to do the join are basically the following:

  a) AHP technique first applied to prioritize the items on a numerical scale, then automatic assignation of the E&QCFFP class from the scale.
  b) E&QCFFP technique first applied to allocate the set of items in functional classes, then AHP applied to refine the first estimation.

The a) case can be considered as a "re-allocation" of a pure AHP estimation on the E&QCFFP classes; here some not-yet-solved problems may rise, as for example how to decide which AHP resulting numerical range should be assigned to a given E&QCFFP class. If we manage to solve this and similar problems, we can obtain a hierarchical representation of the estimated system as in a pure E&QCFFP technique, but with more robustness in the input (nonetheless, this could not result always in a more robust output forecast, due to the fact that E&QCFFP categories necessarily "blur" the exact ratios given by AHP).

The b) case is to be considered more significantly, since it requires firstly an analogical approach, which is usually easier at the beginning for the human estimator, and after that a robust refinement of the estimation in a mathematical way.

Depending on the desired precision or the time at our disposal in doing the estimation, we should decide on which variant to apply to estimate the COSMIC-FFP number: only by E&QCFFP, only by AHP, with the a) case or with the b) case. The last approach should result in the most accurate forecast, still saving us from applying an exact (and more time-consuming) COSMIC-FFP counting procedure. Next section deals more deeply with the b) case.

5   The "b) case": E&QCFFP + AHP

The case is:
1. E&QCFFP to allocate the items in subsets;
1. AHP to revise/refine the estimation.

Note that the first step already provides a first estimation, but its uncertainty could be quite wide, if the estimator dealt with one or more high-level class (e.g. general processes or macro-processes). The second step could be an AHP application on the global set of items from the first step, but since the pairwise ratios involved in such a global application would be of magnitude 10^2 and higher, it would be obviously very hard for a human estimator to provide such estimated ratios in the comparisons. An enhancement is to apply AHP separately on homogeneous subsets of the E&QCFFP items:

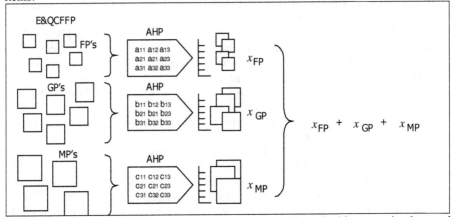

or only on two contiguous subsets per time (avoiding double sums in the total result):

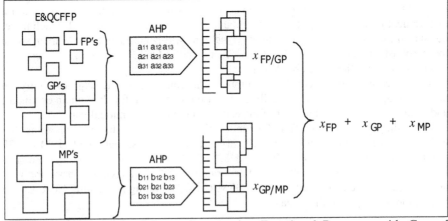

The second variant, mixing and comparing Functional Processes with General Processes, and General Processes with Macro-Processes, would be the more self-consistent and coherent one.

In any case, this approach would maintain the hierarchical representation of the system as firstly posed by the E&QCFFP estimator, but with a more consistent and robust numerical evaluation of each item compared to the others; the final estimated value is a revision of the first, pure E&QCFFP forecast, but with a lower uncertainty range (the original uncertainty range should be reduced, based on the value of the resulting CR). Eventually, some items could be re-allocated in terms of their E&QCFFP category, if the AHP step shows some significant change with respect to their original E&QCFFP allocation.

We should not be too scared of the quantity of different comparisons to perform in every AHP step, since we know from section 3 that not all the comparisons have to be effectively performed, unless the CR is not low enough. So, monitoring the value of the CR after several incremental iterations of the AHP step, we could decide to stop them when the CR satisfies a predefined accuracy level.

When deriving the final estimation result, two approaches are possible: one or more items should be fixed in their C_{FSU} value, as "landmarks", to propagate the number of assigned C_{FSU} to the whole set, or the whole set can be mapped in a "fuzzy" way onto an ordered scale of items, as the E&QCFFP classes, with assigned quantities of C_{FSU}. Future field trials should show which approach is preferable.

The landmarks could be put among the original unknown items to help in both the E&QCFFP and the subsequent AHP step. These landmarks could be taken from a so-called Experience Data Base (or Catalogue of Typical Elements). This catalogue could contain for example all the typical processes or functions that can be identified in a generic project, and their average quantities of C_{FSU}. Once some of these typical elements are identified among the list of items, the comparison matrix (or matrices) would greatly benefit of the relative ratios between them. A generic useful case of "typical element" would be the already cited Typical Process, or CRUD, which is usually very easy to identify and to use as a comparison landmark. In case of more than one landmark, further research is necessary to establish the exact mathematical procedure to fix their values, while propagating the quantities of CFSU through the unknown items.

A special case of application would be when the E&QCFFP step provides a list of items, all classified at the Functional Process level. In this case, the whole set would be taken into account for a unique AHP step, in order to compare directly the quantities of data movements contained in each process; this means that it could be significant to compare directly estimated quantities of CFSU (but still without exactly counting them).

6 Numerical Examples

Several AHP cases have been studied, as depicted in the following tables. In every case, we have $n = 10$ items, and we assume that the comparisons made between the 1st item and each of the remaining items (i.e. the first column/row of the matrix A) are the "best" estimates; eventual inconsistency is put in the remaining comparisons (i.e. between 2nd, 3rd, ..., and 10th item). What differentiates each case is the expected ratio between each of the 10 items. Since the field trials are still to provide actual numbers of C_{FSU} for E&QCFFP, for sake of clarity in the examples we consider the first item always with *unitary size*.

For each case, different inconsistency errors were introduced separately on each pairwise comparison (except for comparisons between the 1st item and the others, assumed as correct) to simulate the human pairwise comparisons: uniformly random ±10%, ±25%, ±50%, ±75%, ±90%, and ±100% errors. For example, the 100% error means that, while the estimator should evaluate "item i is p-times item j" the simulation could put "item i is $2p$-times item j" (doubling the expected ratio, i.e. with a 100% error). For each case and each error range, 1000-samples statistics have been generated; all values are approximated at one decimal. The first column of each table denotes the maximum error for single pair comparison.

Case A: (1,1,1, 1,1,1, 1,1,1,1), Total = 10, $CI_{(n=10,\ max\ ratio=10)}$ =0.65.

Error	λ_{max}	CR	Estimates (average)	Total	$\Delta_\%$
10%	10.0	0.2%	(1.0, 1.0, 1.0, 1.0, 1.0, 1.0, 1.0, 1.0, 1.0, 1.0)	10.3	3%
25%	10.1	1.6%	(1.1,1.1, 1.1,1.1, 1.1,1.1, 1.1,1.1, 1.1,1.1)	10.7	7%
50%	10.3	4.8%	(1.1, 1.2, 1.2, 1.2, 1.2, 1.2,1.1,1.1,1.1,1.1)	11.6	16%
75%	10.8	14.2%	(1.2,1.5,1.4,1.4,1.4,1.3,1.3,1.2,1.2,1.2)	13.1	31%
90%	11.7	28.7%	(1.3,1.8,1.7,1.6,1.6,1.5,1.4,1.3,1.3,1.2)	14.8	48%
100%	15.3	90.3%	(1.5,3.4,3.6,3.1,2.8,2.3,2.2,1.8,1.6,1.4)	23.6	136%

Case B: (1,1,1, 1,1,1, 1,1,1,10), Total = 19, $CI_{(n=10,\ max\ ratio=10)}$ =0.65.

Error	λ_{max}	CR	Estimates (average)	Total	$\Delta_\%$
10%	10.0	0.2%	(1.0, 1.0, 1.0, 1.0, 1.0, 1.0, 1.0, 1.0, 1.0,10.2)	19.5	3%
25%	10.1	1.2%	(1.1, 1.1, 1.1, 1.1, 1.1, 1.1, 1.1, 1.1, 1.1,10.6)	20.2	6%
50%	10.3	4.8%	(1.1, 1.2, 1.2, 1.2, 1.2,1.1,1.1,1.1,1.1,11.1)	21.4	13%
75%	10.8	14.2%	(1.2,1.4,1.4,1.4,1.3,1.3,1.2,1.2,1.2,11.5)	23.0	21%
90%	11.7	29.1%	(1.2,1.8,1.7,1.6,1.5,1.4,1.4,1.3,1.2,11.8)	25.0	32%
100%	15.3	90.1%	(1.4,4.0,4.2,3.1,2.7,2.2,1.8,1.8,1.4,13.2)	35.8	88%

Case C: (1,2,3,4,5,6,7,8,9,10), Total = 55, $CI_{(n=10,\ max\ ratio=10)}$ =0.65.

Error	λ_{max}	CR	Estimates (average)	Total	$\Delta_\%$
10%	10.0	0.2%	(1.0,2.0,3.0,4.0,5.0,6.0,7.0,8.0,9.0,10.0)	55.0	0.0%
25%	10.1	1.2%	(1.0,2.0,3.0,4.0,5.1,6.0,7.0,8.0,9.0,10.0)	55.2	0.4%
50%	10.3	4.8%	(1.0,2.1,3.2,4.2,5.2,6.2,7.1,8.1,9.0,9.9)	56.1	2.0%
75%	10.8	14.2%	(1.0,2.4,3.5,4.6,5.6,6.5,7.4,8.3,9.1,9.9)	58.3	6%
90%	11.7	29.6%	(1.0,2.9,4.1,5.2,6.2,7.1,7.9,8.6,9.1,9.6)	61.8	12%
100%	15.3	95.4%	(1.0,4.6,6.4,8.2,8.5,10.1,9.8,10.0,10.0,9.4)	78.0	42%

Case D: (1,1,1, 1,1,10, 10,10,10,10), *Total* = 55, $CI_{(n=10,\ max\ ratio=10)}$ =0.65.

Error	λ_{max}	CR	Estimates (average)	Total	$\Delta_\%$
10%	10.0	0.2%	(1.0,1.0,1.0,1.0,1.0,10.2,10.2,10.2,10.2,10.2)	55.9	1.6%
25%	10.1	1.2%	(1.0,1.1,1.1,1.0,1.0,10.5,10.4,10.4,10.4,10.3)	57.3	4.2%
50%	10.3	4.8%	(1.1,1.1,1.1,1.1,1.1,10.9,10.9,10.8,10.6,10.6)	59.3	8%
75%	10.8	**14.2%**	(1.1,1.3,1.3,1.2,1.2,11.7,11.3,11.1,10.8,10.5)	61.4	**12%**
90%	11.7	**29.3%**	(1.1,1.5,1.5,1.4,1.3,12.9,12.2,11.7,10.9,10.5)	65.0	**18%**
100%	15.3	**90.1%**	(1.1,2.8,2.5,2.0,1.9,16.5,15.6,14.0,12.3,10.6)	79.5	**45%**

Case E: (1,5,10, 15,20,25, 30,35,40,45), *Total* = 226, $CI_{(n=10,\ max\ ratio=10)}$ =2.36.

Error	λ_{max}	CR	Estimates (average)	Total	$\Delta_\%$
10%	10.0	0.1%	(1.0,5.0,10.0,15.0,20.0,25.0,30.0,35.1,40.0,44.9)	226.0	0.0%
25%	10.1	0.3%	(1.0,5.1,10.1,15.2,20.2,25.2,30.1,35.2,40.0,44.9)	227.0	0.4%
50%	10.3	1.3%	(1.0,5.4,10.6,15.8,20.7,25.7,30.6,35.6,40.1,44.5)	230.0	1.8%
75%	10.8	3.9%	(1.0,6.1,11.8,17.2,22.4,27.2,32.2,35.9,40.0,44.4)	238.2	5%
90%	11.7	8.0%	(1.0,7.1,13.7,19.5,24.6,29.3,33.9,37.6,40.9,44.0)	251.6	11%
100%	15.4	**25.6%**	(1.0,12.3,21.6,28.7,32.3,41.4,41.2,43.5,42.5,42.6)	307.1	**36%**

Note that for uniformly random errors from 10% to 50% we always get acceptable *CR* values, and the final per cent deviation between expected and estimated values ($\Delta_\%$) is always no more than 3-times the *CR* value.

As we stated in section 3, the largest eigenvalue λ_{max} is always $> n$, and increases as the average error in the comparisons increases. Moreover, almost everywhere each item is overestimated with respect to its expected value; exception are cases *C* and *E* (those with the most widespread values), where the 10th item is underestimated and counterbalances the overestimation of the remaining 9 items. However, every estimation is globally *over* the total expected value: this should be taken as a general property, i.e. the AHP estimation is to be taken as an *upper threshold*.

Relevant cases are:

Case A. In this case (all items expected as identical), the more error we put in the simulation, the most error we get in the estimated total. This could be explained as follows: if the set is strongly homogeneous (all items identical) we should not be too "easy" in estimating wrong ratios between the items.

Case E. This case involves a wide range of items, putting together the first item (unitary size) with a 45-times larger item (the 10th). In this case even a strong (random) error up to 90% on some comparisons is "blurred" by AHP to give a 11% deviation for the total estimation.

7   Further Discussion and Conclusion

The examples above are very encouraging, but much investigation has still to be made. For example, very large cases (very high n) introduce difficulties in managing the items. From this perspective, is noticeable that the original AHP deals only with small n; a suggestion is to try to use homogenous clusters of items, and to make comparisons between these clusters. Of course, further research in realistic, field trials is strongly encouraged to test the proposed approach in different situations.

As cited above, the fact that only a single value is to be provided, besides of the relative weight estimates, does not mean that more than one true value cannot be used: e.g., if we know the values of items 1, 2 and 3, this means that we have more confidence in fixing several weights in the comparison matrix; *de facto*, in this way we do use the richer information. A further research theme should be on how to make some landmarks to "weight" more than others, if their value is far more accurate.

AHP is a powerful means for several tasks in the estimation and decision making field. The proposed combination with the E&QCFFP technique can solve those situation in which the only E&QCFFP does not provide good results, especially due to atypical or new situations, not collected in the historical statistics, or when it is used identifying few, high level items, providing too wide ranges of uncertainty.

References

1. Abran, A., Desharnais, J.M., Oligny, S., St-Pierre, D., Symons, C.R.: COSMIC-FFP Measurement Manual. version 2.0, Ed. S. Oligny, Software Engineering Management Research Lab., Université du Québec à Montréal (Canada), October (1999)
2. Meli, R., Abran, A., Ho, V.T., Oligny, S.: On the applicability of COSMIC-FFP for measuring software throughout its life cycle. ESCOM-SCOPE 2000, Munich, April 18-20 (2000)
3. Meli, R., Santillo, L.: Function Point Estimation Methods - A Comparative Overview FESMA 99, Amsterdam, October 6-8 (1999)
4. Saaty, T.L., Alexander, J.M.: Thinking with Models. Pergamon Press (1981)
5. Santillo, L.: Early FP Estimation and the Analytic Hierarchy Process. ESCOM-SCOPE 2000, Munich, April 18-20 (2000)

Measuring the Ripple Effect of Pascal Programs

Sue Black and Francis Clark

Centre for Systems and Software Engineering, South Bank University,
103 Borough Road, London SE1 0AA, UK
Tel.: ++44(0)702 815 7471
blackse@sbu.ac.uk
clarkfh@hotmail.com

Abstract. Recent acquisition of a half million LOC telephone switching system TXE4 [7] written in Pascal has provided a unique opportunity for software measurement. This paper discusses the software implementation of ripple effect measure - REST (Ripple Effect and Stability Tool) focusing on a recent attempt to produce a Pascal parser for REST which will be used to measure the TXE4 system. Ripple effect is a measure of impact analysis: the effect that a change to one part of a system will have on other parts of a system. It can be used in software engineering development to compare different versions of software or during maintenance to highlight software modules which may need attention. The implementation of the Pascal parser has highlighted several significant differences between Pascal and C source code, which are discussed and investigated.

1 Introduction

In this paper we begin with a short introduction of previous work in the area of ripple effect analysis. A description of ripple effect analysis follows with a detailed description of intermodule and intramodule change propagation. Parsing is explained in the next section with some discussion of the differences in parsing C/C++ vs. Pascal source code. Implementation of the Pascal parser with a description of the problems encountered and their solutions are described in section five, section six is an evaluation of the parser with recommendations for further work.

2 Background

Impact analysis is the assessment of the impact a change will have on a piece of software. It can be used to follow the course of the change through a system's variables, functions and programs or to provide a measure of the effect that a change to a certain variable or function may have on other functions within the system. This paper describes an example of the latter type. The ripple effect measures impact or how likely it is that a change to a particular function is going to cause problems in the rest of the program. It can also be used as an indicator of the complexity of a particular module or program.

R. Dumke and A. Abran (Eds.): IWSM 2000, LNCS 2006, pp. 161-171, 2001.

The first mention of ripple effect in software engineering was by Haney [6] in 1972, he used a technique called module connection analysis to estimate the number of changes needed to stabilise a system. Ripple effect as it is known today was first introduced by Yau and Collofello [9] in 1978, it was seen as a complexity measure which could be used to compare various modifications to source code during software maintenance. The ripple effect algorithm has since been modified to compute ripple effect based solely on design information [12]. Detailed algorithms used in the computation of ripple effect throughout the software lifecycle are given in [13]. Attempts to automate the ripple effect measure have had some success: Yau and Chang [11] give an example of a two thousand line Pascal program's ripple effect taking thirteen hours of CPU time to compute. They also present an algorithm which can compute ripple effect faster than this but which treats modules as black boxes, thus not taking information from inside modules of code into account.

Yau and Collofello's algorithm has been reformulated using matrix algebra [2]. This provided us with a much clearer picture of the process by which ripple effect is computed, and highlighted an opportunity for approximation which significantly simplifies the computation. The reformulated algorithm has now been implemented as the REST tool. REST currently computes ripple effect measures for a subset of C and C++ programs, this paper describes the implementation of a Pascal parser which will enable the computation of ripple effect for Pascal programs. Further details of the REST tool can be found in [3].

3   Ripple Effect and Logical Stability

Ripple effect is a measure of how much a module within a program would affect the other modules within that program if a change was made to it. It can be broken down into two main components: *intramodule* change propagation and *intermodule* change propagation.

Intramodule Change Propagation
Intramodule change propagation involves the amount that a variable within a module or function affects the other variables within the function. For example in the following piece of code:

```
1. a := b ;
2. d := a ;
3. return(d) ;
```

a change to the value of b in line 1 will result in a change to the value of a in line 1 and subsequently a change to a in line 2. The value of a will then propagate to d in line 2 which will change to value of d in the return statement in line 3.

The computation of ripple effect is based on the effect that a change to a single variable will have on the rest of a program. Given the piece of code above matrix V_m represents the starting points for intramodule change propagation through a module. These starting points are called 'definitions' by Yau and Collofello and can be any of the following:

1. the variable is defined in an assignment statement;
2. the variable is assigned a value which is read as input;
3. the variable is an input parameter to module k;
4. the variable is an output parameter from a called module;
5. the variable is a global variable;

1. The variable is defined in an assignment statement:
   The first condition can be restated as "a variable on the left-hand-side of an assignment statement" such that in each of the following:

```
a : = 100;
a : = func(b);
```

variable *a* satisfies the condition.

2. The variable is assigned a value which is read as input:
   An example of the second condition in C syntax might be:

```
scanf("%d",&n);
```

or in Pascal syntax:

```
READLN(n:5);
```

There are bound to be numerous means of achieving the reading of an input in any particular language, but the condition will always hold that any variable altered by the reading of an input (a kind of implicit assignment) will be a source of intramodule change.

3. The variable is an input parameter to module k:
   This condition picks up on cases such as the function definition:

```
        void func(int a, int b){......} //(C/C++)
```
or
```
        PROCEDURE func(a,b: INTEGER);   //(Pascal)
```

Here variables *a* and *b* are input parameters to module *func*}. The value that variables *a* and *b* accept upon invocation of module *func* will propagate through *func*} (the current module, module *k*).

4. The variable is an output parameter from a called module:
   This condition warrants careful treatment since there are a number of subtleties to look out for. The theme behind the condition is that within the current module we may invoke another module with a call, such as:
```
        invokeFunc(a);
```

The question we wish to answer is this: Under what circumstances is the value of variable *a* altered by the call to module *invokeFunc*? The answer to the question is that variable *a* is (possibly) altered under the following two circumstances:

(Situation 1) *a* is a pointer variable, or else it is the address in (logical) memory of the variable that is being passed.

(Situation 2) *a* is a reference variable.

To appreciate why, consider the case of passing by value. This involves function calls such as

```
callFunc(a);
```

where the signature of *callFunc* looks like this:

```
void callFunc(int n);        // (C/C++)
```

Here a 'copy' of the integer variable *a* is passed to *callFunc* , meaning that when execution of flow returns to the invoking module the value of variable *a* remains unchanged. Therefore when function parameters are passed by value the condition "output parameter from a called module" does not hold.

On the other hand, suppose the signature of callFunc looks like this:

```
void callFunc(int* n);        // (C/C++)
```
or
```
PROCEDURE callFunc(VAR n : @ INTEGER);
                              // (Pascal)
```

and from within the current module we make the function call

```
callFunc(&a);                 // (C syntax only)
```

Now variable *a* does satisfy the condition. This is because now the (logical) memory address of variable *a* is being passed, which allows the called function to directly manipulate the value of the variable stored at that address. The changes (if any) made to variable *a* will persist even after the called module returns. Thus in this case *a* is an output parameter from a called module, satisfying the conditions for intramodule change.

A similar case, assuming the same function signature for *callFunc*, involves the call:

```
callFunc(p);
```

where *p* is pointer variable. That is, *p* was declared as:

```
int* p;                       // (C/C++)
```
or
```
VAR p : @ INTEGER;            // (Pascal)
```
The condition holds for much the same reason. Variable *p* is a pointer to a logical memory address which allows the called function direct access to the variable and any

changes made to the value stored at that address persist after the called module terminates. The preceding discussion justifies Situation 1; pointer variables or variable addresses passed to a called module are potential sources of output from that module. Situation 2 concerns the passing of variables by reference, since there is nothing you can achieve through the passing of variables by reference that you cannot achieve by passing variables using pointers or addresses. C++ and Pascal do make provision for passing variables by reference however. Given the following variable declaration:

```
        int n;                    // (C/C++)
or
        VAR n : INTEGER;          // (Pascal)
```

then without any further information, the function invocation suggests the variable *a* is being passed by value. In fact if the signature of *callAnotherFunc* looks like this:

```
        void callAnotherFunc(int& n);    // (C/C++)
or
        PROCEDURE callAnotherFunc(VAR n : INTEGER);
        // (Pascal)
```

then the function call is passing an implicit reference to variable *a*. The inclusion of the VAR keyword under the Pascal syntax makes the parameter a reference parameter, while under the C/C++ syntax it is through the presence of the ampersand symbol.

The point is that when variables are passed by reference, they are alterable within the body of the called module or function and the changes persist. Therefore variables being passed by reference are potential sources of output from the called module in the same way as pointer variables/addresses of variables.

5. The variable is a global variable:

Since variables need only satisfy one of the conditions for intramodule change propagation the condition can be restated as "a global variable on the right-hand-side of an assignment" [2]. This is in view of the fact that a global variable appearing elsewhere will be detected under one of the other four conditions. Assuming a global variable *g* has been declared, we are interested in the following C/C++ syntax (similarly for Pascal):

```
        a : = g;
```

Intermodule Change Propagation

Intermodule change propagation is concerned with observing the impact of a module upon other modules within a program. Yau and Collofello \cite{Yau80} term these *interface variables* of a module *k*, defined as the set of variables satisfying any one of the following conditions:
1. the variable is a global variable.
2. the variable is an input parameter to a called module.
3. the variable is an output parameter of module *k*.

These conditions are easily demonstrated:

1. The variable is a global variable:
Global data affects any module using it, and necessarily propagates between modules. Changes to the global's variable itself (a definition) will affect any modules making use of the value of the variable.

2. The variable is an input parameter to a called module:
From within the current module, the variable *a* appearing in the function call

```
callFunc(a);
```

serves as an example of an input parameter to a called module. Whether the variable is being passed by value or reference is not of any consequence since the variable is guaranteed to act as an input to the called module.

3. The variable is an output parameter of module k:
In the function signature/definition

```
void func(int a, int* b, int& c)    //(C/C++)
```
or
```
PROCEDURE func(a:INTEGER; VAR b:@INTEGER;
     VAR c :INTEGER);                //(Pascal)
```

The variables *b* and *c* are output parameters of *func*, while variable *a* is not. The justification for this claim follows the same line of reasoning behind the determination of which variables are output from called modules. Here the only difference is that we are 'looking the other way'; we are looking at the function signature or declaration and are able to determine which parameters will propagate change back to calling modules. In the example above, variable *a* is a 'value parameter' (not an output parameter), while variable *b* is a 'pointer parameter' (possible output parameter) and variable *c* is a 'reference parameter' (also potential source of output).

4   Parsing Program Source Code

This section introduces the concept of parsing and discusses the automation of parser construction. A language consists of a set of words (the vocabulary) and a set of rules describing how the words may be used to construct valid sentences of the language. For formal languages the words are called *tokens*. Before the parser can determine the grammatical structure of the input string, it must be able to recognise the tokens. This stage is called *lexical analysis*. Here the parser checks that each character sequence encountered forms a valid token of the language. A programming language example is the token IDENTIFIER, used to store the value of variables for example. An IDENTIFIER token may be defined in the following way:

IDENTIFIER: *letter,* followed by zero or more *letters, digits* or *underscore* characters

Tokens are grouped under *syntactic categories.* The set of rules (*productions*) describing how the syntactic categories may be used defines the *grammar.* As an example a simple English-based language may include syntactic categories *sentence, subject, verb, object, article* and *noun.* Language tokens may include: 'kicks', 'a', 'the', 'ball', 'girl'. The rules (productions) may then be defined as follows:

```
sentence  →  subject verb object
subject  →  article noun
verb  →  'kicks'
object  →  article noun
article  →  'a' OR 'the'
noun  →  'ball' OR 'girl'
```

Starting at the syntactic category *sentence,* valid constructs of the language are generated by repeatedly applying the production rules.

For example, consider the following parser input string:

The girl kicks a ball

Rule *sentence* matches an element of the set *subject* followed by an element of the set *verb* followed by an element of the set *object.* Rule *subject* matches an element of the set *article* followed by an element of the set *noun.* Rule *article* matches token 'a' or 'the'. Here the parser makes a successful match of the token 'the' before returning to rule *article* to try to match a noun. This strategy proceeds until the whole sentence is either recognised or rejected.

Most parsing methods work *top-down* or *bottom-up.* These terms reflect the order in which new nodes are added to the parse tree during its construction. A top-down parser adds new nodes from the root node (*sentence* in the preceding example) down to the bottom (terminals). Top-down parsers are more easily understood than bottom-up parsers and can be constructed easily by hand, although bottom-up parsers can parse a greater variety of languages [1].

The parser described in this paper is a top-down recursive descent parser. The term recursive descent is derived from the fact that the parser is implemented by means of a set of possibly recursive routines that descend through the parse tree as they recognise the source program. It was built using the Purdue Compiler Construction Tool Set (PCCTS), [8] software which aims to facilitate automatic parser construction. PCCTS works by automatically generating C++ source code from a user-supplied grammar description. From the grammar file with embedded actions PCCTS generates the C++ source code for the language parser, this can then be compiled using a regular C++ compiler. The resulting executable is a working parser. PCCTS is interesting in that it adopts several innovative strategies for parser implementation which are important in their own right. It has already been used in CSSE as part of the implementation of the software tool X-RAY [5] a program structure analyser.

5   Pascal Parser Implementation and Evaluation

This section discusses some of the key issues and problems faced during the practical implementation of the Pascal parser for REST. Analysis of the existing system commenced with locating all embedded ripple effect analysis code in order to understand ist purpose. After this several problems were encountered some of which are highlighted below.

Nested Functions and Procedures in Pascal

In Pascal, functions and procedures can be nested to arbitrary depth. C and C++ have no equivalent syntax. This nesting affects the scope of the variables. Under the existing system, each module is parsed and the data collected during parsing is written out to a number of separate files. When the module has been fully parsed, the output files are closed. Upon parsing the next (if any) module, new files are created to be written to. The problem for a Pascal implementation is the need to 'remember' which module is the outer (enclosing or containing) module so that when the parser reaches the end of a nested module it 'knows' which module it has returned to. Then the parser can restore the information corresponding to the enclosing module, including the correct output files associated with it. The solution in practice is to define the Pascal grammar for procedures and functions recursively. In simple terms this means that upon recognition of a procedure definition say, the parser stacks up the details of any enclosing modules, and retrieves them (pops them off the stack) upon reaching the end of the nested module. In effect each module 'remembers' which module is its 'parent'. Outermost modules have a null 'parent', i.e. they are not nested within any other module.

Detecting Output Parameters from Called Modules

The various means by which variables form potential sources of output from called modules were described previously (condition 4 for intramodule change propagation). This section looks at how the different features of the condition can be detected during parsing. Code snippets of the features satisfying the intramodule change propagation condition (output parameter from a called module) are given below:

```
(1)  func(&x);
(2)  int* p;
     func(p);
(3)  typedef int* intptr;
     intptr p;
     func(p);
(4)  callFunc(x);  //where callFunc has
                   //signature callFunc
                   //(int& n)
```

Code snippet (1) passes the address of variable x to module *func*. Running a test under the C/C++ parser and examining the output reveals that the condition is detected successfully.

Code snippets (2) and (3) pass a pointer variable to module *func*. The difference between them is that (3) declares variable *p* to be of type *intptr*, which by virtue of the preceding *typedef* is an indirect means of declaring *p* to be a pointer variable. The reason for giving both will become clear. We should expect the parser output under the current system to match the output produced for code snippet (1) but it does not produce output for either of these cases. This is because the current parser implementation has no means upon seeing the variable *p* in the function call

```
func(p);
```

of knowing whether *p* is a pointer variable or not.

The solution is to introduce a new boolean variable attribute, which is *true* if the variable is a pointer. The only time to determine if a variable is a pointer or not when the variable is declared. The strategy must therefore be to detect the declaration of pointer variables , so that when the variable is stored the fact that it is a pointer can be saved. Upon seeing the variable in the invocation of a function, the task is then simply a matter of retrieving this information, so that the pointer variables will produce output for the intramodule change condition. The reason for including code snippet (3) follows form this proposed strategy. The reason is that a variable may be declared using *typedef-ed* pointer types. A complete solution must therefore store the same kind of information about types, then upon recognition of a variable declaration using the alias *intptr*, the parser will be able to recall whether the type name is a pointer type or not, and if it is, will treat the variables declared as pointer variables. Code snippet (4) represents the passing of parameters by reference. Looking at the parser output for such cases it is clear that REST does not currently implement this language feature.

The Pascal syntax for the code constructs corresponding to the C/C++ constructs given above are as follows:

```
(1)  //no equivalent syntax in Pascal for
     explicitly passing the address of
     a variable.
(2)  VAR p:@INTEGER;
     func(p);
(3)  TYPE intptr=@INTEGER;
     VAR p:intptr ;
     func(p);
(4)  callFunc(x);  //where callFunc has
                   //signature callFunc
                   //(VAR n:INTEGER)
```

While REST can be forgiven for not currently implementing the passing of reference parameters since the feature is a C++ extension, the feature is necessary for a Pascal implementation. This is because VAR parameters are common in Pascal code. The strategy adopted relies on the proviso that the signature (function name and details) must have been seen by the parser before the function is called. This proviso is necessary because upon function invocations of the form

```
callFunc(n);
```

the only way to determine if variable n is being passed is to have already seen the parameter list details of *callFunc*. This is so that the parser has had an opportunity to remember which of *callFunc*'s parameters are reference parameters. Without access to the information prior to *callFunc* being invoked, the parser can only assume that the variables are being passed by value. For the cases where the function call is made in the same file as the function definition this is not likely to be a problem. Unfortunately it is extremely unlikely that function definitions will be included from external files through the use of compiler directives. Therefore a good general solution would be to pre-process all Pascal code before parsing.

6   Conclusions and Further Work

It can be seen from the research reported upon here that further work needs to be carried out to ensure that REST produces accurate ripple effect measures for Pascal code. There is much scope for further research and measurement involving the TXE4 telephone switching system as the entire project's software and extensive documentation are available for our use. Once the Pascal parser is fully operational we intend to measure the ripple effect of the

Pascal programs from two perspectives. Firstly with a focus on the development of the system, comparison of modules in different stages of development, and secondly from the perspective of software maintenance: is the ripple effect a good predictor of modules of code which are regarded as complex or more *troublesome* than other modules.

Acknowledgements

Sue Black would like to thank Dave Homan at Nortel, New Southgate and Ian King of Advance Micro Computers Ltd for giving the Centre for Systems and Software Engineering access to TXE4 and their extensive personal knowledge of the system.

References

1. Albas, H., Nymeyer, A.: Practice and principles of compiler building with C. Prentice Hall, Europe (1996) 376-380
2. Black, S.E.: A simplified algorithm for computing logical stability. Tech. Report. SBU-CISM-96-19, South Bank University, London (1996)
3. Black, S.E.: REST - A tool to measure the ripple effect of C and C++ programs. In: Dumke, R., Abran, A. (eds.): Software Measurement: Current trends in research and practice. Deutscher Universitäts Verlag, September (1998), 159-172
4. Black, S.E.: Measuring ripple effect for software maintenance. IEEE International Conference on Software Maintenance, September (1999) 38-42
5. Black, S.E., Wigg, D.J.: X-Ray : A Multi-Language, Industrial Strength Tool. IEEE International Workshop on Software Measurement, September (1999) 39-42

6. Haney, F.M.: Module connection analysis-A tool for scheduling software debugging activities. In: Proc. Fall Joint Computer Conference (1972) 173-179
7. Homan, D.: 10 years of software maintenance or crawling through the mire! Workshop on Empirical Studies of Software Maintenance, September (1999)
8. Parr, T.J.: Language translation using PCCTS and C++. Automata publishing company, San Jose, CA 95129, USA (1996)
9. Yau, S.S., Collefello, J.S., McGregor,T.M.: Ripple effect analysis of software maintenance. In: Proc. COMPSAC, (1978) 60-65
10. Yau, S.S., Collefello, J.S.: Some stability measures of software maintenance. IEEE Transactions on Software Engineering 6(1980)6, 545-552
11. Yau, S.S., Chang, J.S.: Estimating logical stability in software maintenance. In: Proc. COMPSAC, (1984) 109-119
12. Yau, S.S., Collefello, J.S.: Design stability measures for software maintenance. IEEE Transactions on Software Engineering, 11(1985)9, 849-856
13. Yau, S.S., Liu, S.: Some approaches to logical ripple effect analysis. Tech. Report. SERC-TR-24-F, University of Florida, Gainesville, FL 32611 (1988)

An Assessment of the Effects of Requirements Reuse Measurements on the ERP Requirements Engineering Process

Maya Daneva

Clearnet Communications, 200 Consilium Place, Suite 1600
Toronto, Ontario M1H 3J3, Canada
mdaneva@clearnet.com

Abstract. Setting realistic expectations for a requirements measurement exercise and assessing the real benefits resulting from the implementation of metrics in Requirements Engineering (RE) is a key challenge for many information systems (IS) organizations. This paper describes how a project team can demonstrate a connection between efforts invested in requirements reuse measurement and business results in Enterprise Resource Planning (ERP) projects. We provide an approach to analyzing and assessing the benefits gained from integrating requirements reuse measurement practices in the ERP RE process. Dependencies between requirements measurement activities and RE activities and deliverables are studied in the context of SAP R/3 implementation projects.

1 Introduction

A typical ERP implementation project suggests a reuse-driven architecture-centric process of engineering the ERP business requirements. For the reuse processes to be planned, and reuse planning to be done at the level of business requirements, reuse measurement practices have to be integrated into the ERP RE cycle [2]. An ERP requirements reuse measurement process is a systematic method of adopting or adapting standard reuse counting practices in ERP RE, measuring the ERP reuse goals, and indicating reuse levels targeted at the beginning and achieved at the end of each stage of the ERP implementation cycle [3]. The main purpose of this process for ERP customers is to learn about their own business, technological and environment opportunities by learning how much reuse their ERP-supported business processes could practice.

In our previous research [2,3,4], we investigated the problem of integrating requirements reuse metrics in ERP RE. We (i) developed a reuse measurement plan that linked the reuse measurement needs to reuse objectives and action items to be taken in ERP RE, and (ii) formulated an approach to measuring functional size and reuse aspects of the business requirements represented in terms of business process and data models.

The present paper mainly addresses the effects of applied requirements reuse measurement on the ERP RE process. The contribution of the paper is towards the

R. Dumke and A. Abran (Eds.): IWSM 2000, LNCS 2006, pp. 172-182, 2001.

systematic approach to assessing both the value-added benefits of the implementation of metrics in RE and the actual usage of measurements in the RE process. Such an approach could serve two different but related purposes: (i) it could be used as a reference model to guide a quick post-implementation assessment of the benefits an ERP organization gets from measuring requirements reuse, and (ii) it could be used as a communication tool to help both business users and IS team members set up objectives to maximize the benefits of the reuse metrics data. For the purpose of this research, we place the requirements reuse measurement activities in the context of implementing the SAP R/3 System, a leading product in the ERP software market [1].

2   Analysis Method

The goals of this assessment study are: 1) to come up with a catalogue of potential benefits the ERP RE process could gain from using requirements reuse metrics, (2) to provide the process architect with a list of issues to consider while conducting a benefits assessment study, and (3) to formulate guidelines for the reviewers of assessment results to help them evaluate the work done. To achieve this, we defined an analysis method based on four types of sources: (i) frameworks for evaluation of the value-added benefits from IT investments [15,18] that helped us keep the global undersanding of requirements reuse metrics data and their usefulness in large, (ii) existing theoretical and empirical work on RE process assessment [6,7,8,9,10]   as well as the RE good practice guide [16] which provided useful insights into the mechanics and the pittfalls behind the assessment of RE process aspects, (iii) the lessons learnt from studies on the application of Function Point Analysis in industry [11,12,14] that gave us initial ideas of what can be expected from using reuse data based on function point (FP) counts, and (iv) methodologies for building lessons-learnt architectures [5,17] that guided us in the process of documenting, packaging and analyzing reuse metrics experiences in our ERP projects.

2.1   Overview of the Processes

This section provides a brief description of the two processes of interest and how they are integrated. The unit of analysis [10] in our study is the Accelerated SAP (ASAP) RE process. It is a project specific process that is engineered, standardized and provided to customer IS-organizations by SAP and ASAP certified consulting partners. The process can be modeled as a spiral with four iterations showing the increasing collection of information by three types of activities: (i) *requirements elicitation* activities which deliver the foundation for the business blueprint and are concerned with finding, communication and validation of facts and rules about the business, (ii) *enterprise modeling* activities which are concerned with the business processes and data analysis and representation, and (iii) *requirements negotiation* activities which are concerned with the resolution of business process and data issues, the validation of process and data architectures and the prioritization of the requirements. In this process, the very first iteration results in a clear picture of the company's organizational structure based on the pre-defined organization units in the R/3 System. The second iteration is to define aims and scope for business process standardization based on the R/3 application components. The third iteration leads to a company-specific business process architecture based on scenarios from the standard SAP process and data architecture components. Finally, the fourth iteration results in the specification of data conversion, reporting and interfaces requirements. The major actors in these activities are business process owners who are actively supported by the SAP consultants and the internal SAP process analysts and data architects.

Furthermore, the requirements reuse measurement (RM) process consists of practices structured in three process areas: planning, implementation and usage [3]. The process is carried out by a process/data architect who is also the key team member responsible for the development of the customer-specific process and data architectures based on reusable components. Reuse measurements are taken at the end of the third iteration once the business process and data models are completed. The results of this process are (i) FP counts that show the size of the reused and the total requirements delivered within the project, and (ii) reuse level rates which show how requirements are reused. The latter are indicators that include the amount of reused requirements as a percentage of the total requirements delivered [2].

2.2   Scope of the Analysis

The ASAP process [1], the RM process [3] and the interactions between the two processes have been analyzed in terms of what metrics data have been used for, how the reuse measurement process changed the RE process, why the change is considered good for the team, and what is the value of 'good'. This was done by means of *experience packages* [5] that we built to capture facts and observations about characteristics of our ERP project context as well as aspects of our RE and RM processes [3].

Next, we considered measuring reuse in ERP RE as an investment that should result in (i) better understanding of what is happening during the RE process, and (ii) better control over what is happening on the project. Requirement reuse measurement itself does not lead to any benefit. It provides us only the opportunity to create value: RM leads to knowledge and the team must think out strategies for maximizing the benefits of our process knowledge. One way to document the processes of using requirement reuse measurements is to build *SAP process knowledge flow models*. These were developed on the basis of typical stakeholders' interaction patterns and specified all business locations, the desired distribution of process knowledge onto these locations, the type of reports to be distributed and the action items that could be taken based on the metrics reports. The analysis of the way the stakeholders consume the metrics data helped us develop multifaceted definitions of the value-added benefits.

2.3   Dimensions of Benefits

As the existing literature in ERP, RE and RM provides no theoretical frameworks that could direct the empirical derivation of impacts that RM may have on a component-based RE process, we modeled the process assessment aspects at a high-level only (Fig. 1). Since we needed dimensions of value-added benefits, we applied the value-chain principle [1] well known in business (re)engineering projects. According to it, everything a RE team does can be categorized into primary and support activities. Primary activities constitute the physical delivery of the business blueprint. These are: requirements elicitation, requirements modeling, and requirements negotiation. Support activities bolster the primary activities and each other by providing knowledge assets, resources and some form of technology to perform a given RE function. We divide them into four areas: process/product quality assurance, decision making/issue management, knowledge management and reuse measurement. Furthermore, we mapped our experience packages and knowledge flow models into the elements of our RE value chain. Each experience package or knowledge flow model was associated to a primary or a support activity. This led us to characterize the benefits on six dimensions: (i) the maturity of the RE process, (ii) the quality of the RE deliverables, (iii) the efficiency of the decision making process, (iv) the communication between the stakeholders, (v) the effectiveness of the RE activities and (vi) the enforcement of knowledge management practices in RE.

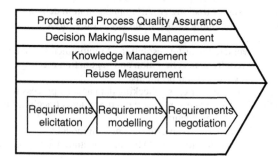

Fig. 1. The RE value chain: components of the assessment

3   The Approach

3.1   Cataloguing Potential Benefits

We define an effect as a benefit that is (a) a property of the reuse data usage pattern the stakeholders follow, or (b) a result of having RM exercise carried out as part of engineering the business blueprint. To ensure the reliability [7] of our benefits assessment, we developed multifaceted definitions of benefit components. The high-level model in Fig 1 was operationalized by listing a set of statements where each statement represents a claim regarding how RM adds value. The components of potential benefits are defined as follows:

- *Maturity of RE process* includes items referring to RE practices that compliment the ASAP methodology and help the team overcome some deficiencies in the standardized ASAP process.
- *Quality of RE deliverables* includes items concerned with quality aspects of five types of deliverables: business blueprints, business process models, data models, project plans and project estimates.
- *Efficiency of decision-making* includes items addressing how RM helps both technical and business decision-makers assess, evaluate, select or compare alternatives in the course of engineering the business requirements.

- *Stakeholders' communication* includes items concerned with the extent to which RM helps the team link the system to the business as well as increases stakeholders' understanding of the ERP impacts on the business.
- *Effectiveness of RE activities* refers to items that show the effects of the RM practices on the requirements elicitation and negotiation activities as well as the improved visibility of the overall ERP implementation process.
- *Enforcement of knowledge management practices in RE* includes items concerned with the extent to which RM promotes the activities of creating, documenting, packaging and sharing ERP RE knowledge.

The items pertinent to each component are given in Fig.2.-7.

▤ Maturity of RE process.
  ▤ RM provides systematic procedures for quantifying fits and gaps between the company's desired state and the R/3 System.
  ▤ RM is a mechanism for tracking ASAP implementation deliverables.
  ▤ RM helps the team build business understanding of and ownership over the R/3 implementation.
  ▤ RM serves as a vehicle for faster resolution of requirements problems and conflicts.
  ▤ RM helps focus requirements elicitation and negotiation meetings.
  ▤ RM helps resolve architectural problems.
  ▤ RM leads to a procedure for cross-checking data against process requirements.
  ▤ RM helps the architect make sure that the requirements tracebility policies are followed as per the ASAP recommendations.
  ▤ RM data serves as an input to an effort estimation model.
  ▤ RM provides a basis for linking SAP implementation /enhancement projects to the business model.
  ▤ RM helps identify bottlenecks in the system, spot reuse problems, assess their impact on the process workflow.
  ▤ RM enables the exploration and the validation of implementation alternatives.
  ▤ RM helps the team better understand the SAP business scenarios.

Fig. 2. Effects of RM on the maturity of the RE process

▤ Quality of RE deliverables.
  ▤ RM helps the team recognize model problems.
  ▤ RM reveals conflicting assumptions.
  ▤ RM helps identify model clashes.
  ▤ RM helps the team track the process model changes and keep the process changes synchronized.
  ▤ RM leads to consistent tracebility information being maintained for all the business processes.
  ▤ RM provides quantitative information on what percent of the package must be changed.
  ▤ RM provides initial understanding of the cost to integrate the package.
  ▤ RM helps identify which essential requirements can be met by the package and which can not.
  ▤ RM contributes to the rapid discovery of non-compliance with standards.
  ▤ RM helps reduce omissions in the business impact analysis document.
  ▤ RM increases the probability of finding poorly prioritized requirements.

Fig. 3. Effects of RM on the quality of the RE deliverables

⊟ Efficiency of the decision making process.

- ▤ RM helps the technical decision makers fine-tune the amount of consulting and implementation resources.
- ▤ RM helps the team realize needs for adjusting deliverables to be produced at a later stage.
- ▤ RM helps decision maker understand what prevents the team from reusing more.
- ▤ RM helps the team assess the degree of difficulty involved in the migration to new releases.
- ▤ RM helps identify processes to be migrated with extra caution.
- ▤ RM serves as input to the assessment of the customization risk in upgrade/enhancement projects.
- ▤ RM is a decision factor in the selection of package implementation strategies.
- ▤ RM is an input to the process of selecting customization options.
- ▤ RM helps the team identify on-site and off-site resource needs in the postimplementation stage.

Fig. 4. Effects of RM on the decision-making process

⊟ Communication between the stakeholders.

- ▤ RM helps us understand in both qualitative and quantitative terms the role of the pre-defined process models in ERP RE.
- ▤ RM helps communicate the value of reuse techniques and reuse processes in ERP implementation.
- ▤ RM creates awareness of the highly integrated SAP components.
- ▤ RM increases the team's consciousness about the cost of customization.
- ▤ RM increases business process owners' understanding of the workflow activities, the information suppliers and inputs, the information clients and outputs, and the data reports and the applications used in support of the business workflow.
- ▤ RM enforces integrated project team planning and communication.
- ▤ RM helps the architect manage the reuse expectations.
- ▤ RM helps the team understand what the benefits of reuse are and when these would be seen.
- ▤ RM enables the team to operate in a problem preventive mode.
- ▤ RM helps arrive at a consensus regarding the use of a formal prioritization procedure.
- ▤ RM leads top clarification of business terminology problems.

Fig. 5. Effects of RM on the communication between the stakeholders

⊟ Effectiveness of RE activities.

- ▤ RM reveals the difficulty of achieving common information across the entire organization.
- ▤ RM leads the team to early assess the strategic implications of their system.
- ▤ RM helps decision makers team realize the SAP impact on the way the company is organized and the day-to-day culture of the organization.
- ▤ RM enables the early development of a strategy for future process modifications.
- ▤ RM helps the team determine how the usage of the system is changing over time – have the users developed better practices?
- ▤ RM helps identify parts of the process likely to be most expensive to change.
- ▤ RM enforces the collection and the maintenance of meta-data about business concepts.
- ▤ RM enforces the collection and the maintenance of meta-data about business activities.
- ▤ RM helps identify requirements that are likely to cause particular dificulties to the configurators.
- ▤ RM is a factor in determining reuse recommendations.
- ▤ RM helps the team define scope for practicing reuse.

- ▤ RM makes the team rethink rejected requirements.
- ▤ RM leads to the identification of reuse constraints.
- ▤ RM validates the needs for customization.
- ▤ RM makes the team analyze and compare options for businesss process standardization and harmonization.
- ▤ RM helps the team determine how reuse fits into the business environment.
- ▤ RM helps the team assess ERP technology limitations.

Fig. 6. Effects of RM on the RE activities

▤ Enforcement of KM practices in RE
- ▤ RM compliments the repository of documentation about the system and the business processes it supports: it is a central record of process specific reuse information.
- ▤ RM helps the team handle the complexity of the reuse process knowledge.
- ▤ RM helps establish a bridge between the company's business language and the SAP standard business terminology in the R/3 Reference Model.
- ▤ RM streamlines the transfer of implementation knowledge from the consultants/architects to the end users.
- ▤ RM provides a foundation for assembling ERP organization knowledge map.
- ▤ RM serves as a process for generating and using ERP reuse knowledge.
- ▤ RM encourages the use of knowledge mapping technology.
- ▤ RM helps the team build an ERP knowledge-oriented organization.
- ▤ RM creates awareness of the benefits from knowledge-oriented technologies.
- ▤ RM encourages knowledge transactions to take place.
- ▤ RM contributed to the development of positive knowledge sharing culture.
- ▤ RM helps the architect build knowledge networks.

Fig. 7. Effects of RM on the KM practices

3.2 Application Procedure

We suggest the assessment be done by the process/data architect on the project who is responsible for leading the metrics planning, collection and reporting efforts. It should take place once the blueprint stage of the project is completed and the business requirements documents are signed off by business process owners.

The following procedure has been devised to carry out a quick assessment of the benefits:

1. Score reuse metrics usage against item lists from the catalogue. Use the knowledge flow models for reference purposes. In case of doubts about whether or not an item is applicable, the architect should move it to an action item list.
2. Review the action items. Resolve uncertainty by collecting feedback on reuse metrics data usage from relevant stakeholders.
3. Quantify the items. Count the applicable items. Use an indicator that includes the applicable items as a percentage of the total items making up a benefit class. The greater the percentage, the more extensively RM had been used and the bigger the bottom-line impact of reuse metrics on the RE process.
4. Build a graphical representation. Use a radar map to show the assessment results.

For example, let us assume that an assessor arrived at the graphical representation shown in Fig. 8. These results indicate that reuse metrics contributed primarily to a more mature RE process, the effectiveness of the RE activities, the improved communication between stakeholders and the quality of the RE deliverables. Some potential benefits that might be sought in the future lie in the areas of information and process knowledge sharing practices and decision making.

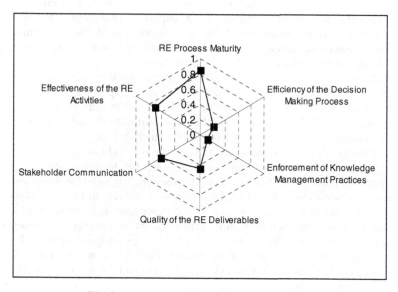

Fig. 8. Assessment of the benefits of RM in RE

3.3   Context of Use

Architects in ERP project organizations may use the approach in at least two ways:

- *Pre-implementation analysis*: a *should/could-be* map may be developed to systematically analyze and define the value the team may want to get from the RM practices. This will help the architect set up a benefits realization process that will run in parallel with the RE process. The immediate advantage of the assessment is twofold: it is a foundation to manage expectations for the RM initiative and make sure that reuse data are linked to action items relevant to the RE process.
- *Post-implementation analysis*: multiple process instances for a set of ERP projects may be assessed and compared to understand the actual usage of reuse data in ERP RE. This will assist the architect in defining how well the benefits realization process works for the project stakeholders and will serve as a basis in the planning of how to maximize the benefits of what the team has already got.

3.4   Issues

The following major issues arise when assessing effects of RM on the ERP RE process:

1. *Poor planning of the benefits realization process.* There is a strong tendency to believe that the process of getting value from metrics data can be done ad hoc. Promoting systematic benefits analysis and process assessment as well as purposeful big picture thinking is an important prerequisite for the correct selection and prioritization of the effects we would like to achieve. The consequences of having to implement the wrong effect are potentially worse than the consequences of not having a benefit at all.

2. *Failure to see that measuring reuse has a business part at all.* In each dimension, there is a business and a technical perspective. The technical one refers to the steps for designing the RM process as part of a larger process, namely the ERP RE process. It is, of course, critical to the reuse metrics success; however, the business perspective which includes steps to make sure RM knowledge is used in the analysis of business, technology and environment opportunities is equally important. Balancing the technical and the business items that make up the benefits components is the key to a reliable assessment.

3. *Generalizability of the results.* In assessment studies, there is a temptation to consider the benefits assessment as an experience that (i) is specific to an organization, and (ii) is highly influenced by a number of organizational environment factors. Since the ASAP process was designed as a standard to be applied in both small and large IS organizations in any industry [1], it is critical to analyze the benefits in regard to this process and not solely in the context of the organization who runs it. We do not underestimate the role of organization-specific factors, like level of maturity or level of experience in using software metrics [4]; however, these are of secondary importance in the context of architecture-centric, reuse-driven ERP project. The architect, of course, should be completely aware of any IS team-specific factor promoting the realization of RM benefits. However, it is the process that matters and because of this it is important to make the benefits explicitly dependent upon the aspects of the standard RE process and relatively independent upon the organizational factors. By doing so, the architect is now able to generalize the assessment results beyond the scope of a specific ERP project and to develop a staged plan for absorbing the benefits in a course of multiple projects.

4   Conclusion

It is commonly accepted that reuse measurements bring value to the RE process. In this paper, we tried to systematically analyze and assess the effects measurements have on the ERP RE process and to translate them into value-added benefits. We sought answers to three basic questions: (1) what are the components of RM benefits in the context of the ASAP RE process, (2) how to assess the process in terms of benefits gained from RM, and (3) what are the major issues arising in carrying out such an exercise. We defined an analysis method that led us to the following contributions:

- a catalogue of six components of benefits has been developed;
- a benefits assessment procedure has been defined;
- major problems/misconceptions with assessment studies has been identified and documented.

When applying the approach in ERP *post-implementation* mode, documented assessment results help the architect ensure that RM remains a relevant and viable part of the ERP project. In case of *pre-implementation* assessment, the approach provides both business and technical perspectives to determine what the RM usage patterns need to be in order to make an impact on the RE process.

It is our believe that the approach would help other ERP teams increase the usage rates of their RM assets while narrowing the gap between expectations of RM and reality. An architect could use the catalogue as a starting point to define organization-specific benefit criteria, set up a disciplined benefits realization process, and plan the capabilities required to realize those benefits.

Further work will be focused on the classification of the benefits based on three types of ERP projects: new implementations, upgrades and enhancements. This will help us refine it to allow for more flexibility and adaptability to the specific needs of the ERP project organization.

References

1. Curran Lad: SAP R/3 Business Blueprint. Prentice Hall, 2nd edition (2000)
2. Daneva, M.: Mesuring Reuse of SAP Requirements: a Model-based Approach. Proc. Of 5th Symposium on Software Reuse, ACM Press, New York (1999)
3. Daneva, M.: Reuse Measurement in the ERP Requirements Engineering Process. Proc. Of the 6th Intrn. Conf. On Software Reuse, LNCS, Springer (2000)
4. Daneva, M.: Practical reuse measurement in ERP Requirements Engineering. Proc. Of Int. Conf. On Computer-aided Information Systems Engineering (CAiSE), Springer (2000) 309-324
5. ESPRIT Project PROFES, URL: http://www.ele.vtt.fi/profes
6. El Emam, K., Birk, A.: Validating the ISO/IEC 15504 Measure of Software Requirements Analysis Process Capability. IEEE Transactions on SE, 26(2000)6
7. El Emam, K., Briand, L.: Costs and Benefits of Software Process Improvement. Better Software Practice for Business Benefits: Principles and Experience, R. Messnarz and T. Tully, eds., IEEE CS Press (1999)
8. El Emam, K., Madhavji, N.H.: Measuring the Success of Requirements Engineering Process. In Proc. Of the 2nd IEEE Int Symposium on RE (1995) 204-211
9. El Emam, K, Quintin, S., Madhavji, N.H.: User Participation in the Requirements Engineering Process: an Empirical Study. Requirements Engineering Journal, 1(1996) 4-26
10. Goldenson, D., El Emam, K., Herbsleb, J, Deephouse, C.: Empirical Studies of Software Process Assessment methods. Elements of Sofware Process Assessment and Improvement, K. El Emam and N.H. Madhavji, eds. IEEE CS Press (1999)
11. Goodman, P., Morris, P.: Forgotten Aspects of Function Point Analysis. Proc. of the IFPUG Annual Conference (1999)
12. Jones, C.: Applied Software Measurement. McGraw Hill, New York (1996)
13. Keller, G., Teufel, T.: SAP R/3 Process Oriented Implementation. Addison-Wesley Longman, Harlow (1998)
14. Longstreet, D., Using Function Points. Longstreet Consulting, http://www.softwaremetrics.com/Articles/using.htm

15. Meyer, N.D., Boone, M.E.: The Information Edge. 2nd Ed., Gage Educational Publishing Co., Toronto Canada (1989)
16. Sommerville, I., Sawyer, P.: Requirements Engineering: Best Practice Guide. Willey, London (1997)
17. Statz, J.: Leverage Your Lessons. IEEE Software, March/April (1999) 30-33
18. Thorp, J.: The Information Paradox: Realizing the Business Benefits of Information technology, McGraw-Hill, New York (1999)

A New Metric-Based Approach for the Evaluation of Customer Satisfaction in the IT Area

Reiner R. Dumke and Cornelius Wille

University of Magdeburg, Faculty of Computer Science, Postfach 4120,
D-39016 Magdeburg, Germany
Tel.: +49-391-6718664, Fax: +49-391-6712810,
{dumke,wille}@ivs.cs.uni-magdeburg.de

Abstract. For the existence and growth of enterprises the protected sales of goods and performances are of decisive opinion. In order to ensure this, the acceptance of the products and performances by the customers is depended on indirect criterion mainly: the customer satisfaction. A lot of criteria and methods with help of the science were or are worked out to "measure" satisfaction or discontent of the customers to the inquiry.

Our paper describes the general satisfaction aspects and their coherence between customer satisfaction, quality and customer loyalty as well as their significance for the development of an enterprise. After the classification of methods for measuring customer's satisfaction different methods for the recording of customer satisfaction are shown. A basic model for customer satisfaction is introduced for recording and assessment at software products using software metrics related to the product, process and resources aspects. This method attemps to measure directly the causes to evaluate their effect to the customer satisfaction.

In order to evaluate customer satisfaction, a tool COSAM was implemented that allows a metrics-based assessment besides the traditional assessment of the customer satisfaction by customer interviews. On the other hand, the tool can be used for experiments of a given level of customer satisfaction to analyse the effects of successful measured aspects such as ISO 9000 certification, a high level of the developer skills or a high level in the CMM evaluation.

1 Introduction

Customer satisfaction is one of the main reasons for controlling the software quality in the software marketplace. The analysis and evaluation of the customer satisfaction is based on a set of orthogonal aspects and intentions (see Figure 1).

Hence, it is necessary to define complex evaluation methods to drive the main indicators, which are addressed to the customer satisfaction on the area of software development and application. On the other hand, customer satisfaction is typically a dynamic measurement and evaluation aspect, which may change from indifference to satisfaction or discontent depended on the predefined situation (see Figure 2).

R. Dumke and A. Abran (Eds.): IWSM 2000, LNCS 2006, pp. 183-195, 2001.

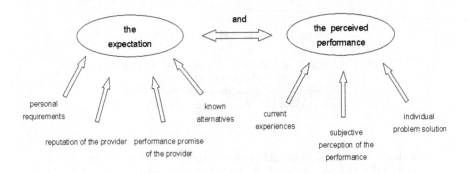

Fig. 1. Aspects in the process of the evaluation of customer satisfaction

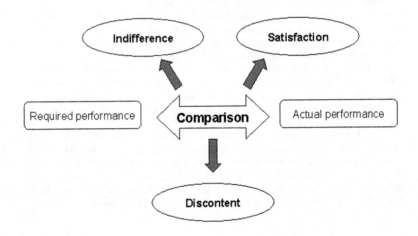

Fig. 2. Dynamic states of customer intention

We will consider the *customer satisfaction* as a result of a complex information process, which is based on the comparison of the required/actual performance evaluation by the customer. The Figure 3 describes the essential aspects of the methods to the customer satisfaction evaluation.

We will not discuss these evaluation methods here and will describe the essential characteristics of the evaluation techniques themselves. A detailed description of these methods is given in [9].

A main aspect of recording the data for the evaluation of the customer satisfaction is included in the kind of the method to register the customer data. Table 1 show the main aspects by [7].

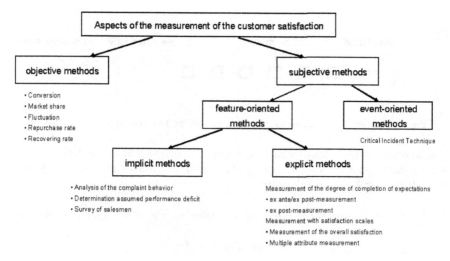

Fig. 3. Evaluation methods of customer satisfaction by [7]

Table 1. Advantages and disadvantages of the method of recording of the customer data

Forms of the Survey Criteria	written survey	personal survey	telephone survey
Response rate	in the tendency low, but strongly	High	high
Costs	small-medium	high	medium-high
Support of Quality control	small (of whom and like the questionnaire filled out)	very well	well
Objectivity of the results	High	very low (influence of the interviewer)	low (influence of the interviewer), may be improved by training
Representation and entry of complex issues	Impossible	very well	well
Acquisition of qualitative back-ground informations	almost impossible	very well	well

Usually, the recording is based on a questionnaire which apply different kinds of scales. A complete form of such a scale for recording customer satisfaction data is shown in Figure 4.

very dissatisfied   neutrally   very contently   not applicable

Fig. 4. Questionnaire scale including the 'neutrally' and the 'not applicable' evaluation

The answers of the questionnaires represent the *satisfaction value* derived using a weight factor for the different aspects the *weighted customer satisfaction*. A simple formula is given by [5] as following

$$Weighted\ customer\ satisfaction\ =\ feature\ weight\ \times\ satisfaction\ value$$

$$as\ K = W \times Z$$

This execution is also called as *measurement* in the literature. Considering all defined features, we can determine the *customer satisfaction index* as (see [2], [3] and [5])

$$Customer\ satisfaction\ index (KZI) = \sum_{i=1}^{n} (W_i * Z_i)$$

This index can be assumed as a basis for customer satisfaction comparing and improving. In order to analyse the influence of the different features of this evaluation, we can use a portfolio description which is shown is the Figure 5.

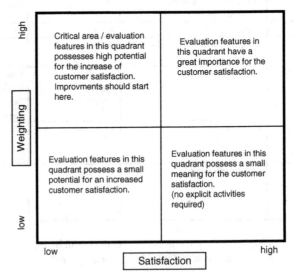

Fig. 5. Portfolio representation of the evaluation features for the customer satisfaction.

An application of this portfolio for three different evaluation features of a software product is given in Figure 6.

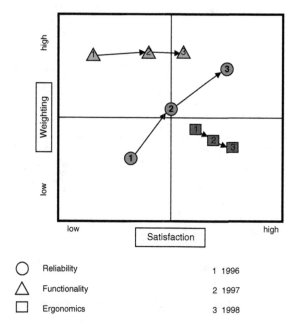

Fig. 6. An example of a portfolio-based evaluation analysis

Another context of the customer satisfaction evaluation is described in Figure 7 and leads us to the reasoning interpretation of the obtained/measured results [4].

Finally, we will show an overview of some practical methods for the evaluation of the customer satisfaction in Table 2 (see the details in [9]).

2   Metric-Based Measurement and Evaluation

The presented methods to estimate the customer satisfaction given in the Table 2 are *evaluations*. The intention of measurement is to quantify the different attributes of evaluation in order to improve the analysis of considered aspects. Related to the customer satisfaction, we must observe the statistical correlation between the evaluation and the possible reasons based on the general characteristics in the IT area shown in Figure 8 (see also [1]).

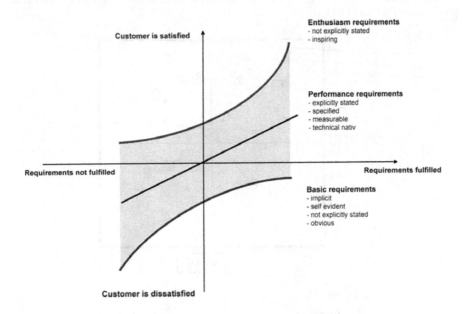

Fig. 7. The Kano model of the customer satisfaction

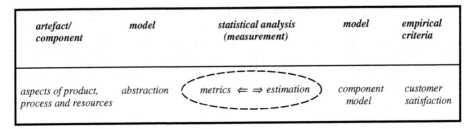

Fig. 8. Metrics-based evaluation

The evaluation models above are based on the questionnaire of the customer. The use of (software) metrics in the sense of Figure 8 can lead to a reasoning of the customer satisfaction. It is possible to proof some of the following hypothesis:

- What are the reasons for customer satisfaction related to the process and resource characteristics?
- Are their any relationships between a high customer satisfaction and a high process level?
- Is it possible to estimate the customer satisfaction based on the characteristics of chosen software metrics solely?

The following new approach will extend the possibilities of 'traditional' customer satisfaction evaluation to apply new kinds of evaluation and supporting the a metrics-based customer satisfaction *measurement*.

Table 2. Aspects of chosen practical methods of the evaluation of customer satisfaction

Practical examples	The McCall Model	User satisfaction evaluation by Hayes	EFQM-Model	Quality assurance ISO 9000	Measurement of the customer satisfaction by Gause and Weinberger	Measurement of the customer satisfaction at T-Nova
Method	*Multi-attribute measurement*	*Multi-attribute measurement Global satisfaction query*	*Multi-attribute measurement*	*Multi-attribute measurement*	*Multi-attribute measurement*	*Multi-attribute measurement Global satisfaction query*
Satisfaction measurement	*no*	*yes*	*yes*	*no*	*yes*	*yes*
Scale		*Nominal scale*	*Ordinal scale*	*Nominal scale*	*Ordinal scale*	*Ordinal scale*
Weighting	*no*	*yes*	*yes*	*no*	*no*	*yes*
Scale		*Ordinal scale*	*Ordinal scale*			*Weighting of the constant totals*
Statistical methods	*none*	*none*	*Evaluation of the degree of completion by percent calculation*	*Calculation of the quality index*	*Calculation of the average of the evaluation of individual features*	*Index of the customer satisfaction arithmetic means*
included components:						
Product	*yes*	*yes*	*yes*	*yes*	*yes*	*yes*
Process	*no*	*no*	*no*	*no*	*no*	*no*
Resources	*no*	*no*	*yes*	*yes*	*yes*	*yes*
Remarks	*Quality model for software products*	*May be used as a basis for a questionnaire*	*Hard and soft factors of software development*	*Customer satisfaction is not explicitly inquired*	*Focus on revealing of modifications of the satisfaction*	*Questionnaires with emphasis on work on the project or product quality*

3   The New Approach of the Evaluation of the Customer Satisfaction

In our new approach, we will chose and classify the customer intentions as an empirical basis for satisfaction evaluation. On the other hand, we will try to map software metrics to the empirical criteria to perform some investigations about the software process characteristics and the customer satisfaction and, finally, that we can work out a metrics-based measurement of the customer satisfaction in the IT area.

This three intentions are described in a simplified manner in Figure 9. The investigations of the mapping between satisfaction aspects and metrics are denoted by *adjustment* of the metrics values related to different ordinal values of the traditional customer satisfaction evaluation.

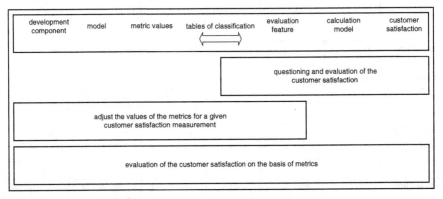

Fig. 9. The three kinds of application of our approach for customer satisfaction evaluation

Therefore, we have defined a set of aspects for the traditional empirical evaluation. These criteria and the optional kinds of software metrics for mapping are shown in Figure 10.

In order to keep the traditional form of the customer satisfaction evaluation, we implemented the following three methods (see also [8]):

- The customer satisfaction index by [5] as

$$KZI = \sum_{i=1}^{n} \left(W_i * Z_i \right)$$

  with W_i as feature weight for feature i and Z_i as satisfaction value for the feature i. The KZI considers the weights of the evaluation features apart from the satisfaction also. It can serve as yardstick for the comparison of the current with past test results of the same product/project or for the comparison of the examined product/project with others.
- The **weighted total satisfaction** by [6] considers likewise the satisfaction and the weights of the evaluation features.

$$Z_{ges} = \frac{\sum_{k=1}^{22} \frac{\sum_{i=1}^{n} \left(EZ_{ik} - \frac{|EZ_{ik} - W_{ik}|}{7} \right)}{n}}{22}$$

with EZ_{ik} as satisfaction of the customer i with feature k and W_{ik} as weighting of the feature k by the customer i.

- The *customer satisfaction index* by [7] as

$$KUZ = 1/n \sum_{i=1}^{n} Z_i$$

with Z_i as satisfaction value for feature i.

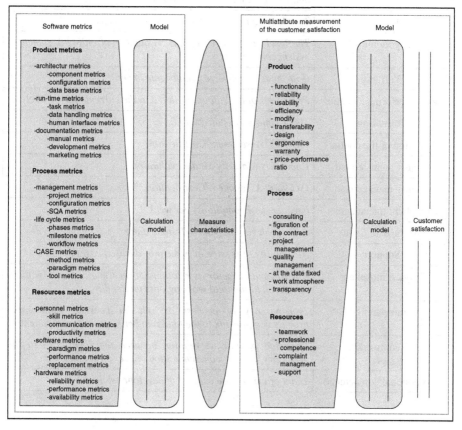

Fig. 10. The empirical criteria and the possible metrics for mapping

For the measurement of the customer satisfaction, we have chosen or defined as a first approximation *one metric* for *one empirical criterion*. The Table 3 includes a general description of this kind of mapping.

Table 3: Mapping of software metrics to the empirical criteria for customer satisfaction evaluation

Empirical criterion	Software metric
Functionality	*Traceability measure as relation between specified requirements and the given requirements in the problem definition*
Reliability	*Mean Time To Failure (MMTF)*
Usability	*Completeness of the documented product components*
Efficiency	*Performance of response time of the considered systems*
Modify	*Neighbourliness of maintenance*
Transferability	*Portability as relation between the effort of new development and the effort for transformation and adaptation*
Design	*Topology equivalence of the designed screens*
Ergonomics	*The level of the help support as number of online-documented system components*
Warranty	*Guarantee of software components in years*
Price-performance ratio	*Price level of the software related to the current market level*
Consulting	*Mean Time To Repair (MTTR)*
Figuration of the contract	*ISO 9000 Assessment/Certification*
Project management	*Capability Maturity Model evaluation*
Quality management	*ISO 9000 Assessment/Certification*
Complaint management	*Frequency of complaints per week*
At the date fixed	*Average deviation from milestone dates*
Support	*Availability of service in percent of the used cases*
Work atmosphere	*Environmental factor as relation between working ours without any break to the total working ours on the day*
Transparency	*Transparency of process as relation between manageable process components to the total number of process components*
Teamwork	*Provision of time as relation between the spent time to the necessary time for communication of every team member*
Professional competence	*Years of experience as level of developer skills*

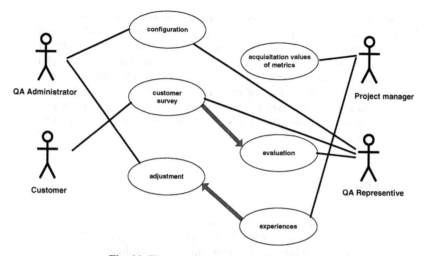

Fig. 11. The user profile of the COSAM tool

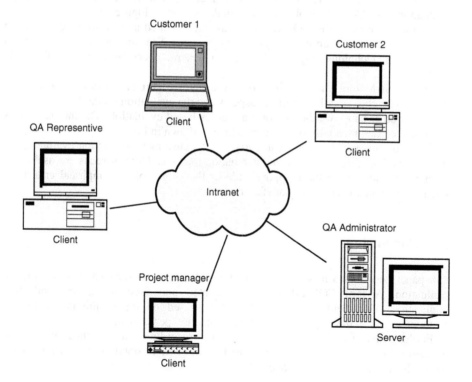

Fig. 12. The distributed architecture of the COSAM tool

On the other hand, it is necessary to map the possible metrics values to the ordinal scale of the empirical criterion. We have chosen a unified ordinal scale for the empirical criterion from *1 (worst)* to *5 (best)*. This aspect is at most indeterminate in our approach. Hence, its tool support requires a high flexibility for the adjustment or tuning the measurement process of the customer satisfaction determination.

Based on this first step of mapping software metrics to the empirical aspects of customer satisfaction, we have defined a default mapping table in order to have a possibility to determine the customer satisfaction based on the different intervals of the metrics values.

4   Tool Support

Our intention of the tool support is based on two general aspects:
1. The implementation of a client/server system to improve the current manual technique for the traditional customer satisfaction evaluation.
2. The implementation of a new approach of the measurement of customer satisfaction based of widely used software metrics.

The general user profile of the implemented system for customer satisfaction evaluation – the COSAM tool – is shown in the following Figure 11.

On the other hand, the COSAM tool was implemented as a distributed system in order to perform a Web-based system application. The authenticity is kept by a special login technique. Figure 12 gives an general overview about the COSAM architecture.

The COSAM tool enables kinds of variants for traditional customer satisfaction evaluation by choosing the empirical aspects and the evaluation method.

On the other hand, we can perform a metrics-based evaluation. The metrics values must be recorded manually in a screen, which is shown in Figure 13.

Based on this recording, we can carry out the customer satisfaction evaluation by using one of the three implemented evaluation methods. Other screens are usable for changing or adaptation the mapping table or the choice of the empirical criteria in order to evaluate the customer satisfaction.

5   Conclusions

Our paper describes a new (measurement-based) technique for customer satisfaction evaluation. A tool COSAM was implemented and used for a first industrial application. This field experiment was only based on the traditional evaluation method and led to the improvement of the evaluation performance.

Further investigation are related to the recording and application of the measurement component of the COSAM tool in order to obtain essential results for the goals their are described above.

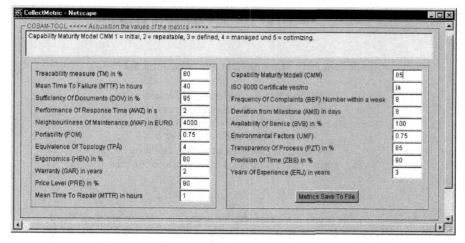

Fig. 13. The COSAM screen for metrics value recording

Acknowledgements

We will thanks the T-Nova company of the Deutsche Telekom for supporting this project and for given the necessary empirical background of our investigations.

References

1. Dumke, R., Foltin, E.: An Object-Oriented Software Measurement and Evaluation Framework. Proc. of the FESMA, October 4-8, Amsterdam (1999) 59-68
2. Hayes, B.E.: Measuring Customer Satisfaction. ASQC Quality Press, Milwaukee, USA (1992)
3. Hierholzer, A.: Benchmarking der Kundenorientierung von Softwareprozessen. Shaker Publ., Aachen, Germany (1996)
4. Kano, N.: Attractive Quality and Must-be Quality. The Journal of the Japanese Society for Quality Control, April (1984) 39-48
5. Mellis, W., Herzwurm, G., Stelzer, D.: TQM der Softwareentwicklung. Vieweg Publ., Wiebaden, Germany (1998)
6. Scharnbacher, K., Kiefer, G.: Kundenzufriedenheit: Ansalyse, Maßbarkeit und Zertifizierung. Oldenbourg Publ. Munich, Germany (1998)
7. Simon, H., Homburg, C.: Kundenzufriedenheit Konzepte Methoden Erfahrungen, Gabler Publ., Wiesbaden, Germany (1998)
8. Talley, D.J.: Total Quality Management – Performance and Cost Measures. ASQC Publ., Milwaukee, USA (1991)
9. Wille, C.: Konzeption und prototypische Implementation der Erfassung und Bewertung von Kundenzufriedenheit bei der Entwicklung, Wartung und Anwendung von Software. Diploma Thesis, University of Magdeburg, Germany (2000)

Utility Metrics for Economic Agents

Dirk Schmelz[1], Margitta Schmelz[1], and Julia Schmelz[2]

[1]Thüringer Kompetenzzentrum eCommerce
tranSIT GmbH Ilmenau, Germany
c/o Friedrich-Schiller-Universität Jena, Germany
mms@informatik.uni-jena.de
[2]Technische Universität München, Germany
schmelz@mathematik.tu-muenchen.de

Abstract. In this paper, a metric view for operating software agents is developed and explained by way of an example of economic trader agents utility. Here, the role of simulation models as a helpful technology for construction and validation of agents in artificial environments is propagated.

1   Software Agents Application

The software agent is a software-based system with capabilities as well to perceive changes in its complex environment and to derive inferences. It solves special tasks by planning, timing and assessing its actions independently and autonomously. An appropriate environment in which the agent operates is often called agent-based system.

It influences the dynamically changing environment by actions. The agent's interpretation of relevant events in its observation range is used for both executing a concrete order and increasing its efficiency. It learns by repeating tasks and interpreting processes. By reason of these capabilities the software agent is an intelligent assistent of a costumer which benefits from the agent's perceptive faculty, adaptability and fitness for work. It works with available technologies for informing the customer and therefore helping in routine activities and providing situation training. Agents solve manyfold problems in practice, for example they help in maintenance of operation systems, in organization of applications or they capture, select and analyze data.

In an agent-based system, there are agents with different tasks. Co-ordination agents organize processes in the system and arrange contacts within agents. User interface (UI) agents provide the connection of users and the system. Ressource agents provide access to data bases. Security agents realize the security policy of the system. Software agents may be static or mobile in the network. Agents with different targets may delegate tasks or problems to the convenient agent type, agents with the same object may be competitive. Moreover, so-called application agents work in different applications.

A special application domaine is the category of economic agents which need some artificial intelligence. These agents move and work in the world of goods and prices. They buy and sell in dependence from the achievable utility. They trade autonomous

R. Dumke and A. Abran (Eds.): IWSM 2000, LNCS 2006, pp. 196-204, 2001.

in a certain degree. The environment of a commercial agent consists in market places, competitors and trading partners and also in an infrastructure from which some trading services are attainable. Different market places can influence themself mutually. More qualified agents can suggest the communication within the market place. In comparison to a simple trader agent they have other tasks, rights and additional abilities. Especially, the mobile agent technology in networks of economy and administration will play an essential role in information systems, in the workflow management and in the electronic commerce.

2   Software Agents in the View of Metrics

2.1   Attributes of Agents

In the chapter 1, we have mentioned some attributes which are rather unknown in the terminology of software metrics. In the center of attributes such as skill of perception, ability of learning and thinking or autonomy of action, we focus on the term of intelligence. The engine for revealing of rules and their exploitation belongs to the technical equipment of an intelligent agent.The agent can have a stable memory that is uncoupled from the environment in dependence on the autonomy degree. So it adapts to the environment using this memory. The intelligence of the agent is beneficial for surviving and augmenting the own performability. The utility of the agent in the operation phase is determined by its fitness in the operation space that is a part of the environment. The statical description of the agent as a software product is aided by the following scheme of [1] :

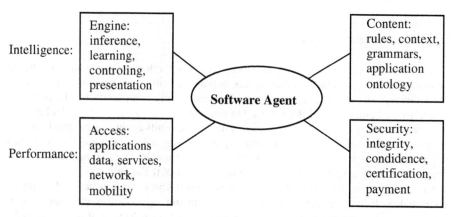

Now, some reflections on the measurement of agent´s productivity follow. Productivity has a direct relation to the utility attribute of the agent. Measures and models of the agent´s productivity are attractive from a manager view especially. Whereas in a common way, the value, that is generated or generable by the agent, and the concrete or expected expenses have to be compared.

A measurable part of this value we call the utility size. For example, a gain of money is a quantified utility. The number of actions given a fix time horizon is useful for the estimation of the action intensity. Sometimes, we research into a classification within a set of action patterns. By such metrics the quantitative behavior of an agent is measurable. The tree below shows a hierarchy of the measurement variables determining the productivity of an agent:

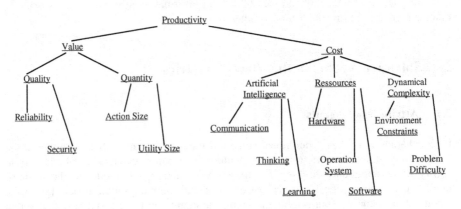

Software Agent Productivity

The attributes in the tree point out the wide requirement spectrum of the software agent subject. The quality of the agent depends on the security attribute strongly. This attribute will be amplified below. The cost aspect is coupled to the attributes of difficulty and strength of environment constraints in conjunction with the routine or the fitness of agents. Additional expenditures emerge from requirement which demand for more artificial intelligence.

2.2   Agent-Based Systems

Each autonomous agent is distinguishable from other autonomous agents in a given environment independently wether agents pursue the same targets or not. That leads to the concept of the multi-agent-system. Some dynamic complexity results from the parallelity and autonomy of the agents. On the one hand an agent is individual and on the other hand it is a part of multi-agent-system. The multi-agent-system produces the complexity of an organism. J. Holland [4] defines the agent as a rule-based input-output element in an environment and it is stimulated by other agents. Its representation governs the following characterization of the agent:

The agent knows its role in the environment. So it knows what it has to do with its functionality. It has capability of interactivity, transfer, aggregation and control with respect to the environment. The agent has mechanism for selection of roles and tasks and it identifys, modifys himself and makes predictions. The agent-based system owns attributes of object orientation and self-organization. System timing and survival ability of the agent type and of a single agent is also interesting. Each agent type

– represents some basic functionality,
– identifys relevant objects and contents,

- controls success of transactions,
- learns rules and roles .

Rocha [6] works on basics and possibilities of realization of semiotic agents. They are charcterized by an incoherent coupling to the environment. They live in an artificial environment which is represented by permanent laws, dynamical requirements and specific start situations. The model of the multi-agent-system is an implicite integration of laws and rules in the application field in which contexts emerge temporary. Rules from this context appears as a set of strategies in which the agent can choose. The interaction between the agent and the environment gives the dynamic complexity of the system that is the connection of static system complexity with operation profiles [8]. In simulated processes, the dynamic complexity is observable. Where, as well the semantic behavior of agents and its reaction in the case of decision as the effect of their decision on the environment is interesting. Particularly, the semantics of artifacts will be visible by simulation.

The idea that artificial environments for judgement and construction of software agents are useful leads to the subject of software metrics. Already before the design of an agent, performance parameters of the type and its intelligence degree could be simulated. The agent ought to be tested as a black box in the environment. This experimental aspect well-known in practical software metrics obtains a reasonable base by the possibility of simulation of the agent's behavior. A validated and data generating duo of agent and environment is beneficial to both testing the applicability of analysis algorithms and developing of control routines.

An essential improvement of communication between distributed objects by mobile agents is expectable in comparison to other client-server technology. The concept of mobility consists in autonomy, activity and parallelity. The agent migration in the net results in lower connection costs. For this reason, the mobility has a positive impact on the economic behavior of the agent. A problem of mobile agents results from unsolved security problems.

2.3   Security in Agent-Based Systems

The attribute of security may be defined nearby the attribute of reliability. Security is a very important attribute with respect to multi-agent-systems. Classification of failure kinds and damage causes can be extended by failure kinds induced from attitudes of the net user. Agents and agent environments need internal and external security services. Security claims and risks come from relations between agent and environment. In [2], two aspects were noted down:

- the aspect of protection and integrity of data,
- the aspect of guarantee of correct behavior of both agents and environment in accordance with their specification.

The first of the two aspects comes from security requirements of computer systems which use specific mechanisms to guarant a minimal level of security. The second aspect means that the specification must not be contradictory and that the implementation satisfys the specification. The agents are not completely autonomous, but, the significant autonomous behavior prevents any complete analysis. The exploitation of the agent as a "Trojan Horse" is even realistic [9].

Like the reliability problem, the security needs a technical and legal concept including their controllability of actions. So access methods for distributed informations and applications must be chosen carefully. From the task delegation from the user to agents and from agent mobility in the net security problems can emerge to that attention has to be paid.

Agents have to develop an own security behavior for their stay on the host. This behavior also has to satisfy the security standard of the chosen host. An administrator agent determines the rights of agents in dependence from their claims and trustworthiness of the agent. Such rights could concern

- how long the agent stays,
- how much safe storage place it has,
- the persistent data generated by the agent,
- permission to start other agents,
- access to local ressources,
- allowed net communication .

Simulation experiments and statistical analysis also could be of interest in relation to security questions. They are useful for testing and validating of security components of agent-based systems.

3   Economical Behavior of Software Agents

3.1   Two Scenarios

In this section, we deal with the application of economically oriented software agents. Exploiting the general ideas that are described in previous chapters we demonstrate the concept and the way of thinking in two simple models.

In the first model [7], the possibility of any agent for advertising of price offers to sell or to buy with respect to a product or a service on a market place is focused. The both quotations of any agent can be interpreted as quantifiable trading interest on a particular time point.

The comparison and utilization of the actual offering situation can be carried out in several ways. As well the last is essentially influenced by the market place. In [7], the given price offers are compared. So for instance, the necessary condition for a succesful transaction : Bid (quotation to buy) > Ask (quotation to sell) can be checked. In the cited paper, there we can find sufficient conditions, too. Furthermore, formulae for the utility evaluation of any trader are derived there and are also presented below.

Another model [5] assumes that the seller of a good knows the actual sell quotations of his rivals and computes his own price offer to sell in dependence on a profit evaluation formula. This behavior of the seller can be interpreted as indirect selling interest in the context of the first model. Whereas, the buying interest is modeled directly in both models. Direct modeling means that a variable of interest is explicitly given in the model. With respect to the utility the second model is a special case of the first model [7]. We call the first model [7] "transaction model" and the second model [5] "selling model". The application of the selling model to information brokering in the internet is only one of several possible applications [5].

In both models, the economic utility is of paramount importance. How we can see in comparison of the two models they use different base types as agents. The pure seller type has another behavior than the trader type. Both agent types are able to work in the same environment, then they will be in competition if both of them want selling. Nevertheless, they have a different view to their environment and this is essentially caused by the qualification for solving of concrete tasks. The extreme seller type is not sensitive to the real traded value of the good. The trader type can play the role of a pure seller type in certain market situations. So we see several kinds of perceptive faculty, but similar economic target of two agent types.

3.2   Economic Utility

The following presentation is coarse and the interested reader can become more familiar with the topic in studying the cited papers. In the two models mentioned above, a good is characterized by an universal value V that is known among the market members. This universal value V we multiplicate with an individually determined interest coefficient γ_i and we get the price offer to buy $V_i = V \gamma_i$, $\gamma_i \in [0,1]$. In the selling model [5], the value of V has to be more than the value of P_j of a seller j, $j \in J$, for any successful buy. The seller j sets his price P_j with a view of the price offers of the other sellers. Whereas he uses algorithms and computing services for the evaluation of a suitable price P_j and a suitable time point to advertise his quotation [5]. The utility by selling an information good to n prospective buyers in I with the interest coefficients $\gamma_i \in [0,1]$, $i \in I$, is modeled by

$$S_j = \sum_{i=1}^{n} A_{ij} [\gamma_i P_j - P_T] - P_S, \quad i \in I, \ j \in J, \quad I,J \quad N, \ I \cap J = \varnothing.$$

Here, A_{ij}, $A_{ij} \in [0,1]$, is used as an indicator of trade agreement of the seller and the buyer. The parameters P_T and P_S represent seller's costs as transaction costs and costs for purchasing the good from a producing source.

The utility of consumer i caused by buying the good from seller j is given in the following:

$$B_i = \sum_{j=1}^{m} A_{ij} [\gamma_i (V-P_j) - P_c], \quad i,j \text{ see above.}$$

The seller agent is able in decision making because of exploitation of convenient algorithms from which costs can emerge supplementary. A seller agent will be able to increase its endeavour if it is not successful for a sequence of time points. Sometimes, the agent trys avoiding direct confrontation with rivals. The buyer agent has to pay costs P_c.

If there are positive utility values for the seller and the buyer given the values of P_j, γ_i, P_c, P_T, P_S, we will enjoy a successful transaction or we can say a trade agreement.

In the transaction model [7], we have in a sense a symmetrization of sellers and buyers. The trader who is authorized in trading on this market place can advertise a price offer to buy and a price offer to sell simultaneously. In addition to the universal value V, we have there a further universal parameter P. We achieve an individual interest quotation to sell when we evaluate the product $P_{i*}=P\,\gamma_{i*}$, where γ_{i*} is an individual interest coefficient to sell. If we have m sell actions and n buy actions of trader j, we will compute his utility by:

$$U_j = \sum_{i=1}^{m} S_{ij*}(a)\,[-\,V_{\,j*}+P_{ij*}(a)-C^*] + \sum_{i*=1}^{n} S_{i*j}(a)\,[\,V_j-P_{i*j}(a)-C],\ i{\neq}j,\ i,j \in T,$$

$$T = \text{set of traders on the market place.}$$

Here, C and C* are trade dependent costs of the buyer or seller respectively. The nomenclature S_{kl} are binary indicators for successful transactions again, $S_{kl} \in [0,1]$. These indicators correspond to the indicators A_{ij} in the seller model. An index that is accompanied by a star * points out the trader as the seller. The same index without star * points out the trader as the buyer. Hence, the first part of U_j is the utility of trader j that is achieved by buying and the second part of U_j is achieved by selling. A trader can not sell and buy simultaneously and can not trade with his own.

The term $P_{ij*}(a)$ can be chosen as a weighted mean of quotation to buy $P_j=P\,\gamma_j$ and quotation to sell $P_{i*}=P\,\gamma_{i*}$:

$$P_{i*j} = [a\,\gamma_{i*} + (1{-}a)\,\gamma_j]\,P\ =\ a\,P_{i*} + (1\text{-}a)\,P_j,\qquad a \in [0,1].$$

In an analogous way we can compute :

$$P_{ij*} = [a\,\gamma_i + (1{-}a)\,\gamma_{j*}]\,P\ =\ a\,P_i + (1\text{-}a)\,P_{j*},\qquad a \in [0,1].$$

The difference V − P can be an indicator of interesting process features especially when we think of the parameters P and a as determined by the market place and observed by the traders.

3.3   Black Box, White Box and Types of Traders

With the aid of interest coefficients we can use the black box principle for testing of agents. The interest coefficients can be interpreted as the agents outfit in the environment. In this case, the interest is generated by distribution assumption. The realization of interest coefficients stands for real values or constructively achieved white box model values. The simulation experiments with trader agent model that were carried out in 7 involve the following components:

engine	random variable generator, time series methods, utility metrics, visualization instruments, graphs;
memory	internal system state data, individual roles and strategies;
access	market data, further environmental data;
security	modeling of disturbances, with failure interpretation;

In this place, we remark upon self-modification and type characterization. On the base of the two original types depicted in sections 3.1 and 3.2, we investigate a situation where and how the pure seller agent´s repurchasing interest could grow up. It compares its previous prices with other sellers prices in its proper way. It is interested in capability to contemplate in the view of a buyer. Now, we suggest that the seller directs his attention using his operation and comparison techniques not only to selling-price , but to buying-price. Whereas, we assume that the seller is in a position to observe the buyer rules and buyer view of the world with respect to interest setting. As a buyer he goes another way for getting positive utility in the same article category. As a buyer he is interested in a low buying price. So we guess that the trader type is better in cooperation in a natural way. In a situation where the selling business is quite bad, the pure seller could with his new knowledge and an actual full purse change from the seller party to the buyer side. The reason for activity in inquiring into rules of permanent or temporary type realization can be arisen from the agent or the environment.

4   Summary

In chapter 2 and 3, we have seen that not only principles of specification but also possibilities of observation, interpretation and selection are needed in the artificial environment. In such environments, agents can exist which are equiped with

- asynchronous behavior;
- situation adapted communication;
- shared knowledge expressed in public languages;
- ability of self-assessment.

The development and application of metrics that aid in construction and operation phase of complex agent systems are a challenge in the domain of software metrics. Here, the validation of applicability of new metrics and models is an important issue. The changing success of agents is dependent on environment constraints such as the agent roles diversity and the number per role realizations.

Economic agents are a demonstration example of artificial agents. Mainly, they have to consider a seed capital in money and goods. Network flow controlling makes interactivity and transfer measurable. The way of utility computation as an evaluation base provides a wide decision spectrum of the establish economic systems in which agents are defined and work with effect on their environment.

The examples of the trader models in section 3.1 show that more or less flexible agents can be created for buying and/or selling. Empirical substantiated arrangements of structural market place complexity yield appraisals for necessary application of mathematical methods. Experiments with the selling model (Kephart et. al. 6/1998) indicate that myopic optimization in price competitions can provide unending cycles of disastrous price "wars".

In the trader model [7], commercial agents can make price policy with respect to their actual money-good-situation and risk aversion. Other agents are able to observe and stimulate the dynamic trader behavior. First results in this context come up to the expectations of the usefulness of such model for experimenting with agents in artificial environments which replace the real world.

Further experimental targets of research concern for instance:
- realistic bandwith of good categories;
- different models of market places,
    trading rules, completations;
- risk factors and boundary effects.

In conjunction with the actual problem of concrete agent-based system architecture implementations it remains to be seen wether there will be a self-assessment component of the achievable economic utility.

In each case, such a component would have an algorithm for computation of utility size.

References

1. Caglyan, A.K., Harrison, C. G.: Intelligente Software-Agenten, Grundlagen, Technik und praktische Anwendung in Unternehmen. Carl Hanser Verlag München, Wien (1998)
2. Fünfrocken, Stefan: How to Integrate Mobile Agents into Webservers. Proceedings of the WET-ICE'97, Workshop on Collaborative Agents in Distributed Web Applications, Boston, MA, June (1997)
3. Hanson, J. E., Kephart, J.O.: Spontaneous Specialization in a Free-Market Economy of Agents. Artificial Societies and Computational Markets Workshop (at the Second International Conference on Autonomous Agents, Minneapolis/St. Paul) (1998)
4. Holland, J. H.: Hidden Order: How Adaption Builds Complexity. Addison-Wesley (1995)
5. Kephart, J.O., Hanson, J. E., Sairamesh, J.: Price-War Dynamics in a Free-Market Economy of Software Agents. Proceedings of ALIFE VI, Los Angeles (1998)
6. Rocha, L.M.: From Artifical Life to Semiotic Agent Models. – http://www.c3.lanl. gov./~rocha (1999)
7. Schmelz, J.: Transaction Processes among Autonomous Traders. Workshop on Mathematical Finance, 4.-7.10., Konstanz (2000)
8. Schmelz, D., Schmelz, J.: Growth Models for Software Reliabilty. In: Metrics News, Journal of the GI-Interest Group on Software Metrics, Otto-von-Guericke-Universität Magdeburg, 3(1998)2, 48-55
9. Schmelz, M.: Sicherheitsprobleme bei der Arbeit mobiler Agenten. Zuarbeit zum Jahresbericht 1998 des Thüringer Kompetenzzentrums eCommerce, unpublished, Friedrich-Schiller-Universität Jena (1999)

QF²D: A Different Way to Measure Software Quality

Luigi Buglione[1] and Alain Abran[2]

Software Engineering Management Research Laboratory
Université du Québec à Montréal
C.P. 8888, Succ. Centre-Ville
Montréal, Québec, Canada
[1]Tel: (39) 338.95.46.917, Fax: (39) 06-233.208.366
`luigi.buglione@computer.org`
[2]Tel: +1 (514) 987-3000 (8900), Fax: +1 (514) 987-8477
`abran.alain@uqam.ca`

Abstract. Quality Function Deployment (QFD) technique has been developed in the context of Total Quality Management, and it has been experimented in the software engineering domain. This paper illustrated how key constructs from QFD contributed to an development of a second version of a Quality Factor (QF) for a qualitative software evaluation, considering three distinctive but connected areas of interest, each of them representing dimension of performance:
- **economic dimension**, the perspective is the managers' viewpoint;
- **social dimension**, the perspective is the users' viewpoint;
- **technical dimension**, the perspective is the developers' viewpoint.

This new version of the original QF technique, referred to as QF²D (Quality Factor through QFD), has the following features: it can be used for both a priori and a posteriori evaluations of the software product; it makes usage of the set of quality sub-characteristics proposed in the new upcoming ISO/IEC 9126:2000 standard it has a variable number of elements taken into account the three viewpoints for the evaluation; it offers the visual clarity from QFD for external and internal benchmarking. An implementation of this new version of this technique in quality models is also discussed.

1   Introduction

Measurement and assessment, both of products and processes, are becoming one of the most important topics in the software engineering community. They are being increasingly recognised as being fundamental to objectively assess and to set realistic targets to improve organisational performance, with a view both to resources allocation and functional process areas implementation – or improvement, in order to reach optimal qualitative levels [1].

Measuring its own projects performance levels becomes then a strategic component for a proper planning and development of the software organisation.

But in order to do that, in the evaluation you must consider the viewpoints of multiple company *dimensions ,* all part of the software production process, such as:

R. Dumke and A. Abran (Eds.): IWSM 2000, LNCS 2006, pp. 205-219, 2001.

- the Economic one, represented by the managers' viewpoint;
- the Social one, represented by the users' viewpoint;
- the Technical one, represented by the developers' viewpoint.

Nearly the totality of software engineering literature takes into consideration only the first and the third viewpoints cited above. Because of a growing involvement of users with information technologies, the second viewpoint must now play an essential role in software assessment, because they are the real users of these products and it is increasingly necessary to meet their software quality requirements because only considering the three dimensions at the same time and with the same weight it is possible to obtain correct and complete assessments.

Referring to product quality, specifically of software, it must be interpreted in the light of the concept of **purpose of use**, considering both internal attributes (product characteristics) and the external ones (aim of the use). From the different possible definitions of quality, we refer here to "the totality of features and characteristics of a product or service that bear on its ability to satisfy stated or implied needs" [28]. Therefore, software quality assessments take into account multiple and distinct viewpoints such as the three ones discussed above:

- the **management**'s one, who is "interested in the overall quality rather than in a specific quality characteristic [...] and need to balance the quality improvement with management criteria" [34];
- the **user**'s one, whereas software quality is given by all the properties right to satisfy correctly and efficiently the present and future real needs of who buy and use it;
- the **developer**'s one, whereas software quality is given by the "conformity to functional and performance requirements explicitly fixed, to development standards explicitly documented and to implied characteristics supposed for every software developed in a professional way" [39].

One of the most powerful tools for collecting and prioritising multiple requirement sources in Industry during last thirty years has been Quality Function Deployment (QFD) [45]. This paper presents how key concepts from QFD were used to develop a new version of the Quality Factor (QF) for software [8] which we developed to consolidate into a single value for quality, relevant to three viewpoints, using an open weight scale methodology permitting any appropriate value ranges rather than an arbitrarily set of weights. This new version is referred to as QF2D (Quality Factor through QFD). a method able For external comparability of results, we have chosen the international software engineering standards (ISO/IEC 9126 and 14598 standard series to build the tools for QF calculation.

Section 2 discusses Quality Models and foundations for the QF. Section 3 presents QFD and its applications in the software field. Section 4 provides the description for the new improved technique, QF^2D, and finally Section 5 summaries the state of the art and shows future directions for this study.

2   Quality Models & The Quality Factor (QF)

A Quality Model (**QM**) is defined as "the set of characteristics and the relationships between them which provide the basis for specifying quality requirements and evaluating quality" [28] or as a "structured set of properties required for an object of a class to meet defined purposes" [19]. The goal of this paper is, as already said, to present a quality value, expressed by QF. But QF represents the output of a qualitative evaluation process based on a QM.

The benefit of QMs is given by the decomposition of the valuable object (both a process, a product or an organisation) in a list of its characteristics, sub-characteristics and measures and it is applicable both to predict/assure/verify the achievement of a defined goal about the object before/while/after producing it.

The best known QMs for software are those proposed by Boehm et al. [5] and McCall et al. [36], which formed a basis for the 1991 ISO standard (ISO/IEC 9126[1] [2]). It is possible to classify QMs depending on their number of layers:

- **2 layers** (Boehm and McCall): a set of characteristics, further subdivided into a set of sub-characteristics;
- **3 layers**: with specific measures for each sub-characteristic measures.

In the description of their QM various the authors have used different terms, and for consistency, we use in this study the ISO terminology (Table 1).

Table 1. Terminology of Quality Models

Layer	Boehm [5]	McCall [36]	ISO [34]	IEEE [27]	Dromey [17]
1	H-Level Charact.	Factor	Characteristic	Factor	H-Level Attribute
2	Primitive Charact.	Criteria	Subcharacteristic	Subfactor	Subordinate Attribute
3[3]	(Metric)	(Metric)	(Metric)	Metric	

Another classification of QMs is based on the number of relationships between the first two layers:

- **1:n relationship**, as in ISO/IEC 9126 - every characteristic has its own set of sub-characteristics;
- **n:m relationship**, as in McCall's Factor-Criteria Model (FCM) - every sub-characteristic is linked to one or more characteristics.

---

[1] 6 characteristics and 21 sub-characteristics compose the current standard, released in 1991. The new updating version (not always International Standard) has foreseen -27 sub-characteristics for Internal and External Quality against 6 characteristics plus 4 additional characteristics for the Quality in Use [29, 30, 31, 32].

[2] We have not listed IEEE Std 1061-1992 [27] in the text because it does not propose a pre-compiled checklist, but just furnishes in Annex A an example list of factors, sub-factor and metrics specifying that "these tables are not exhaustive. There are many possible sets of factors, sub-factors and metrics that can be used". By the way, this standard lists the same six ISO characteristics and 18 sub-characteristics with a strong overlapping with the 21 ones in the ISO model.

[3] The brackets for "Metric" on the third table row indicate that the model architecture does not formally mention that layer, even if it exists and is needed to make evaluations.

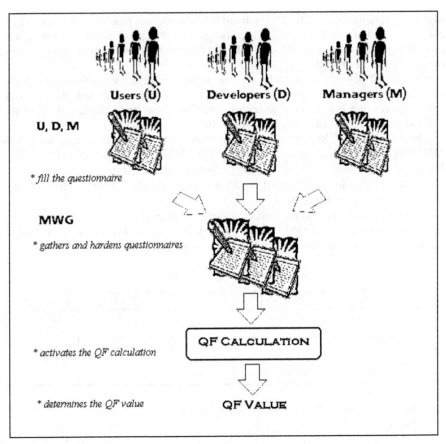

Fig. 1. QF procedure flow

In our previous work for the definition and calculation of a Quality Factor (QF), we did not defined our own QM but selected the ISO quality model. Thus, we designed a procedure to calculate a Quality Factor for software (QF), which returned a value which originality and added value is derived from the comparison between users', developers' and managers' opinions about the project being assessed [8]. Figure 1 shows the high-level procedure flow. First, the questionnaire is submitted to both users and developers and managers, who express their quality opinions. Then, the Measurement Working Group (MWG), responsible for the management of the procedure, gathers and consolidate these opinions and, through the QF calculation procedure, obtains the final quality value for the project being assessed.

The QF technique was tested in a large Italian company in the Utility sector, and the results obtained indicated a strong alignment with their own techniques to evaluate software quality issues. These results were proposed as examples in [8], with people interviewed from three groups (users, technicians and managers) answering the questionnaire from distinct company sites.

The main limitation observed in the used of the QF method was that it is applicable only for evaluation purposes; however, in a production process all the phases of the lifecycle should be covered.

The successful experimentation with software n of a powerful tool as QFD was a positive stimulus in order to use it, improving the basic idea behind QF. The other substantial difference in this new version is the introduction of the new upcoming ISO/IEC 9126 version, including a set of internal, external and quality in use metrics. This is very useful for the three stakeholders groups of interest in order to determinate in a better way the most critical product attributes in their viewpoint. QFD permits to summarise all data in a graphical way through the HoQ and enormously helps in evaluating the current situation and taking decisions.

3   Quality Function Deployment (QFD)

Quality Function Deployment (QFD) method originated in the late '60s in Japan and was developed as a means of translating customer requirements (the so-called "*Voice of the Customer*") into appropriate technical requirements throughout the development and production of a product. In the '80s this method was introduced in North America and its initial focus on the product was extended to the whole production chain (the "4 phases of QFD": HoQ (or Design), Parts (or Details), Process, Production) [15, 16, 24, 42, 44].

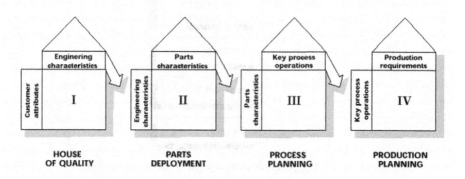

Fig. 2. 4 QFD phases [23]

QFD includes a series of matrixes, as documented in Mizuno and Akao [45], which are the tools used to represent data; the most commonly used matrix is the "House of Quality" (HoQ – in the terminology of the American Supplier Institute – ASI) or "A1 Matrix" fin the terminology of the Growth Opportunity Alliance of Lawrence GOAL/ QPC) described in [23], those structure is presented in the following figure.

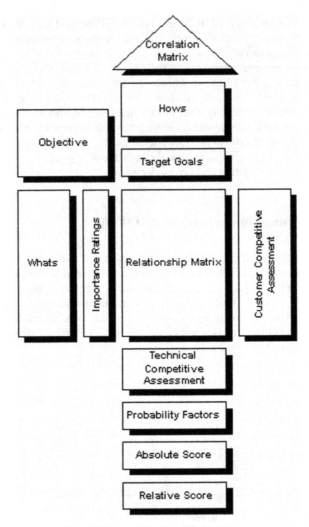

Fig. 3. House of Quality (HoQ) structure

Basically the HoQ presents the intersection of two dimensions, the horizontal one (the WHATs) and the vertical one (the HOWs). Referring to product development, the WHATs identify the characteristics of the product and/or service desired by the customer while the HOWs identify the way to achieve the WHATs. For a detailed explanation about the HoQ and how to fill out the matrix, refer to [21, 25, 44].

The relationship matrix, that is the central part of the HoQ, represents the heart of the system, presenting the prioritisation of the WHATs through the attribution of importance ratings. This rating is calculated by multiplicating each WHAT importance level (normally measured using a Likert scale) by its intensity relationship with the HOWs, using symbols with an associated weight. In Figure 4 some of the symbols and weights most often used in QFD literature are presented:

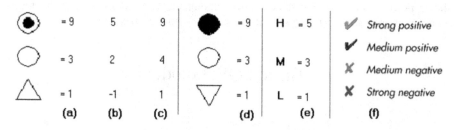

(a) Mizuno & Akao [45]
(b) Eriksson et al. [18]
(c) Conti [14]
(d) QFD/Capture Software [40]
(e) Hrones Jr et al.[26]
(f) Hauser & Clausing [23]

Fig. 4. Different QFD symbols and weights

In various quality models and case studies, the authors tend to design their own sets of weights, thereby making comparisons difficult across case studies. Because of the large awareness of QFD , the mapping to the QFD weights and symbols with ISO/IEC 14598-1 standard [33] is illustrated in Figure 5 (as in Figure 9).

Mark	QF²D Symbol	Rating	Global Rating
3	●	Excellent	
2	◎	Good	Satisfactory
1	○	Fair	
0	Blank	Poor / Absent	Unsatisfactory

Fig 5. QF²D symbols and weights

This matrix approach in QFD represents a good communication tool: it allows for a balanced consideration of requirements and provides a mechanism to communicate implicit knowledge throughout the organisation. But is the means and not the end: the real value is in the sharing of communication and decision-making of information and priorities among people of the numerous functional departments involved in product development, from Marketing to Product Support. QFD helps development personnel in maintaining the correct focus on most relevant requirements, minimising the misunderstanding of the customer needs. For these reasons, QFD represents an effective communication and quality-planning tool [23]. For example, QFD has been used in the manufacturing industry with great achievements, leading to significant reductions in overall project costs (e.g. 50%), project cycle time (e.g. 33%) and major increases in productivity (e.g. 200%) [21]. During the '80s this method was experimented in software development environment, and was referred to as Software QFD (SQFD): SQFD [22] is an adaptation of the HoQ scheme, considering the Technical Product Specifications as the HOWs of the matrix. A peculiarity is that SQFD does not use the "roof" of the House (the "Correlation Matrix" in Figure 2) that shows positive and negative relationships among the HOWs, since here the major focus in on processes. Figure 5 shows a basic SQFD model structure[4].

Basic SQFD model

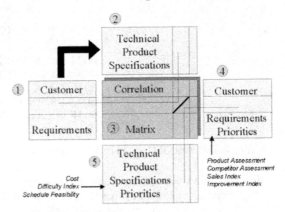

Fig 6. Basic SQFD model [22]

Some of the QFD adaptations for the software field are listed next:

- The Distributed QFD (DQFD) [4, 26] by Digital Equipment Corporation (DEC): a tailored version in 1992, optimised for local and global groups involved in defining product requirements,;
- Zultner Project QFD: an "essential minimum method to identify high-value needs, product characteristics and project tasks, quickly" [46]. His main focus is on shortening project schedules by a more efficient risk management using well-known quality tools through the application of the Theory of Constraints by E.M. Goldratt;
- Eriksson, McFadden and Tittanen [18] study on the need to join process and product analysis to check whether the user requirements concerning both the product and the project issues were correctly determined and to get the customers' acceptance of these points;
- Richardson [41, 42] QFD-based model: a tool to aid the implementation of a Software Process Improvement (SPI) action plan for SMEs, using Bootstrap as the reference SPI model. SPI/HoQ is the name of this HoQ that gives the organisation the full list of priorities to follow to reach greatest improvement in their software processes;
- The "Matrix of Change" (MoC) project by the Massachusetts Institute of Technology [6, 44], which shares similarities with Richardson's model. This

---

[4] Another application of QFD to Software Engineering is presented in [35], in particular for the Software Requirement selection.

MoC can help managers identify critical interactions among processes, providing useful guidelines for Change Management[5].

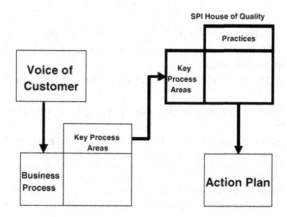

Fig. 7. The SPI/HoQ matrix cascade

4   QF²D: Description and Advantages

As introduced in Section 1, for software Quality Management field there could be significant benefits in software   to use some of the same methodologies and techniques, such as QFD' developed in the manufacturing field.. This lead to the redesign of our Quality Factor through the use of the Quality Function Deployment, joining the two into the QF2D (Quality Factor through QFD); note that the procedure to compile the HoQ matrices is similar to the one in QFD.

As a reminder,   the original QF technique allows the integration of different opinions and ratings from several organisational viewpoints to obtain a single and final quality value; however, any source data and intermediate results are of course not explicitly available in the consolidated final quality figure. A manager could need, first of all, an overall index value of quality and then, multiple levels of details to understand the relationships across the multiple variables, that is he will then need to access all sources of data for each different perspectives. Several level of analysis can be taken into account, with respect to the aim of evaluation and the level of granularity desired.

---

[5] As already said, QFD methodology is more than the HoQ, since it incorporates a lot of tools as the Voice of the Customer Table, Affinity and Tree-diagrams, comparisons in pairs, Pareto Analysis etc. in order to analyse customer needs and satisfaction, gathering and examining market information etc. This reasoning has been put in the majority of QFD software tools. [25] lists the most used ones, determining at all the characteristics of the "perfect" QFD software tool. It follows a typical result screen from the QFD/CAPTURE tool [40]. Another software product to consider in addition to this starting list is **GFP** (*Governo dei Flussi dei Processi*), described in [13, 14].

Such a weakness in the initial design of QF will be eliminated with the introduction of the key concepts of HoQ and its related matrices for traceability of intermediate results and calculations.

The following features from QF have been implemented in this new version of QF²D :

- multi-perspective evaluation (E, S, T) of software quality;
- evaluation of QF on a percentage scale in order to obtain an immediate/intuitive understanding of results;
- usage of the ISO/IEC 9126 and 14598 series for software quality attributes and evaluation.

The following features from the HoQ usage have been implemented in the new version of QF²D:

- implementation not only for the assessment phase but also for the development / maintenance phases;
- simplification of the QF method;
- summarisation of all data in one table;
- usage of histograms to prioritise in a visual way most relevant sub-characteristics and requirements-features of the products to be evaluated.

In addition, while QF was using the 1991 version of ISO 9126, it has been updated in QF²D with the 2000 version of this standard[6], which means that its basis has increased from 21 to 31 quality sub-characteristics (this of course implies that there will be no direct convertibility across results from QF and QF²D).

It must be stressed that QF²D represents an extension of the original idea and how the new structure, based on a variable number of the quality requirements of the software product (in D/M matrix) or of the quality of implemented features (in A matrix). Figure 8 illustrates the structure of the two matrixes of QF²D, the D/M matrix (*Development / Maintenance*) and A matrix (*Assessment*), that define the life cycle of software product.

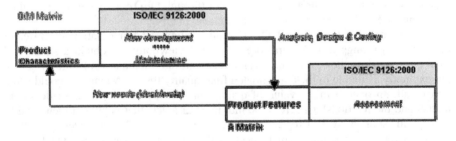

Fig. 8. D/M and A matrices and QF²D lifecycle

The first matrix allows to quantify the target goal for the quality of the software product , and defined from the viewpoints (E,S,T) on the basis of the ISO   product quality characteristics, and corresponding quality sub-characteristics. These quality goals and quality indications will be taken into account in the development of the

---

[6] It must be noted that the new 9126 series has as a main input for part 4 the ISO 9241-11 standard, providing guidance on usability aspects.

software product. Next, the software will be analysed, designed, coded, tested and evaluated.

In the second matrix, the list of the product features delivered will be matched against the ISO sub-characteristics list, now with aim to assess the product. The passage of values between the two matrixes allows to provide feedback based on testing (from D/M to A matrix) and new requirements (from A to D/M matrix). In this way QF2D gives a company the opportunity to monitor the quality of a software product in a dynamic way along all its life cycle time. Figure 9 illustrates the structure of the two matrixes with the three viewpoints dimensions (E,S,T) on the left (*n* possible people per each group), together with their sets of quality requirement (Targets DES$_i$) Then for each, the priority is assigned on a Likert scale (from 1 to 5), and then the assignment of the ratings of the sub-characteristics.

		PRIORITY (1-5)	ISO/IEC 9126-x SUBCHARACTERISTICS					INTERNAL / EXTERNAL COMPARISONS	% VALUES	
			Char 1			Char n				
			SubChar 1				SubChar n			
E	M1	DES1								
				•		◎	•			
				○						
						◎				
	Mn									
S	U1	DESx								
				•		◎	•			
				○						
						◎				
	Un									
T	D1	DESy								
						•				
						○				
			◎		•					
			◎							
	Dn	DESn								
		Sum							TCV		
		Mx									

Fig. 9. A sample D/M matrix[7]

Table 2 presents the elements in the matrices of QF2D that are either similar or different depending on the lifecycle phases. For example, in the rows of the development/maintenance matrices, the requirements are the objects of evaluation, while in the Assessment matrices, it is the features of the software product itself that are being evaluated. On the other hand, for all types of matrices, the elements of the columns, the list of the 2000 ISO/IEC 9126 standard sub-characteristics (parts 2, 3 and 4) are the same for all matrices. For all the relationship between target goals in the requirements and the quality sub-characteristics is expressed using the ISO/IEC

---

[7] A matrix presents the same structure than the D/M matrix. The difference resides in the third column, containing the list of most *relevant features perceived* in the produced software (assessment scope) in place of the requirements (new development / maintenance scope).

14598-1 [33] scale (from 0 to 3), rather than the usual QFD graphic symbols used in the HoQ.

Table 2. D/M and A matrices : a comparison

	D/M MATRIX	**A MATRIX**
SLC phase in which is used	• Requirements • Maintenance	• Testing
Object of analysis	Product (via process) through a TQM approach	
Whats (*rows*)	Requirements – REQ	Product Features - PF (after coding)
Hows (*columns*)	ISO/IEC 9126:2000 sub-char	ISO/IEC 9126:2000 sub-char

Note that some variables (concepts and names) used in the new version of QF2D are the same than in the initial version of the QF technique. For instance, the variable **TCV** is the **T**otal **C**haracteristic **V**alue and represents the total value for one of the quality characteristics listed in the ISO/IEC 9126:2000 standard in the consolidation of the opinions from the three interest groups (Economical, Technical and Social) after filling the QFD matrix. Whistl TCVmax represents the maximum value assumed by TCV if all respondents were to rate every quality characteristic at the maximum value. The final quality value obtained from such calculation is be named QF^2D and it is equivalent to the QF value in the QF technique (in fact, the two models share the same formula).

The sum of column totals represents the TCV variable, ranging from a minimum of 0 and a maximum of x*465, where x is the total number of target goals in the requirements.: In fact, the multiplication of the maximum level of priority (5) by the total number of sub-characteristics (31) by the maximum relationship value (3) would produce a resulting value of 465 and would correspond to the selection of all sub-characteristics with maximum value.

Being TCVmax = x*465, QF formula is the same, that is $QF^2D = \dfrac{TCV}{TCV_{max}}$, that allows expressing QF2D on a percentage scale. At the WHAT and HOW bottom side, numeric values are expressed in a graphical way through histograms, at the aim to give in a while which are the most relevant sub-characteristics and desiderata requirements for the production. The comparison are comprehends internal and external reference values that give the possibility to trace the trend of software product quality over time referring to its further versions as well as the capability of the company to produce a quality software with respect to competency.

In summary, the advantages of this new improved version of QF are:
• use of the new ISO/IEC 9126 standard series;
• not only a assessment of the software product at the end of the development phase, but a broader assessment throughout the development cycle, with a feedback loop;
• use of the ISO/IEC 14598-1 evaluation scale to express relationships in the HoQ table;
• a greater granularity in the whole product evaluation, at the sub-characteristic level.

5   Conclusions and Prospects

The initial QF model was designed to address the need to obtain a more objective software quality assessment which would include the different aspects - technical, economic and social - that live together in every organisation, but which was often not seen in a unitary view. This paper has presented its subsequent version referred to as QF2D (Quality Factor through QFD), a method to measure in a quantitative way software quality. This method is based on a multi-dimensional view of software quality, using different stakeholders' viewpoints, and on the   application of IT standards like 9126-x and 14598-x about software quality attributes definition and evaluation. Joining QF and QFD allows to obtain an evaluation that covers the whole software product life cycle, providing useful   information for the management of quality, from the design to the production to the maintenance phases, and this through the use of two HoQ-based matrixes. QF2D can be used both as a single quality measure and in conjunction with quantitative evaluations as in [7, 9, 10].

But QF2D framework could be also used to focus on a particular perspective and a much more in-depth analysis. For example, for an in-depth assessment of usability, another standard such as ISO 9241-11 standard would be used, considering every characteristic as a separate dimension.

Finally, it must be noted the integration among QF/QF2D techniques and the QEST/LIME models [9, 11]. In fact QF2D, as QF, can be used separately or jointly with these two software multidimensional performance models, as the assessment technique for the qualitative project/project phase evaluation.

References

1. Abran, A.: Quality – The Intersection of Product and Process. The 6th IEEE International Software Engineering Standard Symposium (ISESS'95), Montréal, Québec, Canada, August 21-25 (1995)
2. Basili, V.R., Rombach, H.D.: The TAME Project: Towards Improvement-Oriented Software Environment. IEEE Transaction on Software Engineering, 14(1988)6, 758-773
3. Basili, V.R., Weiss, D.M.: A Methodology for Collecting Valid Software Engineering Data. IEEE Transaction on Software Engineering, 10(1984)6, 728-738
4. Berga, E., Krogstieb, J., Sandvoldc, O.: Enhancing User Participation in System Design using Groupware Tools. IRIS20 Conference Proceedings, Hankø Fjordhotel, Norway, August 9-12, URL: http://www.ifi.uio.no/iris20/proceedings/20.htm (1997)
5. Boehm, B.W., Brown, J.R., Lipow, H., MacLeod, G.J., Merrit, M.J.: Characteristics of Software Quality. Elsevier North-Holland (1978)
6. Brynjolfosson, E., Austin, R.A., van Alstyne, M.: The Matrix of Change, Massachusetts Institute of Technology. Working Paper # 189, URL: http://ccs.mit.edu/papers/ CCSWP189/CCSWP189.html, January (1997)
7. Buglione, L., Abran, A.: Implementation of a Three-Dimensional Software Performance Measurement Model. Technical Report, Université du Québec à Montréal (UQAM), to be published (2000)
8. Buglione, L., Abran, A.: A Quality Factor for Software. Proceedings of QUALITA99, 3rd International Conference on Quality and Reliability, Paris, France, 25-26 March (1999) 335-344

9. Buglione, L., Abran, A.: Multidimensional Software Performance Measurement Models: A Tetrahedron-based Design. In: Software Measurement: Current Trends in Research and Practice. R. Dumke/A. Abran (eds.) Deutscher Universitats Verlag GmbH, (1999) 93-107

10. Buglione, L.: Misurare il software. Quantità, qualità, standard e miglioramento di processo nell'Information Technology, Franco Angeli, ISBN 88-464-1729-1 (1999)

11. Buglione, L., Abran, A.: LIME: A Three-Dimensional Software Performance Measurement Model for Project Management. 2WCSQ - 2nd World Congress on Software Quality, Yokohama (Tokyo Bay Area), September, 25-29 (2000)

12. Conti, T.: Diagnosi Trasversale: Fondamenti concettuali della metodologia e descrizione del programma che la implementa. TQM s.a.s., 29 Agosto (1996)

13. Conti, T.: GFP: Governo dei Flussi di Processi – Guida per l'utente. TQM s.a.s., 20 Giugno (1996)

14. Conti, T.: Organizational Self-Assessment. Chapman & Hall (1997)

15. Crow, K.: Customer-Focused Development with QFD, DRM Associates. URL: http://member.aol.com/drmassoc/QFD.html

16. Dean, E.B.: Comprehensive QFD. URL: http://akao.larc.nasa.gov/dfc/qfd/cqfd.html

17. Dromey, R.G.: A Model for Software Product Quality. IEEE Transactions on Software Engineering, 21(1995)2, 146-162

18. Eriksson, I.V., McFadden, F., Tiittanen, A.M.: Improving Software Development Through Quality Function Deployment. 5th International Conference on Information Systems Development, ISD96, Golansk, Poland, URL: http://www.helsinki.fi/~tiittane/qfd.htm, September 24-26 (1996)

19. Fusani, M.: Quality Models for Software Evolution Instruments. Int. Seminar on Software Measuring & Testing, IEI-CNR/Qualital/SSSUP "S.Anna", Pisa, Italia, December 12 (1995)

21. Guinta, L.R., Praizler, N.C.: The QFD Book: The Team Approach to Solving Problems and Satisfying Customers through Quality Function Deployment. Amacom Books, ASIN 081445139X (1993)

22. Haag, S., Raja, M.K., Schkade, L.L.: Quality Function Deployment: Usage in Software Development. Communication of the ACM, 39(1996)1, 41-49

23. Hauser, J.R., Clausing, D.: The House of Quality, Harvard Business Review. May-June (1988) 3-13

24. Herzwurm, G., Ahlemeier, G., Schockert, S., Mellis, W.: Success Factors of QFD Projects. Proceedings of the World Innovation and Strategy Conference, Sydney, Australia, URL: http://www.informatik.uni-koeln.de/winfo/prof.mellis/ publications/qfdsf.zip, August 3-5 (1998) 27-41

25. Herzwurm, G., Mellis, W., Schockert, S., Weinberger, C.: Customer Oriented Evaluation of QFD Software Tools. University of Cologne, Germany, URL: http://www.informatik. Uni-Koeln.DE/winfo/prof.mellis/publications/qfd-tools/qfd-tools.htm

26. Hrones, Jr. J.A., Jedrey, Jr. B.C., Zaaf, D.: Defining Global Requirements with Distributed QFD. Digital Technical Journal, 5(1993)4

27. IEEE: Std 1061-1992: Standard for a Software Quality Metrics Methodology (1992)

28. ISO: International Standard 8402: Quality - Vocabulary (1986)

29. ISO/IEC: International Standard 9126: Information Technology - Software product evaluation – Quality characteristics and guidelines for their use (1991)

30. ISO/IEC JTC1/SC7/WG6 FDIS 9126-1: Software Engineering Product Quality - Part 1: Quality Model, N2228 (19/11/1999)

31. ISO/IEC JTC1/SC7/WG6 PDTR 9126-2: Software Engineering Product Quality - Part 2: External Metrics, N2263 (31/01/2000)

32. ISO/IEC JTC1/SC7/WG6 PDTR 9126-3: Software Engineering Product Quality - Part 3: Internal Metrics, N2265 (31/01/2000)

33. ISO/IEC JTC1/SC7/WG6 PDTR 9126-4: Software Engineering Product Quality - Part 4: Quality in Use Metrics, N2268 (02/02/2000)

34. ISO/IEC JTC1/SC7/WG6, DIS 14598-1: Information Technology - Software product evaluation – Part 1: General Overview (3/6/97)
35. Karlsson, J.: Towards a Strategy for Software Requirement Selection, Department of Computer and Information Science. University of Linköping, Sweden, Thesis (1995)
36. McCall, J.A., Richards, P.K., Walters, G.F.: Factors in Software Quality. Voll. I, II, III: Final Tech. Report, RADC-TR-77-369, Rome Air Development Center, Air Force System Command, Griffiss Air Force Base, NY (1977)
37. Natale, D.: Qualità e quantità nei sistemi software: teoria ed esperienze. Franco Angeli Informatica (1995)
38. Ouyang, S., Fai, J., Wang, Q., Johnson, K.: Quality Function Deployment. Technical Report, University of Calgary, Alberta, Canada, URL: http://www.cpsc.ucalgary.ca/~johnsonk/SENG/SENG613/Project/report.htm
39. Pressman, R.: Software Engineering: a beginner's guide. McGraw Hill (1988)
40. QFD/CAPTURE homepage (http://www.qfdcapture.com)
41. Richardson, I.: Quality Function Deployment: A Software Process Tool? 3rd Annual International QFD Symposium, Linkoping, Sweden, URL: http://www.csis.ul.ie/staff/ItaRichardson/intlqfd.htm, October (1997)
42. Richardson, I.: Using QFD to Develop Action Plans for Software Process Improvement. SEPG98 Conference Proceedings, April (1998)
43. Sorli, M., Ruiz, J.: QFD: una herramienta de futuro. Labein (1994)
44. The Matrix of Change (MOC) Homepage. http://ccs.mit.edu/moc/
45. VV.AA.: QFD: The customer-driven approach to Quality Planning and Deployment. S. Mizuno & Y. Akao (Eds.), APD (1994)
46. Zultner, R.E.: Blitz QFD: Better, Faster and Cheaper Forms of QFD. American Programmer, 8(1995) 24-36

Using FAME Assessments to Define Measurement Goals

Dirk Hamann[1], Andrew Beitz[1], Markus Müller[2], and Rini van Solingen[1]

[1]Fraunhofer IESE, Sauerwiesen 6, Technopark II, 67661 Kaiserslautern, Germany
[2]Fraunhofer IESE, Luxemburger Str. 3, 67657 Kaiserslautern, Germany
{hamann, beitz, markus.mueller, solingen}@iese.fhg.de

Abstract. Although assessment-based approaches and measurement-based approaches are often considered as competitors, they compliment each other very well. Assessments are strong in identifying improvement objectives within a relatively short time frame, but are weak in guiding the actual implementation of the proposed changes. Measurement, however, supports very well in supporting actual changes and providing feedback on the effects of these changes, but has a difficulty with selecting the right goals. In this paper, we suggest an approach in which focused assessments are used to identify improvement goals and to use goal-oriented measurement to guide the implementation of the actual changes.

1 Introduction

Today's software industry is confronted with major challenges:
- the amount of IT application in society is increasing rapidly,
- the demand for innovative, complex and integrated IT solutions is high,
- the expectations for software quality are high,
- the amount of money spent on IT/software is exploding.

However, the amount of skilled software developers only increases slowly, and the productivity of these developers appears to maintain quite constant. To increase the productivity of software development, while maintaining the required quality levels and preferably reducing the time-to-market is one of the current challenges in the IT domain. This sets ambitious but not very easy goals for industry.

One of the ways to achieve these goals is in making software development processes more effective and efficient. This is done through continuous improvements to the software process, often addressed under the term 'software process improvement', or shortly SPI. Several well-known approaches are available such as the CMM, SPICE, ISO9000, GQM and the Balance Scorecard. These approaches have similar objectives and share the fact that they all try to focus software development to those aspects that are relevant and are therefore worth the improvement investment. The differences between these SPI approaches are mainly in 'how' they achieve their objectives.

SPI approaches can be classified in several ways. One way is to classify them over 'measurement-based' and 'maturity-based' improvement approaches [3], [28], [26].

R. Dumke and A. Abran (Eds.): IWSM 2000, LNCS 2006, pp. 220-232, 2001.

Maturity-based improvement approaches are based on a normative model that is assumed to contain 'the' best way of developing software. By assessing an organisation, using this model, it becomes possible to identify the 'maturity' of that organisation, and to propose relevant improvements towards the ideal situation according to the normative model. The measurement-based improvement approaches collect and analyse data of software development practices to increase understanding within a specific context and to make improvements based on this current situation, e.g. current problems, past experiences, project results, etc.

Although these two streams of improvement approaches are often considered as competitors, they complement each other well [28]. Assessments are strong in making a fast overview of strengths and weaknesses and setting improvement targets, however, are weak in actually guiding the implementation of the changes and giving feedback during this implementation. Measurement programmes are strong in continuous feedback, learning and optimisation of improvement activities, but highly depend on selecting the right goals for the specific environment. However, measurementbased approaches often have only minor support in identifying and selecting these goals.

It is therefore recommended to combine maturity-based and measurement-based improvement approaches during industrial improvement programmes. In this paper we provide a possible way to do that by using focused assessments (FAME) to identify improvement and measurement goals and by using GQM measurement programmes to support the improvement implementations.

2   Assessments

Efficient and cost-effective development processes are vital for IT businesses. Businesses need to constantly strive for process improvement in order to survive in today's competitive environment. Before process improvement can be initiated, a measure of the current set of processes needs to be established. One way to do this is to compare the organisation's current set of practices with a set of best practices derived from industry. This way, organisations learn what works best from other organisations and may then choose to adopt these practices themselves. An assessment is one approach to comparing organisational processes with industry best practices. They provide a disciplined examination of the processes within an organisation. An example of best practices that can be used for assessment purposes is the international standard for software processes. The result of an assessment provides a profile (see Figure 1 for an example) of which processes that are being performed in an organisation and how well they are being performed.

Although assessments are widely used within industry, there are critical problems that still remain. Assessments are typically expensive and often not well connected with the organisations real problems and needs. It is difficult to build an improvement programme from an assessment without first establishing which processes are most relevant for the businesses. Not all best practices in the standards may be relevant for all organisations, as every organisation is different in what they produce or sell. Assessments need to select processes to assess based upon the business and the desired improvement. Using a fixed list or guessing the processes to assess are not good selection approaches. A structured way is required to select processes that are relevant to the business and is used in achieving the desired goals of the improvement program. If a process is not relevant then time and effort is wasted on assessing and improving a process that will have little or no impact on product quality or on the way the organisation develops the product. Therefore, it is important to select the right processes to assess.

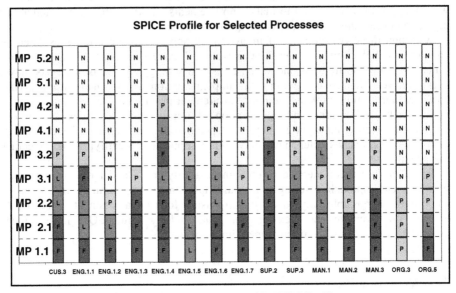

Fig. 1. Example of a Spice (ISO 15504) Profile

3   Background

The assessment method presented in this paper, in FAME[TM1] (Fraunhofer IESE Assessment MEthod) [5], uses a common framework of best software engineering practices. The common framework used is ISO/IEC TR 15504 (also known as SPICE) [23], [16], the upcoming international standard for software process assessment. This framework can be used by organisations involved in planning, managing, monitoring, controlling, and improving the acquisition, supply, development, operation, evolution and support of software.

ISO/IEC TR 15504 has widely been recognised and used around the world. A number of established methods, like BOOTSTRAP [7] and CMMi [27], already use this framework. ISO/IEC TR 15504 has also been validated internationally in the SPICE trials [29] where it has proven useful for performing assessments. The SPICE trials are the most extensive joint effort of Industry, the Public Sector, and Academia to collect and validate process assessment knowledge. Research into the SPICE trials

---

[1] FAME is a registered trademark of the Fraunhofer Institute for Experimental Software Engineering (IESE), Kaiserslautern, Germany.

is leading to a better understanding of how to improve assessments and provide better guidance towards process improvement. The results of this analysis, along with research at Fraunhofer IESE, are constantly being incorporated into the development of FAME™.

Other research programs have also contributed to the development of FAME™, like the PROFES project [9]. The PROFES project was set up within the European ESPRIT IV framework programme to support technology transfer to industries that have strong product-related quality requirements, such as the embedded systems industry. The results from this project help defining explicit relationships between process and product. These results have been analysed and used in the FAME™ project to regard business needs when performing a focused assessment. A focused assessment is an assessment that only assesses selected processes and the capability of those processes. The greatest benefit in performing a focused assessment is that time is not wasted assessing irrelevant processes that will not impact the organisation. FAME™ scopes an assessment, to select only the most relevant processes, by using the techniques discussed in this paper.

4   FAME: The Fraunhofer Assessment Method

FAME™ is an advanced assessment method that contains features that address the problems faced by industry today in software process assessment. It allows you to apply either a SPICE [16] or a BOOTSTRAP Assessment [7], and uses the standard assessment model of the upcoming standard for software process assessment (ISO/IEC TR 15504) [23].

Using FAME™ has the following benefits:

- allows you to perform either a SPICE or a BOOTSTRAP Assessment;
- focuses on relevant business processes to guide process improvement efforts;
- provides a cost-efficient and reliable method to show a better return-on-investment for the improvement program;
- provides a tailorable approach for performing assessments;
- provides an approach that allows an organisation to compare its results with similar businesses that is based upon ISO/IEC TR 15504;
- provides a method that is applicable for small to large organisations.

FAME™ contains supplementary added value elements that have been developed through practical experiences from the worldwide SPICE trials and from Fraunhofer IESE research results. These added value elements are the Business Focus, Efficiency, Reliability, and Benchmarking.

4.1   The Added Value Elements of FAME™

The added value elements were developed because of a strong need from industry to make assessments more cost effective and be more tightly coupled with a process improvement program. Each added value element and its relevance is discussed below:

1. Business Focus: If the organisation wants to develop an improvement plan from the assessment then the Business Focus element should be used with the FAME™ assessment. The goal of the Business Focus is to select the right processes for the right business. This allows the assessment to be focused and the most relevant processes to be targeted for the improvement program.

2. Efficiency: If the organisation is currently spending a lot of money performing an assessment or has little cost to spend on the assessment effort then the Efficiency element should be used with the FAME™ assessment. Efficiency looks at the factors you need to consider when performing a low cost assessment with maximum coverage of processes.

3. Reliability: If the organisation needs to benchmark or compare with other assessment results to show process improvement effort then the Reliability element should be used with the FAME™ assessment. Reliability looks at approaches and factors to consider for producing repeatable and accurate assessment results. This is very important for determining the right processes to improve. The desired level of reliability required can be determined based upon the needs of the organisation.

4. Benchmarking: After the FAME™ assessment, it can be a difficult to determine or justify which processes to improve. Benchmarking is one technique that shows you where to focus the improvement effort based upon the needs of the organisation. It allows an organisation to compare its processes with other projects or organisations to search for which best practices that leads to better performance. The Benchmarking element in FAME™ [6] contains state-of-the-art techniques, such as OSR (Optimised Set Reduction) [11], for more versatile benchmarking.

4.2   Tailoring a FAME™ Assessment to the Business

FAME™ offers a tailorable approach in performing assessments. No one assessment approach can cover all possible situations. Each organisation will have different needs in performing the assessment and the method provides approaches for most organisational needs. Some other reasons for performing an assessment are:

- to define the process improvement program
- to use the results in marketing the organisation
- to determine the capability of a supplier organisation
- to provide feedback on how well the organisation is performing
- to identify risks related to software processes within the organisation

FAME™ puts it's value added elements to work by offering a number of different assessment types for the different needs in performing an assessment. In this paper, only the focused assessment type will be discussed for developing improvement programs. The flexibility of FAME™ allows it to be integrated into the selected improvement framework of an organisation. The method does not prescribe a particular approach to process improvement. Instead, there are any improvement approaches, such as QIP [1], GQM [2], [28], or PROFES [9], to select from and use with FAME™. FAME™ is used primarily to identify the software process strengths and weaknesses – the starting point for an improvement program.

5   Focused Assessments

It is obviously interesting for an Assessor to know which processes at least to assess (and potentially improve) if an organisational unit has certain goals in mind. Normally an Assessor makes these choices based on his/her expertise but our intention is to regard business focus more formally. At the moment, this is a developing research area, and there is not very much validated data available, but there are some promising techniques and ideas on how to proceed in practice.

There are two principal directions on how to select assessment purpose with direct business focus:

- Process performance driven: These are goals such as Time-to-Market, Schedule or Productivity that are related to the performance (or outcome) of the processes.
- Product quality driven: The reference model for the product quality driven goals is the ISO 9126 [22] standard that defines six product quality characteristics (Reliability, Maintainability, Portability, Usability, Functionality and Efficiency) and their refinement into Sub-Characteristics (Figure 2).

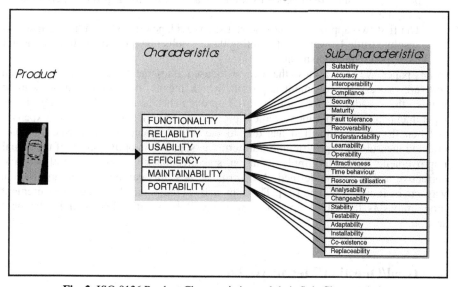

Fig. 2. ISO 9126 Product Characteristics and their Sub-Characteristics

Using explicit product quality goals or performance goals existing dependencies are retrieved to show a set of candidate processes for selection. The most suitable processes are then selected for a focused assessment, depending on the assessment context. In this way the organisations business goals are considered explicitly, and assessment contains only those processes that are important for achieving the business goals. We use the following approaches in FAME™ assessments to determine the relevant processes to select from the product or performance goals:

- Product-Process Dependency (PPD) Modelling: Based on product quality goals, the related processes are identified using a PPD repository.

- Study on Influential Processes: The related processes are selected based upon the desired performance goals that have been derived from the SPICE trials.
- Experience based Heuristics: Simple heuristics are used to select the most relevant processes based on a collection of Assessor experiences between the processes improved and the resulting performance.

We consider all three approaches described above useful in scoping an assessment by selecting the right processes to assess. Each approach has certain advantage over the others described. They mainly differ in the type of business focus offered and the bases in deriving such results. The PPD modelling work [21] and the influential processes study [14], [15] are based on empirical research, and the Heuristics approach is based on Assessor experience. However, when using any of the above approaches, the Assessor must take care in using the results. They must take into consideration the following factors:

1. The results are conservative which means that there may be other processes that are associated with a product/performance measure.
2. It is not stipulated that an organisation must assess and improve all resulting processes identified in order to improve a corresponding product/performance measure.
3. The first two approaches include statistical evidence that should not be taken as absolute truth. However, interpreting these results may provide additional insight when planning assessments.

In this paper, we look at how the idea of focused assessments can be integrated in a software process improvement approach, which means, that a focused assessment builds the roadmap for follow-up improvement actions. Succeeding it is recommended to set-up a measurement programme to collect data about all expenses and benefits the organisation has due to the improvement program. Such a goal-oriented measurement programme, furthermore, supports in optimisation of the actual improvements during the implementation, since feedback is provided on effects and corrective action can be defined. A description how this can be done in an efficient way can be found in [8] and [28]. The approach we recommend for such measurement programmes is the GQM approach, which will be shortly described in the next section.

6   Goal/Question/Metric Method

'Measurement' is the process by which numbers or symbols are assigned to attributes of entities in the real world in such a way as to describe them according to clearly defined rules [19]. Measurement can be used on both a software development process and a software product. It can be used to measure quality characteristics of a certain software product, or to measure effects of a certain software process. Software measurement is the continuous process of defining, collecting, and analysing data on the software development process and its products in order to understand, control and optimise that process and its products.

In the Goal/Question/Metric (GQM) method a systematic approach is represented for tailoring and integrating goals to models of the software processes, products and quality perspectives of interest, based upon the specific needs of the project and the organisation [2]. The result of the application of the GQM method is the specification of a measurement system targeting a particular set of issues and a set of rules for the interpretation of the measurement data.

By using GQM a certain goal is defined, this goal is refined into questions, and metrics are defined that should provide the information to answer these questions. By answering the questions, the measured data can be analysed to identify if the goals are attained. Thus, by using GQM, metrics are defined from a top-down perspective and analysed and interpreted bottom-up, as shown in Figure 3.

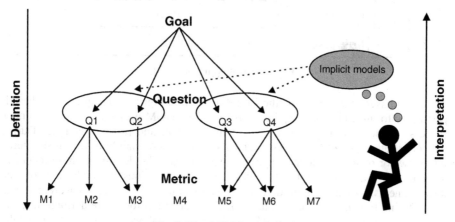

Fig. 3. The GQM Paradigm [2]

The GQM model is started top-down with the definition of an explicit measurement goal. This goal is refined into several questions that break down the issue into its major components. Each questions is then refined into metrics that should provide information to answer those questions. Measurement data is interpreted bottom-up. As the metrics are defined with an explicit goal in mind, the information provided by the metrics should be interpreted and analysed with respect to this goal to conclude whether or not it is attained.

GQM trees of goals, questions and metrics are built on knowledge of the experts in the organisation: the developers [2]. Knowledge acquisition techniques are used to capture the implicit models of the developers built during years of experience. Those implicit models give valuable input to the measurement programme and will often be more important than the available explicit process models.

Carrying out GQM measurement in industrial projects requires a step-wise approach. The recently described GQM method contains four phases:

- The Planning phase, during which a project for measurement application is selected, defined, characterised, and planned, resulting in a project plan.
- The Definition phase, during which the measurement programme is defined (goal, questions, metrics, and hypotheses are defined) and documented.
- The Data Collection phase, during which actual data collection takes place, resulting in collected data.
- The Interpretation phase, during which collected data is processed with respect to the defined metrics into measurement results that provide answers to the defined questions, after which goal attainment can be evaluated.

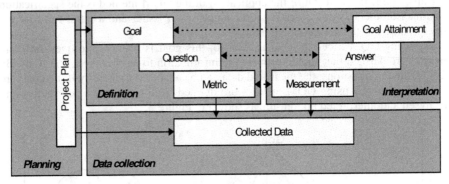

Fig. 4. The GQM method [28]

The four phases of the GQM method are illustrated in Figure 4. The planning phase is performed to fulfil all basic requirements to make a GQM measurement programme a success, including training, management involvement and project planning. During the definition phase all GQM deliverables are developed, mainly based on structured interviews or other knowledge acquisition techniques. The definition phase identifies a goal, all questions, related metrics and expectations (hypotheses) of the measurements. When all definition activities are completed, actual measurement can start. During this data collection phase the data collection forms are defined, filled-in and stored in a measurement database. Then the 'real work' can start: using the measurement data. During the interpretation phase, the measurements are used to answer the stated questions, and these answers are again used to see whether the stated goals have been attained.

6.1   Measurement Goals

The first step in the definition process is the definition of formal measurement goals. These measurement goals are derived from the improvement goals set in the assessments. All people participating in the measurement programme should be involved in the definition of measurement goals. Without this involvement, people's commitment to the measurement programme is at risk, as it may no longer be clear to them why measurement is applied. Templates are available that support the definition of measurement goals by specifying purpose (what object and why), perspective (what aspect and who), and context characteristics [2].

Measurement provides a valuable tool for understanding the effects of actions that are implemented to improve a software development process. Examples of measurement topics and measurement goals are [25] [19]:

- increased understanding of the software development process;
- increased control of the software development process;
- increased capacity to improve the software development process;
- more accurate estimates of software project costs and schedule;
- more objective evaluations of changes in technique, tool, or methods;
- more accurate estimates of the effects of changes on project cost and schedule;

- decreased development costs due to increased productivity and efficiency;
- decrease of project cycle time due to increased productivity and efficiency;
- improved customer satisfaction and confidence due to higher product quality.

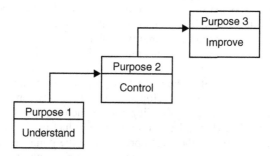

Fig. 5. Three types of measurement goals

Software measurement data is interpreted by people to provide information that can be applied for three different purposes (Figure 5). In the first place, the data provide visibility of the current development process and the characteristics of the software products. This visibility is required to reduce complexity and increase *understanding* of the process and products. Understanding means determining the different variables that exist during execution of a process. Once basic understanding has been established (the variables are known), the collected and analysed data can be used to *control* the process and the products, by defining corrective and preventive actions. This means that the relationships between the process variables have to be determined. Once these relationships are known, they can be used to control the process. Furthermore, based on analysis, the collected measurement data can be used to assess the process, and therefore, act as an indicator of development process problem areas, from which *improvement* actions can be identified. Improvements can be made by influencing or changing process variables and their relationships. This hierarchy of measurement goals is illustrated in Figure 5. It does not mean than an organisation will not improve when focusing on understanding goals. It only implies that it is impossible to talk about improvement/optimisation without knowing how things work or knowing how to control things.

6.2   Linking Assessment Output to Measurement Input

All information gathered during an assessment should be used as input to a measurement programme to link the two activities and to save time and effort. The assessment results can be used for two different purposes in the follow-up measurement activities. On the one hand, the identified weaknesses in the organisation's development process (based on the business goals and needs), which are the main target for improvement activities, should be used as starting point for defining measurement goals (see section 6.1). On the other hand, much information about the company's processes and products is collected during the assessment, which should be used to set-up and execute the measurement program. In order to derive the questions and related metrics for the measurement programme according to the GQM paradigm, a description of the company's processes and products is needed (e.g., [12], [13]).

Our experience has shown that it is possible to collect the necessary information to set-up a measurement programme already during an assessment (see e.g., [20]). Usually, assessment tools store only information about the assessed processes itself (e.g., scores and ratings for base and management practices in SPICE). We developed our own tool with an extended functionality, which allows us to capture additionally to the process-related information all relevant information about the key work products during the assessment.

All this information can then be used to set-up a first model of the company's processes and products. We have developed an interface between our assessment tool and the Spearmint™ [4] process-modelling tool, which we use for building process models including product flows. This process and product model is than used to ease the definition of the metrics in the GQM process and the point-in-time when they are collected. This ensures consistency between the metrics and furthermore, helps to avoid the definition of unnecessary metrics or metrics, for which in practice no data can be collected.

7   Summary and Conclusions

Our approach as presented in this paper is based on the experience from several assessments and improvement programs (e.g., [18], [20]). Based on this experience, we suggest to focus the assessment on the process areas which are particular important for the company and which are related to the organisations business goals and needs. We developed a method including concrete steps called FAME™, which considers all these things. After applying the assessment, a goal-oriented (GQM-based) measurement programme should be started to guide the implementation of the proposed changes, to provide feedback and to enable context specific optimisation.

First experiences in applying FAME™ in combination with GQM have shown that it is an efficient way for companies to better understand where their strengths and weaknesses are, where they should start with their improvement efforts, and which fully supports the implementation of changes in the specific project or business unit. We will continue our work to establish full methodological and tool support for software projects and organisational processes.

References

1. Basili, V., Caldiera, G.: Improving Software Quality by Reusing Knowledge and Experience. Sloan Management Review (1995)
2. Basili, V.R., Caldiera, C., Rombach, H.D.: Goal Question Metric Paradigm. Encyclopaedia of Software Engineering (Marciniak, J.J., editor), Volume 1, John Wiley & Sons, (1994) 528-532
3. Basili, V.R., Weiss, D.M.: A methodology for collecting valid software engineering data. IEEE Transactions on Software Engineering, 10(1984)6

4. Becker-Kornstaedt, U., Hamann, D., Kempkens, R., Rösch, P., Verlage, M., Webby, R., Zettel, J.: Support for the process engineer: The Spearmint approach to software process definition and process guidance. In: M. Jarke, A. Oberweis (eds.), Proceedings of the 11th International Conference on Advanced Information Systems Engineering, LNCS 1626, Springer (1999) 119–133

5. Beitz, A., El Emam, K., Järvinen, J.: A Business Focus to Assessments. Proceedings of the SPI Conference, Barcelona (1999)

6. Beitz, A., Wieczorek, I.: Applying Benchmarking to Learn from Best Practices. 2nd International Conference on Product Focused Software Process Improvement, Oulu, Finland, June (2000)

7. Bicego, A., Khurana, M., Kuvaja, P.: BOOTSTRAP 3.0 – Software Process Assessment Methodology. Proceedings of the SQM '98 (1998)

8. Birk, A., Hamann, D., Hartkopf, S.: A Framework for the Continuous Monitoring and Evaluation of Improvement Programmes. 2nd International Conference on Product Focused Software Process Improvement, Oulu, Finland, June (2000)

9. Birk, A., Järvinen, J., Komi-Sirviö, S., Oivo, M., Pfahl, D.: PROFES- A Product-driven Process Improvement Methodology. Proceedings of the Fourth European Software Process Improvement Conference (SPI'98), Monte Carlo, Monaco, December (1998)

10. Bøegh, J., Depanfilis, S., Kitchenham, B., Pasquini, A.: A Method for Software Quality Planning, Control, and Evaluation. IEEE Software 16(1999)2, 69–77

11. Briand, L., Basili, L., Hetmanski, C.: Developing Interpretable Models with Optimized Set Reduction for Identifying High-Risk Software Components. IEEE Transactions on Software Engineering, 19(1993)11

12. Briand, L., Differding, C., Rombach, D.: Practical Guidelines for Measurement-based Process Improvement. Software Process–Improvement and Practice, 2(1996)4, 253-280

13. Bröckers, A., Differding, C., Threin, G.: The role of software process modeling in planning industrial measurement programs. In: Proceedings of the Third International Software Metrics Symposium, Berlin, IEEE Computer Society Press, March (1996)

14. El Emam, K., Birk, A.: Validating the ISO/IEC 15504 measures of software development process capability. Journal of Systems and Software (2000) 119-149

15. El Emam, K., Birk, A.: Validating the ISO/IEC 15504 measure of software requirements analysis process capability. IEEE Transactions on Software Engineering (To appear) (2000)

16. El Emam, K., Drouin, J., Melo, W.: SPICE: The Theory and Practice of Software Process Improvement and Capability Determination. IEEE Computer Society (1998)

17. El Emam, K., Goldenson, D.: SPICE: An Empiricist's Perspective. Proceedings of the Second IEEE International Software Engineering Standards Symposium, August (1995)

18. ESPIRT Project No 23239. PROFES. URL: http://www.profes.org

19. Fenton, N.E., Pfleeger, S.L.: Software Metrics, a rigorous and practical approach. Thomson Computer Press (1996)

20. Hamann, D., Derks, P., Kuvaja, P.: Using ISO 15504 Compliant Assessment Combined with Goal-oriented Measurement for Process Improvement at Dräger Medical Technology. International SPICE Conference. Limerick, Ireland, June (2000)

21. Hamann, D., Järvinen, J., Birk, A., Pfahl, D.: A Product-Process Dependency Definition Method. Proceedings of the 24th EUROMIRCO Conference: Workshop on Software Process and Product Improvement. IEEE Computer Society Press, Vasteras, Sweden, August (1998)

22. ISO/IEC. Information technology – Software product evaluation – Quality characteristics and guidelines for their use. ISO/IEC standard 9126. Geneva, Switzerland (1991)

23. ISO/IEC ISO/IEC TR 15504-2: Information Technology – Software Process Assessment – Part 2: A Reference Model for Processes and Process Capability. Technical Report type 2, International Organisation for Standardisation (Ed.), Case Postale 56, CH-1211 Geneva, Switzerland (1998)

24. Maclennan, F., Ostrolenk, G.: The SPICE Trials: Validating the Framework. Proceedings of 2nd International SPICE Symposium (1995)

25. Möller, K.H., Paulisch, D.J.: Software Metrics: A practitioner's guide to improved product development. London, Chapman & Hall (1993)
26. Niessink, F.: Perspectives on improving software maintenance. Siks dissertation series 2000-1, Free University Amsterdam, The Netherlands, March (2000)
27. Software Engineering Institute (SEI). "A" Specification for the CMMI Product Suite. URL: http://www.sei.cmu.edu/cmm/cmmi/specs/aspec1.4.html#refs
28. van Solingen, R., Berghout, E.: The Goal/Question/Metric Method: a practical guide for quality improvement of software development. Mc Raw-Hill (1999)
29. SPICE Project Trials Team. Phase 2 Trials Interim Report. URL: http://www.iese.fhg.de/SPICE/Trials/p2rp100pub.pdf, June (1998)

Mapping Processes Between Parallel, Hierarchical, and Orthogonal System Representations

Francis Dion[1], Thanh Khiet Tran[1], and Alain Abran[*2]

[1] Epsilon Technologies inc., 1200, Boul. Chomedey, Laval (QC) Canada H7V 3Z3
fdion@xpertdoc.com,
tkhiet@yahoo.com
[2] Université du Québec à Montréal
Département d'informatique
C.P. 8888, Succ. Centre-ville
Montréal (Québec), Canada H3C 3P8
abran.alain@uqam.ca

Abstract. The importance of software system representation through models and visual diagrams is increasing with the steady growth of systems complexity and criticality. Since no single representation is best suited to address all the documentation, communication and expression needs of a typical software development project, the issues related to conversion and coherence between different representations are having a significant impact on team productivity and product as well as process quality. This paper explores the types of relationships that exist between representations and the impact they have on mapping, generation and synchronization processes. We propose a characterization of those relationships as being parallel, hierarchical or orthogonal. Examples and comments on mapping or transformation processes and automation prospects in the context of software size measurement are also provided.

1 Introduction

In the field of software development and maintenance, we need models whenever the systems we are working on become too complex to be instantly and completely grasped by all involved individuals.

Models and diagrams are used for specifying, visualizing, constructing, and documenting the artifacts of software systems, as well as for business modeling[1]. They are tools for stakeholders to communicate their understanding about the system. They can be used to broadly or precisely specify the work to be done. They can serve as blueprints for construction or as a basis for cost and schedule estimation. They can also be used as input for automated size measurement, property validation, code generation and a host of other purposes.

---

[*] Professor and director of the Research Lab. in Software Engineering Management
[1] Adapted from [1], page xi.

R. Dumke and A. Abran (Eds.): IWSM 2000, LNCS 2006, pp. 233-247, 2001.
© Springer-Verlag Berlin Heidelberg 2001

Local Rules:
Differences Between Organizations Usage of Model Elements

The choice of what models and diagrams one creates has a profound influence upon how a problem is attacked and how a corresponding solution is shaped. Furthermore, the same model elements can be used differently to express different concepts or different levels of abstraction from one organization to another.

Those variations are imputable to many factors, including:

- Organizational culture.
- Available experience and expertise.
- Tools and tools usage.
- Corporate or personal goals and objectives.

Every complex system is best approached through a small set of nearly independent views of a model[2]. No single representation of a system can efficiently express or communicate all needed perspectives on that system. A diagram that is well suited for a specific need or task could be too low level, too high level or conceptually too distant to be used in another context.

Since models and diagrams are capable of expressing the details of a system from a number of perspectives, one of the recurring issues faced when applying modeling surrounds the management of "Enterprise-wide" modeling efforts and models. Specifically, there are concerns about models that exist at different level of abstractions, and how to manage these different models[3].

The cost associated with the independent production of many representations for the same system can be quite substantial. The evolution of the system itself is also likely to be an issue in terms of maintaining the coherence of loosely related representations. It thus seems reasonable to look for ways to somehow relate those representations together. By examining the nature of their relationships, we should be able to assess the potential to produce one representation as a function of another one. In some instances, the mapping would be straightforward and the process would be easy to automate. Other mappings, though, would be much less obvious and require human intervention.

This paper presents a categorization scheme for the relationships between representations in order to assess their potential for systematic mapping. This classification is a fuzzy set of three categories representing decreasing correspondence between elements of the representations. The categories are: parallel, hierarchical and orthogonal.

Please note that, although the examples in this paper are mostly UML diagrams, we believe the concepts and ideas presented here to be as applicable with any other modeling technique and even across notations.

---

[2] [1], page 1-3.
[3] Adaped from [2]

> **Definitions**
>
> A **model** is a simplified representation of a system or a process. A system can be represented by any number of models. A model could also represent a class of systems or processes.
>
> A **view** is a specific expression of a model. It can be seen as a window on the model, exposing part or all of the information it contains in a format that is suitable for some specific use or user. A single model can be expressed through many distinct views.
>
> A **diagram** is a graphical view, by opposition to a textual or tabular view.
>
> Despite their definite differences, these concepts are more or less interchangeable in the context of this paper. To avoid unnecessary confusion, the term "representation" is use here to mean either one of them.

2   Relationships between Representations

When considering the ease and usefulness of establishing a mapping between two distinct representations, one must be able to understand and characterize the relationships that exist between them. To that effect, we suggest the use of the following categories:

- The representations are **parallel** if they express roughly the same concepts at the *same level of abstractions*.
- The representations are **hierarchical** if they express roughly the same concepts but at *different levels of abstraction*.
- The representations are **orthogonal** if they express *unrelated (or at least not directly related) concepts* of the system/unit.

Those categories are not crisp classifiers. They are fuzzy symbols expressing a relative positioning across a continuum from perfect isomorphism to complete independence. As we intend to demonstrate in the following sections, they are useful conceptual tools to assess the potential for systematic mapping between two specific representations.

2.1   Parallel Representations

Two distinct representations of a system or unit are said to be parallel if they express roughly the same concepts at roughly the same level of abstraction.

The mapping or conversion process between parallel representations should be straightforward and easily automated since their information content is identical and their differences lie mainly in the way this information is organized and presented.

Another implication of this definition is that either one could be obtained as a function of the other and that they could both be expressions of the same internal representation.

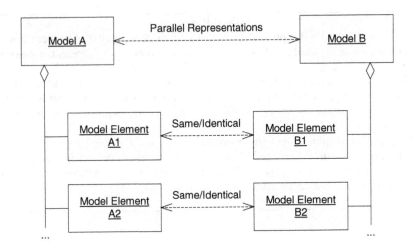

Fig. 1. Illustration of a parallel relationship between to representations

One example of parallel representations is illustrated by the well-known isomorphism that exists between *collaboration* and *sequence* diagrams in the UML notation. Both are instances of the abstract *interaction* type of diagrams and one form can readily be converted to the other without any loss of information. Many modeling tools directly support this transformation.

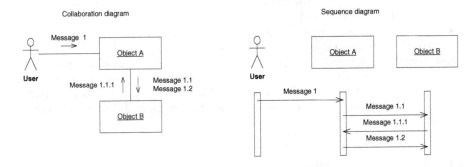

Fig. 2. Example of isomorphic collaboration and sequence diagrams

Another less obvious parallel relationship exists between the model of a class and its representation as a use case diagram. The use cases represented here are not those of the overall system but rather of the users of the class, usually other classes or components.

Class diagram for Class A   Use case diagram for Class A

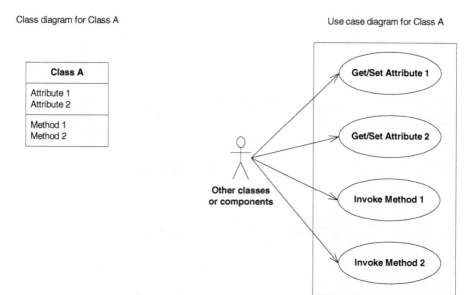

Fig. 3. Example of a parallel relationship between a class an a use case diagram

3   Hierarchical Representations

Two distinct representations of a system or unit are said to be hierarchical if they
express roughly the same concepts but at different levels of abstraction. In other
words, one of the models or diagrams presents a detailed view of the system while the
other is a more synthesized, bird's eye view of that same system. This type of
relationship is especially emphasized by top down methodologies where one goes
from a high level specification to detailed specification to high and low level design
and so on all the way down to implementation. Each level needs to be traceable to its
predecessor while adding new, more detailed information. Such models or views
could share the same internal representation, although at least one of them would use
only part of the available information.

In contrast with parallel relationships, hierarchical transformations require human
intervention or comprehensive heuristic rules to either "fill-in-the-blanks" (when
moving top-down) or select the significant elements (when moving "bottom-up").

A use case diagram and the various collaborations which represent the detailed
specifications of the use cases are a good example of a hierarchical relationship.

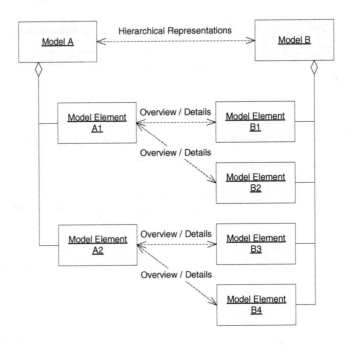

Fig. 4. Hierarchical representations

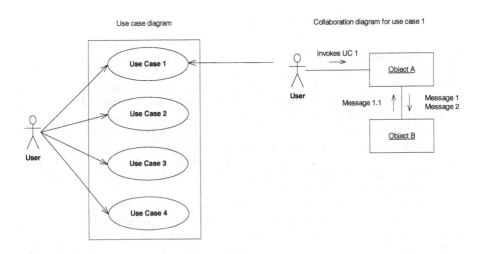

Fig. 5. Hierarchical relationship between a use case diagram and a collaboration diagram

Another example of hierarchical relationship can be found when one diagram represents a summarized view where much of the details of the other one have been "folded", either by way of generalization or by packaging together similar features.

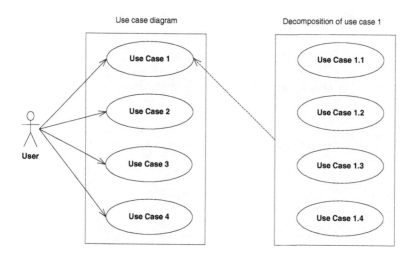

Use case diagram

Decomposition of use case 1

Fig. 6. Hierarchical relationship expressing a generalization between use cases

4   Orthogonal Representations

Two distinct representations of a system or unit are said to be orthogonal if they express unrelated or at least not directly related concepts of the system/unit. This means that their respective items diverge not (or not only) by their form or level of details but by the nature of the objects they represent.

When a purely orthogonal relationship exists between two representations, it can be assumed that there is no systematic mapping by which one could be derived from the other. More common would be situations where only a partial mapping is possible, requiring human intervention or very sophisticated heuristics for such a transformation to be performed. In some situations, a hierarchical or parallel relationship exists but cannot be fully determined because intermediary "levels" are missing, because extensive optimization and reuse have blurred the initial structure or because the representations have not been kept in synch and therefore are linked to visions that have diverged over time.

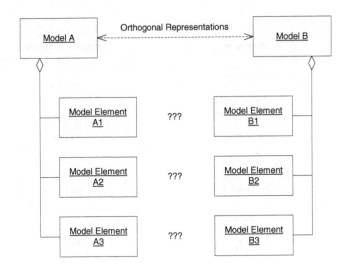

Fig. 7. Orthogonal representations

5   Application to the Measurement Process

We would now like to put this discussion in the practical context of the C-FFP software functional size measurement process.

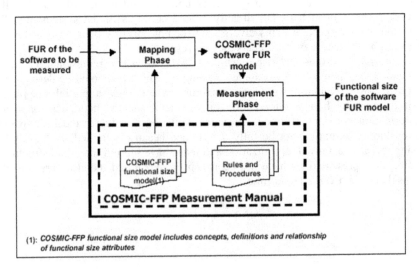

Fig. 8. COSMIC-FFP Measurement Process Model[4]

---

[4] Taken from [3], page 13.

The COSMIC-FFP method applies measurement to a generic model of the software functional user requirements onto which actual artifacts of the software to be measured are mapped[5]. The COSMIC-FFP mapping phase takes as input the functional user requirements of a piece of software and produces a specific software model suitable for measuring functional size. In many situations, those functional user requirements have to be obtained from alternate sources, like architecture and design models[6].

This measurement method essentially consists of making a model of the software in which the functionality has been breaking down into series of data movements between layers separated by boundaries. Those series are called "functional processes" and the data movements are classified in four categories: Entries, eXits, Reads and Writes (see [2] for details).

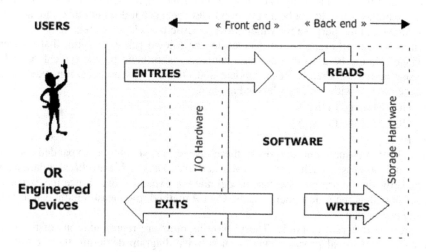

Fig. 9. Generic flow of data through software from a functional perspective

One of the first mapping challenges that should be addressed in the context of this measurement method is: "How can the C-FFP software model elements be expressed in terms of the UML notation elements?". As demonstrated by Bevo et Al. in [1], most C-FFP software model elements map directly to UML notation concepts as follows:

C-FFP software model elements		UML notation concepts
Functional Process	<=>	Use Case
User or Engineered Device	<=>	User
Data Group	<=>	Class
Data attribute	<=>	Attribute

---

[5] Idem.
[6] Ibidem, page 13 and 14.

The following elements, on the other hand, do not lend themselves to any obvious mapping:

C-FFP software model elements		UML notation concepts
Functional Sub-Process (Entry, eXit, Read and Write)	???	Scenario
Layer	???	Package

One way to view this mapping is to consider, for example, that a use case, in any model coming from any organization, should always be mapped to a functional process and that a data group can only be identified by a class in an UML diagram. This, we believe, would not be a very good view because it does not take into account the context and the purpose for which those specific models were created.

Suppose that an organization decided to use a local rule specifying that the verb "manage" should be used in a use case name as a shorthand for the typical "CRUD" database activities: Create, Read, Update and Delete. This organization would then produce models with use cases labeled as such:

- UC1 Manage Entity X
- UC2 Manage Entity Y
- Etc.

For C-FFP measurement purposes, these use cases should be expanded as four functional processes each, one for each activity. Thus a **hierarchical** relationship exists between the original use case model and the expanded one. Since the expanded model **parallels** the requirements of the C-FFP method, the measurement can then be readily performed.

Here is a different example. These two diagrams are representations of the same use case / functional process. One is an activity diagram depicting the algorithmic features of the process while the other is a sequence diagram illustrating the data movements coming in and out of the component realizing the process (as for C-FFP measurement). Although they both represent the same function, they do so through very different, almost **orthogonal** sets of concepts. In this example, there is no indication that the "Check references values" activity really represents a read on the database. Only a deep understanding of the system documented, or the use of agreed upon conventions, would allow such a mapping to be performed.

5   Conclusion

The increasing role that models play in modern software development and maintenance activities makes it more and more important to understand the dynamics of their relationships.

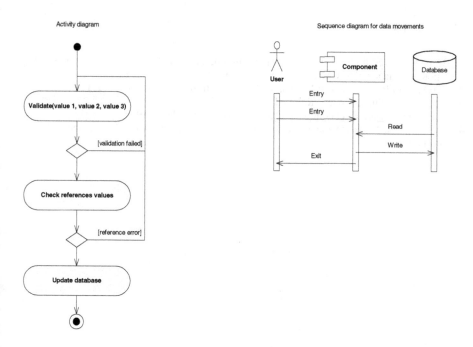

Fig. 10. Orthogonal relationship between two representations of the same functional process

Although it is possible to express almost any aspect of a system using the same model elements, this in itself is not enough to guarantee a simple, straightforward adaptation process that would allow any model to be used as input for every task. We believe that the characterization of representations' relationships presented here could serve as a conceptual framework to guide us on the assessment of mapping, transformation and generation potentials.

Future research directions on this topic include the exploration of the concept of "orthodoxy" versus local rules in modeling as well as more formal and complete specifications of the mapping processes between representations.

Acknowledgements

The authors wish to thank France Cano and Sylvain Hamel for their comments on the first drafts of this paper.

References

1. Bévo, V., Lévesque, G., Abran, A.: Application de la méthode FFP à partir d'une spécification selon la notation UML. In: Proc. of the IWSM, Lac Superieur, Kanada (1999)
2. COSMIC-FFP Measurement Manual. Field Trials 2.0 Version, October (1999)
3. Schulz, T.: Multiple Models. Rational Software,
   http://www.rosearchitect.com/mag/archives/9901/extreme.shtml (1999)
4. OMG Unified Modeling Language Specification, Version 1.3, Object Management Group, June (1999)

Author Index

Lecture Notes in Computer Science

For information about Vols. 1–1920
please contact your bookseller or Springer-Verlag